AGAINST THE WIND

THE RISE OF
KAMEHAMEHA THE GREAT

CHRIS WEATHERHEAD

Although this is a work of fiction, it is based on historical facts and events to which is added myth and imagination. Many characters evolved from actual historical persons and others based on historical research of the culture and customs of the place and period. The dialogue is completely imagined and created from my research except for George Vancouver's captain's log entries regarding his good relationships with King Kamehameha, his regent, Ka'a humanu, John Young and Isaac Davis. The battles and political intrigue are taken from actual facts and lives of people involved.

Cover Art: "Kamehameha's Fleet Sails to Battle" by Francy Walsh

ISBN: 1735508608
ISBN-13: 9781735508603

Acknowledgements

I am forever grateful to my best friend, husband, writer/scholar/actor/producer/director, Clarence Felder, who in his own quest for knowledge, led me to this tale. Great appreciation goes to my mother, Gwendolyn Steelman-Weatherhead, who read my original screenplay of this story just prior to the onset of Alzheimer's disease and made me promise never to give up on this project. When she passed on, my elder sister, Penny Giles-Fagan, suggested it be a novel, which pushed me through the last twenty years to finish the manuscript before her death.

During years of research, I was aided by kind and considerate staff of the Bishop Museum and many local libraries on three islands. Historians and linguists, John Papa I'I, David Malo, Mary Kawena Pukui, Esther Mookini, Ralph S. Kuykendall and others offered many pieces of the puzzle. I owe great respect to explorer, Captain George Vancouver, for his honest and detailed Captain's log. Of the many historical participants I attempted to bring to life, Ka'ahumanu is one who continues to amaze me with her strength of character while being mistress, strategist, advisor and regent to the mercurial king. She then ruled very wisely for thirteen years after his death. The women of Hawaii owe her their freedom and liberty.

Along the way, were my brilliant copy editor/ mentor, Susan Craft, layout guru, Eileen Easler and marvelous design/marketing director, Rich Carnahan.

Several true friends encouraged me through decades of various versions of the book while I was directing and producing theater and film projects. They are, Deidre Smith-Weber, Michael Easler and Lee Reynolds.

A major debt of gratitude I owe to artist, Francy Walsh, whose life at sea and relationships with many native peoples in the South Pacific, gives the book cover and interior art its unique statement. Karen Deloach's battle maps are essential in giving perspective to Kamehameha and his war journeys.

Dedication

To Gwendolyn Steelman-Weatherhead, for motherly support... also to Clarence and Penny, deep gratitude.

Contents

Preface

My love of all things Hawaiian began in 1957, as a nine-year-old girl, after World War II, when my family was heading to Japan, where my Dad was flight captain for U.S. Military Air Transport Service. He had flown secret missions in the Pacific for the United States Air Force during the war, and fell in love with Hawaii for various reasons, including escaping death there.

This visit was the first of many. Whether on Oahu, the big island, or Maui, the astounding rise of Kamehameha, king of the islands, captured my interest. This book began with a serendipitous moment. In the 1980s, I went with my actor husband, Clarence Felder, to Hawaii to shoot a TV series. On a break, we visited my father on the Big Island. While there, my husband discovered a mysterious old photo down a dark hallway in the King Kamehameha Hotel in Kailua/Kona. That photo inspired me to research every book I could find on ancient Hawaiian culture and customs for the next four years. I developed many personal opinions about the king from Hawaiian historians as well as ship's logs of famed explorer, George

Vancouver. Many others revealed intriguing facts about the rise of Kamehameha the Great and his astonishing personality.

Although this is a work of fiction, it is based on historical facts and events to which myth and imagination are added. Main events are available to study, and all but a few characters are real people who lived through the upheaval in the Hawaiian Islands from 1790 to 1796. There are supernatural aspects included in the king's culture, which I felt were essential to his journey.

Who was this man, sometimes called the "Napoleon of the Pacific"? In my opinion, he was a mercurial visionary, Herculean leader, jealous lover, brilliant military strategist, and always, an enigma.

There were five major people with Kamehameha on his wild ride to rule all the islands; one extraordinary woman, two insidious enemies, and two surprising friends. Here is my take on this unparalleled man.

Chris Weatherhead,
Folly Beach, SC,
5/17/2020

The Kings' Courts

KING KAMEHAMEHA

KA' A HUMANU
KING'S CONSORT

KAHUNA LANI
CHIEF PRIEST

KAOANA
HIS NIECE

PALOA
MEMBER OF ROYAL FAMILY

LAMAKUA
CHIEF OF STATE

NAHENA
AUNT OF KAOANA

MAPALA
LOYAL GENERAL

KIANA
A GENERAL AND

RIVAL TO
KAMEHAMEHA

KING KA-HE-KILI

(REIGNING & ELDEST KING OF HAWAIIAN ISLANDS)

KAPAHILI
OLDEST SON

KALANI-KUPULI
SECOND SON

KEOUA
NEPHEW

KEAWE
NEPHEW

KIWALO
COUSIN

KONA CHIEF
ALLY TO KAHEKILI

KAILUA CHIEF
ALLY TO KAHEKILI

Private Hut of King Kamehameha

Island of Hawaii, 1790

The massive, dark hand squeezes his throat. Thoughts cloud. He smells the hot, stinking breath of his deadly rival, King Kahekili, and sees one squinty eye gleam at him with victory. His enemy's face is a fleshy map riddled with deep scars and tattoos. Kamehameha grits his teeth. Panic spreads through him like waves pounding a rocky shore. He grunts in agony, slamming his head against his attacker's temple. The repulsive grin only expands as a drop of sweat courses down Kahekili's cheek. Flashes of black swirl through Kamehameha's mind. His clutch on Kahekili's arm weakens. His fingers claw into his rival king's skin.

Kamehameha bolts up from his afternoon nap, chokes and grabs his throat. In his prime at thirty-five, the king of the vast island of Hawaii, blinks, rises and focuses on blue sky through the thatched window. The breeze bathes him in sweet comfort like a woman's gaze, but he cannot trust it – his mind still fights the chaos in his nightmare. Palms rustle outside his royal hut. He takes a deep breath, but another image of Kahekili crashes into his thoughts. His hand clutches his throat again.

Wait. He chuckles and rubs his hand, his fingers numb from clenching. He stares at the glow of the afternoon sun on the back of his hand. With every deep breath, Kahekili's face fades.

Gone now. Children giggle outside – their tangled, happy cries mingle with rolling surf. At the entrance of his hut he watches them slide down a slope on ti leaves.

All is well. Rest. He falls back on his cot and picks through skeins of his dream for what was important and what was not. Sea birds herald

King Kamehameha

an intruder. Kamehameha shields his eyes. Far out on the sea, he spots a three-masted vessel, a large moku pe'a, sails toward Maui. He muses at this sight, which, since the time of Kapene Cook, killed on his island ten harvests ago, is not yet common, but no longer a shock to anyone.

Ah…what now? He wonders. His people believed Kapene Cook was their god, Lono, until they saw blood running from him, life draining out of him.

Many other strangers have come to my shores, but why these oyster-skin ones come this day? Will there be honest trading or some dark purpose from which I must defend my people? Mysteries.

He stretches up his huge frame to vent the tension. *Was this dream a warning? An omen connected to that ship?*

His mother told him to listen to the voice within. She believed he was descended from the gods. He owed her consideration of that possible truth. He stares at the strange vessel. It plows through waves. His eyes narrow.

I Rise

A conch shell's high-pitched call announces the king will speak. All his subjects are gathering to hear Kamehameha declare his plan for the next season. Everyone who can walk or be carried crowd in and jostle on the shore below their temple, the *heiau*. Every eye searches for sight of their beloved king of the large island of Hawaii.

It is a throng separated by strict tradition. The king's Ali'i royal chiefs cluster in ornamented brightly colored orange, red and blue feather cloaks and helmets, land-owning nobles who can trace their lineage back to early kings.

Many kahunas in priests' robes of tapa cloth and finery signify their high stations as healers, seers, and masters of many crafts, stand in the front row. Gathered behind the high echelons is the largest class, Commoners, who wear their best, bright loincloths, are freed from their work in the fields of the Royal Ali'I and glad to be resting.

In a separate area wait all the women. Elder women have higher honor, younger women behind them. Hundreds of subjects stand in awed silence as wind sings in the palms. Hiding in bushes and undergrowth, the Untouchables, the *kau-va*, slaves of every kind, stare in silence.

A cheer explodes from the assembly as they see their king appear on the slope. Kamehameha's hand gestures to the entire throng as he moves to the highest spot. "My people! I assure you, I will be king of all the islands! We have lived in fear of Kahekili and his vicious armies for too long. All generations before me suffered under warlords on every island – names many of you know, each fighting to be king. Yes, they had powerful mana. However, my war god, Ku-Kaili-moku, has guided me to be king of this great island of Hawaii. And not only this, but soon all the islands." A loud cheer goes up.

"Ku-Kaili-moku is a hungry god and often exacts

a price of many lives. A true and lasting peace is my dream for all our islands. Each one here knows how many have died in the wars. The gods have given us good crops now. For this time of harvest there is needed rest for you and your families. Time to watch our children play. But, do not be fooled, my people! War will come again, and soon. Many of you have told me you long for my dream. Ka-he-kili and his sons remain a constant threat. Let this next season of war be the time the Evil One will be destroyed at last. We will have our peace!"

Ali'i and Commoners inspired by his wisdom and power, wave arms, women draping strings of the most magnificent magenta, yellow and pink flowers, on the slope in front of him, bowing and singing.

However, a few chiefs stand aloof, sullen. One whispers, "Kamehameha continues silent about foreigners coming too often. He speaks only of one enemy, Kahekili. Kapene Cook has been dead for ten harvests, but many other oyster ones come, more and more. What about these enemies with no souls in strange clothes who arrive in those ships? I do not trust any of those pasty-skinned beings. They must be destroyed."

Another grumbles, "Yes, which gods have sent them, and for what purpose?"

They confer away from the king's ear.

Kamehameha and his retinue move up the lane. His subjects prostrate themselves. After he has passed, they rise and creep away.

The angry chiefs continue. One speaks low, "If we kill all those in the ships, they will stop coming."

Another says, "No. They have valuable metal and goods. We should at least trade with them for the metal first, then kill them."

They focus on a quiet chief, listening. "What is your opinion, Kiana?"

Kiana, an extremely handsome and quick-witted fellow, with an arrogant air, waits a moment, smiling. "Hmm... kill or trade? Trade or kill?" He holds a finger to the wind. "I say we do both, as we see fit. As you know, I have sailed with some of these foreigners and do not see anything inside them, only their ghostly flesh, magical ships, and magnificent cargo. I fear weapons they call *musskets,* sticks with burning sand – which can rip off your arm or leg in one instant. Or cannonballs that roar from the sides of their hulls destroying anything in their path. If we cannot kill them all, we must find a way to get these foreigners in our control."

They consider his advice.

Above the group on the slope, Kamehameha

stands with his minister, Lamakua. "My king, they're plotting again about the foreigners."

Kamehameha rubs his chin. "I know. They think I am not aware of their ignorant chatter." He gazes at the giant, green mountains. "I see beyond foreigners – beyond their ships and cargo, beyond even the weapons they bring. Lamakua, sometimes before sleep, I see visions of a very long season of peace and rest. My mother told me to believe that. I have put down the rebellion in the district of Kau on this island. But, many of Kahekili's followers still live there. They give gifts to me, but I know secretly they remain in support of him. Kahekili has stopped fighting for Kau until spring. His sons are not yet powerful enough to take over all the islands, and he is still most feared, reigning over Oahu, Maui, Molokai, and Lani. Such fools! They think I cannot beat him. Idiots. I will prove them wrong. I will kill him myself."

3

The Eleanora

American Brigantine and Captain Metcalfe

The sea slaps against a ship's hull. The *Eleanora*, rests in calm water. It is a half-moon night, 1790, in the harbor at Ma-a-lea Bay on the island of Maui.

The *Eleanora* is a merchant ship out of Boston, and her crew has the misfortune of being captained by an American tyrant, Simon Metcalfe, a man marked for tragedy. He's taken care of the *Eleanora* just enough to keep her seaworthy, and the crew has been hammered by him from Boston

10

to Shanghai. They are eager to get home and out of his sight.

One of the most anxious, Seaman Dolph Peters, is on watch in a skiff off the starboard. As the moon charms the waters around him, Peters composes a poem in his mind for his beloved Irish lass back in Belfast. So mesmerized is he by dancing moonbeams on the bay and evening seabirds, so caught is he in a memory of the soft erotic embrace of his wife, he doesn't hear a canoe of natives as it slices through the water behind him. He doesn't feel the chill of death approach. His eyes sparkle as his mind snatches a rhyme to aid his stumbling metaphor as sea sirens sing and palms sway in the wind. The attack upon him is done so quickly his soul is still dancing with his lass when death cuts in.

The natives shove the body into the bottom of the skiff and slice the line. Peters' fingers twitch and create a small wake in the moonlit bay as the skiff is towed toward shore.

Inside the *Eleanora*, the drunken crew enjoys an overdue rest.

Their lanterns cast an amber glow on the dark backs of the natives as they move away through the bay. The skiff, glides behind the natives' canoe and disappears from sight as sailors onboard begin a frisky shanty:

Ohhhh, when laddies go a fishin, son,
then ladies go a–courting…
And courtin' ladies ever sigh
'til every man be done–in…
Har, har, hee, hee…

The lusty ditty floats on moonbeams into Peters' dying mind.

A loud-mouthed sailor onboard complains about Metcalfe's ban on native women. Several sailors bang tankards on the table. "After all these months, Metcalfe himself should feel the loss of tasty sweets of women in these waters – he is a bloody bag of wind with his ridiculous rules!"

Captain Simon Metcalfe is in his cabin in a quiet panic about his sister ship, the *Fair American,* a schooner he left his young son in charge of as captain. Metcalfe is prepared to sail at any moment. He fears something must have happened.

In the middle of a storm on the way from Shanghai, Metcalfe's son, Thomas, an eighteen-year-old well-meaning innocent, agreed to meet in a bay in the Hawaiian Islands. His father, Simon, is convinced the meeting place shouted back by his son across the high waves was "Keala-ke-kua Bay on the island of Hawaii", but since the *Fair American* has not yet appeared, he is now confused

John Young

about which bay to sail to next. Not willing to admit his puzzlement, he has come to Ma-a-lea Bay on Maui from Kealakekua, but still no sign of the *Fair American*. Not sure of the best action, Metcalfe pours over maps and charts. His patient and trustworthy English Bo'sun, John Young, has orders to keep things quiet.

Young has been the only equalizing force on the two ships during this entire voyage. He's a wise and hearty middleweight of forty, with an honest face and piercing gaze. John sits in his cabin, calmed by a time of solace, while the men enjoy their rum. His mind drifts out on the high seas as he reads what he has just written.

Bo'sun's personal log, Jan. 17, 1790,
MA-A-LEA BAY, MAUI,
Sandwich Isles, Hawaii

I dream Captain's dreams. It is not that I find my position on this ship of Bo'sun unsatisfactory, but even as a boy, I dreamed continuously of being at the helm of a ship, sailing to beautiful islands and fighting sea battles. Those boydreams were foolish – and in them I only sailed to dream islands.

They did not prepare me for the truth of the worlds and strange souls I have encountered.

*God has guided me to many shores of mysteries I
cannot fathom. The flowers in my stiff English
child dreams were never pulsing red as they
do on this side of the world – the waters never
shimmered turquoise, and people were never so
generous and innocent as I find these to be in
my life as a mariner.*

Nor was I prepared for the eyes of the females.

*My boy's dreams left me sweating with panic,
raising my sword and fighting monsters on land
and sea; but I know now, the monsters are in
the flesh of a man, and in his mind and soul.
They need forgiveness of the Almighty.*

*However, I made my choice of this life in
great oceans. They are for me as land is to
others. Had I done my father's will and become
a professor of medicine, I would have no doubt
impaled myself upon my surgical instruments or
at least heaved them out the nearest window as
I ran to the shore. I reflect upon this day of my
birth, many years, deep waters and continents
later, I should perhaps have more complaints,
and many would think me daft, but not having
encountered anything more unsettling than
storms, diseases, surly crewmates, angry natives,
curious women, and gnats, I find myself more
desirous than ever of exploring all the new*

*horizons ahead in my goal of Captain. This
world is so strangely peopled I hunger to know
all its secrets. I devoutly wish to soon command
my own ship. Once back in London or even
Boston, I will earnestly seek it.*

*Post Script. A thought of Nottingham.
Perhaps becoming a Captain would finally
make my father and what few relatives I have
left somewhat content, and possibly even a bit
puffed up on account of it.*

A knock at Young's cabin door pulls him from his log. "Sir, the skiff – Peters – And the line cut, sir!" is all that muffles through. Young closes his journal. Moments later, John steps onto the deck. "You say Peters' line was cut?"

The old seaman limps to the starboard side. "Yes, sir. See, a clean cut. No sign of the skiff or Peters." Several other sailors walk up, concerned.

Young swears under his breath and pounds the railing. "I'll tell the Captain. Get back to your posts."

Captain Metcalfe, half-dressed, storms on deck. "Mister Young, what is this? More chaos? Can we not change a watch without raising the dead?"

Young hauls up the skiff's cut line. "Peters has disappeared, sir. And the skiff. See?"

Metcalfe's right hand flexes, his jaw clenches. "Bloody hell. Send a party." Young is dubious. "I think Peters would be the last man to desert, sir. He's happily wed and a good father." Metcalfe snorts. "I've seen happier husbands toss away wife, children and all manner of life for these women. Take three men. Be quick, Mister Young." Metcalf stares into the night. He tries to shake off a bad feeling. "Always something new to stab ya – wooden-headed sailors – or savages. Blast…"

4

Kamehameha Naked at Pu-u-ko-hola

At the king's temple, dawn has not broken. In the darkness, the tall, impressive figure moves up the lane. Scores of bodies fall before him in rapid succession of obeisance. The predominant sounds are the king's feet on leaves as dozens of bodies land. The koa'e bird screeches at the arrival of the massive royal presence at the temple gates.

After gates close, his subjects lift their heads and feel the rush of quiet joy after danger has passed.

In the temple, the king stands silent, staring at the wooden image of his war god, Ku-Ka-ili-mo-ku. He gazes into the god's huge open mouth, a powerful grimace lined with teeth, framed by horrible extended eyes and massive headdress. He kneels. "Yes, my sacred guide, you are my strength and you will make my army fierce. We will bring great honor to your name as *snatcher of islands*. But, I am weak before you. My heart is no match for you."

He removes his thick, bright yellow feather cape and stands up, all seven feet, naked in the first glow of dawn. With eyes closed, his mind searches the void seeking the voice of his god. He is the highest royal Ali'i leader of his people on this island – agile, supple, entirely fearless, except in the presence of his deity. His eyes pop open, dark pools of peril set in a rocky countenance fissured with battle wounds, framed by plaited-shoulder-length hair. His eyes bore into the fierce image in front of him. Around his neck hang royal ornaments, a walrus tooth gift from a Chinese ship captain surrounded by sharks' teeth, fastened by lengths of human hair. He kneels in the glow of dawn, a phalanx of bold tattoos curve down his back, weaving a pattern with royal designs across his deep, dark brown skin. He removes the necklace.

He rises and walks into a pool, submerging in his bath of purification, a necessary and pleasant ritual, and moves from the water's embrace to the altar. He bows again and speaks, "Naked I come. Now I stand before you my god, stripped of all my trappings of royalty. My heart is bared to you. Fill me with the wisdom and patience of the owl. Give me your searching eyes to see hidden plans of my enemies. Let me see the sure path you have laid before me. Give me the fire of your will. Honor me with your swift arm, your shark's mouth, and the wings of your spirit to see the day of victory. Make me worthy to wield the power of your sacred laws and the shining feather cloak. You can see where I am weak. Punish me, train me, mold me, and fill me with your thunder until your lightning shoots from my spear into the hearts of evil ones, dashing them to pieces before your feet!"

He falls to the ground in humility and awe.

5

Revenge

The next day, on the coast of Maui, Captain Metcalfe in his cabin, charts his course back to the Americas when Young knocks. "Enter," Metcalfe roars. Young steps in.

"Where is he?"

"Captain, we have searched. Shores north and south reveal nothing. No one in the village seems to have any knowledge of the skiff or Peters."

"I am not fooled. Blast. We can't find our sister ship and now this?"

Young is cautious. "It has a bad look to it, sir. Rutgers is still questioning the chief and his men. We think they are hiding something."

"It's far more than petty thievery now, Mister Young. Remember Cook, Lad. It started like this. They caught him weak. And I won't have it." He grabs his waistcoat and heads for the cabin door. "They will not fool this captain. Call all hands."

As Young and Metcalfe arrive on deck, Rutgers returns with other sailors in the punt.

Metcalfe growls from the railing, "What did you find?"

"Sir, they say they know nothing."

Metcalfe peers through his scope at the chief and those assembled on shore. They smile and wave. A sailor stands near one of his small cannon. "Load that and prepare to fire."

The sailor loads the cannon.

Young offers. "Sir, let me go ashore. I will warn them their village could suffer destruction if they don't help us. I am sure that will get results."

Another sailor grabs a lamp and lights a tip of rope. "Where should I aim, sir?"

Metcalfe studies the villagers through his scope. "I know what will get results. Fire at that hut. Fire!"

The cannon blast splinters the side of a hut. Natives shout and run for cover.

"That should get results." Metcalfe gloats.

A brief silence. All eyes watch the hut, now

ripped apart by the blast. It is a silence that will last far longer in the memory of John Young.

A woman staggers out of the hut, screaming as she carries the lifeless body of a small child, covered in blood. Young closes his eyes. The woman collapses on the shore.

Metcalfe barks, "Young! Now go talk. I am sure I've piqued their interest. Tell them there are more cannon balls if we don't get answers. Bloody murdering thieves."

Young and several men hold muskets and push off in the punt.

Once onshore Young hurries to the chief. He and another sailor speak in broken Hawaiian. The chief speaks and gestures in panic.

Shortly after, Young arrives on board, stunned.

Metcalfe barks, "Are ya dumb, man? What?"

Young gathers himself. "They heard only rumors, sir. I told them we had to get the truth or their village may suffer more harm. Then they asked would it be enough to save them for us to 'get *part of* the skiff'. I pressed them further. They said they had been told the skiff was torn up for nails, sir."

"Torn up? *For nails?* What about Peters?"

"After that a kahuna said he was quite sure they could bring back 'some of Peters' clothes', sir."

Metcalfe's eyes widen. "Some of his – what? Who did he say has done this? Who?"

"Some men from Olowalu, the next village north of here." Sweat drips from Young's face.

Metcalfe's fist slams on a barrel. "You believe him? You sure?"

John sighs. "I suggest we go to Olowalu, sir, and offer a reward for some distinguishing item of Peter's. Otherwise they could incriminate themselves out of greed for a reward."

Metcalfe squints toward the villagers. "Killing my shipmen for *nails*?"

Young adds, "To make weapons. I think we are caught in preparations for a war here."

"War? They shall have it, by God." Metcalfe fumes. "We sail to Olowalu. Call all hands, Mister Young."

Behind undergrowth, two trusted spies of Kamehameha study the men on the *Eleanora*.

Wakana, the higher authority with sharper eye, taps his partner, Makena. "I wish we could go in the village. I know the burning log was sent onto shore. But, I cannot see where it landed. Can you understand any of what they are speaking?"

Makena checks in his scope. "They speak too fast. Their language is hard enough when they speak slowly, but this is gibberish. They must have aimed at villagers. Is there some way to help those on shore without revealing we are king's men?"

Wakana stands. "Look – they are setting sail. We must watch them, then get to Lamakua by nightfall to tell the king - not go in the village. The king will have us killed if we admit why we have come. Hurry, they catch the wind."

The village of Olowalu is a cauldron of activity as the *Eleanora* sails into view. Men in canoes have just brought in a fine harvest of fish. All help get it on shore.

Children tussle and splash in the water. Women weave mats on the edge of the beach. They talk and giggle.

A man runs onto the shore from his canoe. He calls to the group hauling fish, "Get ready! A big ship comes. They will trade with us! They called to me from my canoe. But, you must return clothes of the foreigner to them. They will even give us a reward. They say they understand how it happened and are desperate for provisions. But, we must give them the oyster man's clothes to make sure they get what they are looking for."

The ship sails into the harbor and an anchor is

thrown. The sailors call out to the villagers, who clamor into canoes.

Metcalfe calls from the ship, "Trade. Meki. Meki. Reward!"

A sailor questions Young under his breath, "Is he not going to question them first?"

Before Young can reply, Metcalfe comes between them. He shouts and gestures to the villagers to paddle to the ship. "Meki! Reward!"

Young and several sailors look away, refusing to join in deceiving the villagers.

Canoes laden with joyful natives head toward the starboard side. The women wear and carry bright yellow and pink flower leis.

The lead canoe has two men, one holds high a huge flat basket with something protruding from it. Dolph Peters' crumpled brown hat perched atop a pole completes the chilling vision. Metcalfe's sneer freezes. He puts the scope to his eye.

Young is dubious. "What is it, sir?"

Metcalfe's eyes tighten. "That is what's left of Peters... a basket of bones and a hat." He hands the scope to Young. "See for yerself, Mister Young. Now where is yer grand 'understanding'? Who would they be hauling off next, aye, boys, if we don't teach 'em a lesson?"

Young looks through the scope. Hairs on the

back of his neck rise as his mind weaves a macabre scene he would like to crush. He fears the worst. He hands the scope to Metcalfe. "We offered a reward, sir, those could be any bones."

Metcalfe rages. "Have we not proof warriors from here stole that skiff, Mister Young?"

"Yes, sir. But, if we investigate we might find other facts."

Metcalfe waves to the natives, now very close. Young imagines blood spurting from beautiful brown bodies. Metcalfe demands, "Smile, dammit. You told them the larboard is kapu, right?"

Young urges. "Sir, what if they did not kill Peters? What if someone else did?"

Metcalfe growls. "Mister Young, the first man resisting will be flogged for insolence." He waves to the natives. "Aloha. Aloha! Reward. Come." He mumbles, "Savage demons."

Out of sight of the Hawaiians on the starboard side, sit the cannons. Sailors crouch behind them in readiness. The natives' canoes begin to swarm round the starboard side. They paddle into the trap. At least fifty are within range.

The exuberant natives in the first canoe hold the wrapped pile of remains up higher for the Captain to see.

Metcalfe signals the cannon. "Fire!" *Boom.*

The *Eleanora*'s broadside blasts four guns at once.

Young watches in horror. In his mind, the musket balls and langrage shot seem to move through the air, slowed by strings of his heart which yearn in vain for the deadly weapons to miss their mark. The images of unsuspecting faces of natives in shock and fear will roll forever in his memory like hungry sharks, even to the days of his dying.

The natives in the middle canoes shatter in a fountain of flesh, wood, and bright red blood. Young closes his eyes.

Metcalfe raises his hand. "Again. Fire!"

Boom. Cannons blast. Natives in droves are hit with more cannon balls. They howl and die in the water. Survivors paddle in panic, to turn round as fast as they can. Some sailors shout insults, but most look away. Chaos reigns as natives dodge the blasts and head for shore, bloody and mangled.

Metcalfe shouts, "That's for Peters, ya thieving bastards! You want iron? There's iron for ya. Right in yer guts. Cast off. Hoist away lads. Set sail for the *Fair American.* The price is paid."

Young hangs his head, sickened by the devastation.

Red flower petals drift onto the water in the

bloody bay. They land near a hand cutting a red wake. The hand is connected to a small, lifeless native girl as she floats in the current. Her long hair bobs up and down in the outgoing tide. The *Eleanora* catches the wind.

Branches are brought back together as they reveal the hand of Wakana, the messenger. He whispers to his partner as tears course down his face, "…we must get to the king…"

6

The Fair American

Kona Bay, Island of Hawaii

A ribbon of sun glitters across the Kona Bay on the island of Hawaii, where the missing schooner, the *Fair American*, is becalmed, halted in its efforts to meet its sister ship, the *Eleanora*. A pin-eyed petrel seabird luffs near then settles onto a yardarm. The bird stares at the men, like a patient spirit of death. He watches the sailors mend a sail.

The mariners glance up for any sign of a breeze. They return to their work and listen along with an old salt, Thackary, as a sailor tells a tale.

Isaac Davis, is a Welsh mariner of low rank, thirty-six, shy, handsome, and muscular, with a shock of black, curly hair. His voice is edged with warmth, and as he talks, his aqua blue eyes sparkle as much as the sun dances on the water in the bay.

"So, when I first heard the story in the Bible of Father Abraham and his son Isaac, I was horrified the Almighty would exact such obedience. My heart was with Isaac, him being my namesake. What must have gone through his mind as his father's knife was raised? You see, Thack, now I've taught myself reading, I read this again and again and I find it the clearest image of our complete powerlessness in the face of our Maker. To me, He is like...the wind." He looks up. "Who knows where it comes from? Or why it can be gone so quickly?"

"No one knows, lad, but I need no reminder it has gone!" Thackary snorts.

Davis searches the horizon. "If I do all I can to better myself to go up from seaman. If one day I stand on the deck as a first mate, I would feel a blessed man. But, my greater goal now must be to listen for the call, as terrible as it might be, to go up the mountain of God and perhaps lay my most precious possession on His altar."

Thackary's face cracks into a wry smile. "That's a thought, lad. Yer most precious possession? Would that not be yer volume of Shakes-beere?"

"Yes. I value it highly. But, next to the word of the Lord, my wife and my honor are most precious to me." Davis scowls. "We should be half-way to England now, not lookin' for the bloody *Eleanora.* Old Metcalfe's likely gone to Maui to cheat some more natives and not one thought of us. I have no kind words for him. But, if it weren't that his son was such a an honorable young Captain and I need to get home so badly, I would have jumped ship in Shanghai."

Thackary glances toward the young captain who stands at the helm out of earshot. "He's alright, young Metcalfe, but not a captain yet. He's a good heart, just doesn't know much. I'll be glad to be free of 'em both. Him and his slimy father."

Captain Thomas Metcalfe, Simon's son, shouts to Isaac Davis, "Any sign of the *Eleanora*?"

"No, sir. And not a whisper of wind."

A grizzled sailor calls as he repairs rigging, "The *Eleanora* is a hearty ship. It would take a lot more than that storm to get her. She's probably also becalmed in a bay nearby." He wipes sweat off his neck.

Isaac Davis

Young Thomas Metcalfe wanders near and listens as the bird takes flight.

"Yes. Very likely." Thackary chuckles and points to the sky. "Hey, Isaac, was that an albatross?"

Isaac squints. "No, just a hefty plover.

A burly man calls, fueled by fear, "Shut yer face with damned talk of *albatrosses.* Bringin' bad luck on us."

Thackary bellows, "Oh, be glad we have a chance to repair the damage from the storm." He approaches the young captain, "Sir, I heard yer Captain father yell to us through the gale we were to meet at Kona Bay. This bay and the little Kona are the only two on this side of the Island. We could be very close to them, sir."

A sanguine seaman shouts to Young Metcalfe. "Yer father–I mean, Captain-the-elder—is a hardy sot, sir. Perhaps the pleasures of a native girl are keeping him."

Young Thomas Metcalfe ignores this and drifts away.

Davis confronts the seaman. "Mister Laird, those opinions would do better stayin' in yer stringy mind, sir."

Laird stares him down. "If you weren't so intent upon betterin' yerself, Mister Davis, reading all that Shakes-beere, you might not be such a pigfart."

Davis bristles. "Thank you for including me, sir. I was under the impression you were the only pigfarting man among us."

Laird lunges for Davis, but Davis lands the first punch.

The sailor is knocked flat on the deck, but is halfway back up to launch again when a sailor shouts from the mainmast, "Canoes off larboard, Captain."

Davis and Laird abandon their fight to watch several canoes head for their schooner. Other sailors arrive at the railing. Thomas Metcalfe grabs his telescope to study the natives.

A seaman assures Davis. "Don't see any weapons. Friendly appearance."

Thomas orders Davis, "Mister Davis, load water barrels. Stand by. I will talk to them first."

Davis grabs the first barrel and tosses it into the dinghy.

One of the natives yells to the crew, "Aloha a Kona. Ali'i send welcome to mokuJ. Water - wai? Food?"

The lead islander matches his expression to the warm smiles of the other natives.

Young Thomas Metcalfe leans over the side. "Yes. Water. I am Kapene Thomas Metcalfe. Water – wai – close? Kokoke?"

The natives seem impressed with Thomas's knowledge of their language. "Yes Kapene, on side Mauna-pa-pali."

Thomas is confused. A sailor steps forward. "He says on the slope of the mountain, sir." The natives gesture for them to come. Thomas hails the Bo'sun, "McCuffy, you and Billings take the first watch. We will come back before sundown."

Thomas, Davis, Laird, and three other seamen leave in the dinghy and follow the natives in canoes.

As the *Fair American* slips from view, Isaac Davis ponders. *I should have taken another musket in case...* A lazy dolphin takes his thought and runs on a wake with it. *There are three weapons among us, and we each have knives if any trouble comes.* His mind relaxes.

An hour later, on a steep trail up the mountain, Davis sweats under the weight of the water barrel he carries.

"A damn bloody hike," the sailor in front of Davis tosses back to him.

He groans and lifts his eyes. "Something ahead." They come upon vast temple grounds at the edge of a cliff. The wind hits them with a blast. Davis is grateful. Sweat pours into his eyes.

Seven rock levels of the temple rise before them. The tallest is equivalent of a two-story structure. The pristine coast looms into view. Davis is astounded at its beauty. The wind is filled with perfume of plumeria blossoms, and at once the load Isaac carries feels lighter.

Young Captain Thomas Metcalfe smiles as he sees a man who appears to be the chief of the village. Several priests stand nearby, all with expressions of warm welcome. The voice of the chief sails out over the group, "The gods have brought you!"

Thomas steps toward him, as the others stay behind. "Greetings. I am Kapene Thomas Metcalfe from the *Fair American*, sister ship to the *Eleanora* from Boston."

Seeing a chance to rest, the sailors put their barrels down. As they do, from all sides at once, warriors descend on them, beating them with clubs.

Cudgels land on Thomas first. The look of surprise on his face as he spins and falls, will haunt Davis often in later years. He reaches for his pistol, but the next moment is a blur as he is hit. The other sailors attempt to fight, but are outnumbered as natives explode upon them, filling the air with shouts of rage.

Davis, with his last shred of wits, smashes his barrel into several warriors. They scatter, but only briefly. He seizes this chance and runs into the brush. So excited is the chief and priests to be clubbing the captain of the white ship and hoisting young Metcalfe in the air, the order to go after Davis is delayed enough to give him a head start.

The wind howls as sailors' bodies are thrown into a pile.

The chants of the priests and the last cries of Davis' mates mingle in his ears as he runs for his life down the mountain. *Why did I not watch better, listen to my hunch? Thackary was right, Metcalfe was too young.*

Davis registers chunks of his skin being ripped as he hurls himself through thickets and brambles back toward the ship. From somewhere close behind him, he hears natives call to each other as if in a spat about who will get him first. He gasps for breath, sees a new path and hurls himself down it. He runs, stumbles, and rolls his way through the undergrowth. The bay appears through the trees. His mind spins. He jerks off his shirt, leaping forward.

7

Hell Bay

The sun slides lower on the horizon as McCuffy tosses his knife into the center of a chalk circle. He watches Billings swab the already double-clean deck, bored, anxious for the others to return.

From behind them, natives push off from the shore in a canoe.

Davis dashes from the undergrowth at the side of the bay and rushes toward the water. He stumbles across the jagged terrain and dives in.

Moments later, two warriors arrive from the underbrush at the rocky shore. "Look. He's swimming," one warrior shouts.

"He'll sink. Oystermen can't swim. They always die in the water."

This was true. Most sailors couldn't swim. Swimming however, was one of the few unique abilities Davis had always prided himself on – a result of encouragement from a Scottish uncle who made him stroke through icy lochs in his youth. Davis gains speed.

"You fools," a third warrior cries out. "He's getting away. Get the canoe." He dives in after Davis as the other two hurry down the side of the rocks to the shore.

Davis lunges forward like a porpoise and looks over his shoulder to see a warrior not far behind. He shouts with all he can muster, "Billings! Billings!"

Billings, coils a line at the stern, hears muffled shouts, but cannot tell from where.

The two warriors in the canoe skim over the bay toward Davis, now at a reef. He climbs on it, determined to run to the end of the point where he can jump off and head for the ship. He leaps across the volcanic rock and winces as the soles of his feet are shredded by sharp lava.

Davis can see the *Fair American* and even make out Billings, but the pain in his feet slows him down. A sideways glance confirms the swimming warrior lags behind, but other warriors in the canoe are closing in.

He stumbles and calls into the wind, waving his hands, "Billings. Billings. Help!"

Billings stops and looks through his scope, amazed at the sight of Davis, bloody in a silent scream being overpowered and pulled out of view on the point.

"McCuffy, it's Davis under attack!" Billings can't pull himself from the scope. "Mac, look!"

Billings' shout falls on deaf ears. His blood turns to ice seeing McCuffy slumped over the railing. That sensation is the last he feels as his throat is cut. Several natives crawl over the rail and onto the deck.

Thackary returns topside and yells, "What's all the caterwaulin'?"

From behind him, two natives grab his arms, as another strangles him with a rope. The beautiful piece of whalebone he had carved flies from his hands and bounces onto the deck. The sound of bodies splashing over the side of the ship mingle with indifferent screams of gulls overhead. All is quiet.

8

The King's Consort

A most formidable, attractive and powerful young woman, Ka'a-humanu, the highest royal Ali'i daughter in the Hawaiian kingdom, sits on a large tapa mat on a ledge by the sea on the island of Kauai. Her warm brown eyes are her loveliest feature and just now sparkle with delight. She is mischievous, as well as being riddled with a grand wit, passion and intelligence. Her easy confidence is woven with a silvery laugh as she regales her handmaids with a favorite tale. She carves a beautiful pattern on a wooden block, one to be inked and multiplied onto tapa cloth similar to what adorns her ample dark brown body.

Ka'ahumanu, queen consort

All around her, women make flower lei necklaces like ones already hanging round their necks in fountains of bright petals perfumed with scents of plumeria, pikake and ginger.

"No, it is very true. From the time I was five-years-old I was promised to Kamehameha. He had twenty years then and was one of the most fierce warriors in the islands. He could catch spears thrown at him at great speed – catch them in mid-air and throw them back at his attackers with the swiftness of a hawk."

An older royal aunt laughs. "We heard of these things, but I thought maybe those stories to be 'enhanced' perhaps like the size of fish, or a male member."

A burst of laughter fills the air.

Ka'ahumanu is annoyed. "Oh no, the stories of his prowess are all too true. Unfortunately for me, even ones about his anger are true. You do not want to feel his anger." On the heels of this confession, a delicious twinkle rolls across her eyes. "Ah...but, when I stood on a hill with my father as a young girl watching him fight, I could not breathe, he was so powerful, I fell into a faint."

The group erupts with more female amusement.

"My brothers picked me up and teased me. I have never been the same since that day. I am sixteen now and he still takes my breath away. But, in spite of his power over me, I am the owner of Great Kamehameha's heart. Do not be fooled. I don't know why the gods have given me this sway over him, but there is not one woman in this sea, who can make him as happy as I can. In this I am quite sure."

One of the handmaids takes some bright yellow petals and tosses them into the pond nearby as she challenges Ka'ahumanu, "I think we would all agree, but will Kamehameha fight Kahekili after the Makahiki harvest?"

Ka'ahumanu sighs and gazes up at clouds as if reading the future. "If that scorpion, Kahekili, will take the white stone, then Kamehameha will leave him alone for a while. But, if he takes the black stone, Kamehameha will gladly go to fight him. And we will win this time."

The others chime in, "How can you be so sure? Kahekili has many more men and has won so many battles. He is terrifying."

Ka'ahumanu tosses down her work in a rage. "You are all so foolish. He has no fear. Do you understand? When there is no fear, anything may be accomplished. Even if there were fear, he would overcome it. That is the highest form of courage, is it not?"

The women, stung and intimidated, fall silent.

Ka'ahumanu rises and strides down the slope. Her powerful spirit seems to affect even the breeze around her. As she walks along the shore, the adoring wind lifts and flutters her coverings then swirls ever upward, high above her.

It careens past the peaks of Kauai, past massive green towers of thick vegetation, past churning waters of the channel, races along the high cliffs to the slopes of Maui's Haleakala crater, then curves over to Hawaii's volcano peak, Mauna Loa.

Both mountain peaks loom high above thick cloudbanks like two kings locked in a deadly stand-off. A frigate bird screams.

9

Valley of the Kings,
Island of Hawaii

The frigate bird descends, swooping into a clump of palms on a slope where many chiefs sit listening to Kamehameha on the island of Hawaii. The bird sits in stoic silence, observing the massive warrior addressing the assembly.

Kamehameha's eyes probe the soul of every man. "I will send news by the full moon. When the battle comes, you will know as thunder follows lightning. Then you must leave in an instant. You have prepared for this battle all winter. You have prepared for it all your lives. My friends, this is our time, we must seize it. We must take all the islands or die as slaves of Kahekili."

Guards on the perimeter shout, "Wakana and Makena return from Maui." The two messengers run to the center of the council and fall prostrate.

"Our king. Our King…" they moan, facing the dust.

Lamakua the king's minister, steps forward. He is a thin man seasoned with many more years than Kamehameha, but has the demeanor of a wise and thoughtful servant. "Quickly. Good news or bad, Wakana?"

Wakana howls, "Bad, my king, for the people at Olowalu. Many die. Oystermen threw fire on their canoes from logs in the side of their ship. Blood flowing in the water, little ones wander, crying…" He cannot finish.

Shocked voices crackle through the council of chiefs. They are hushed as Kamehameha lifts his hand. "I see the gods have judged the people of Maui for serving Kahekili and his thick-headed sons. They warn us with this news against such a fate. We must act to defend our people here." Kamehameha gestures to Lamakua. "Let the messengers rest. Feed them. We will hear more later."

Attendants take Wakana and Makena away.

Kamehameha looks out to sea. Lamakua comes near. "There is more to this. I feel it, Lamakua. Much more. Who are these foreigners? We must find them, and punish them."

Lamakua is silent, yet his eyes meet the kings in silent agreement.

Kamehameha leaves the area.

Lamakua, stares down. The council, stunned, waits for his opinion. He cannot think of anything to say.

10

Floating Coffin

The ghost schooner, the *Fair American*, floats in the rising tide in the wide Kona bay. Nearby, warriors drag Davis onshore as they strangle and beat him with heavy clubs, grunting in their task. One man jumps on Davis' neck, trying to break it. But, somehow Davis continues to breathe as blood spurts from his mouth.

A conch horn trumpets from behind the assailants. Seeing their chief, they prostrate themselves. Davis' bloody body thuds onto the sand.

The chief of Kailua and a group of his attendants move closer to the white man. The chief studies Davis. "They say this man has the spirit of a fish. They saw him swimming, which is rare for the oyster beings. The gods may be with him." He peers down close to Isaac's face.

Davis struggles to focus on the chief, who leans even closer. Davis whispers, "I… friend… maika'i… good…maika'i. I maka la-una…please… a'ohe…" His head drops, his mouth open as he chokes.

The Kailua chief looks at Davis for a long moment then says into his ear, "Aloha Kaua *We may be friends.*" He rises and pronounces his judgment, "I will send this foreigner to the gods. They will decide. If they send him back, he is a friend and is to live. Go."

Davis's bleeding body is placed in a canoe. Small images of gods are put in with him. The warriors scoop some salt water with coconut shells and splash it on his wounds as they shove the canoe into the bay. The vessel catches the tide and floats toward the sunset.

Hours later, fingers of light from the last of the sun caress Davis' still body as the canoe moves further out to sea. Trickles of his blood create a shiny red pool below his mouth as he murmurs, "Forgive my trespasses…as I…forgive… forgive…"

11

Kealakekua Bay, Hawaii

Drums beat from the king's temple as priests complete their dawn ceremony.

A small boy, Opa, lame, but clever, shouts as he stumbles on the rocks for a better look, "Foreigners. Look. They come!"

The head kahunas of the village stare out to sea, concerned.

The *Eleanora* at full sail swiftly enters the bay, south of Kona. On the deck, John Young shouts orders to the crew as Metcalfe grins, confident his savagery at Olowalu was proper revenge for the demise of Peters. He has returned to the urgent search for his son's ship.

Captain Metcalfe muses, "So, I reckon somewhere in this large bay is the very spot where the fine and noble Captain Cook was killed in a short, bloody attack eleven years ago. Monsters."

John Young sings out, "Trim the mainmast - Knot those lines!"

Metcalfe approaches Young. "Mr. Young, if you are going ashore, best be about it and be back. I'll take over now."

Young grabs a leather pouch and hurries to the side. "Yes, sir. Thank you, sir. I'll return by dawn."

Metcalfe stops him. "Again, who is this native here in Kona village?"

Young climbs down the ladder to a skiff, "A sailor and carver, sir. When we stopped on the way to Canton, I made his acquaintance. He is very trustworthy."

Metcalfe scowls and pins him with his gaze. "Remember, Mister Young, the reason to be ashore is to find out what you can about the *Fair American*. With this size village, someone has likely seen the ship or heard of where they have anchored. Find out what you can."

Young salutes. "Yes, sir, if I hear anything, I'll return at once."

From a distance, Opa, the strange boy, chews at his thumb in excitement as he peers at the skiff bearing Young pulling onshore. He runs with others to meet it.

Mana'oi, a middle-aged Hawaiian, waits with many natives on the beach.

Young catches Mana'oi's eye and yells, "Mana'oi. Aloha. Aloha!" Young leaps into shallow water and greets Mana'oi in a handshake.

Mana'oi's gentle eyes are overpowered by his toothy, white smile. "Aloha, Bo'sun John. You are well, my friend, I hope?"

Young grabs him in another handshake. "Yes, yes, well – and I see you are."

They move up the beach, natives crowding them. As Young enters the village, he doesn't notice the studied behavior of the villagers who watch his every move.

Mana'oi and Young approach Mana'oi's hut.

Young stops at the entrance. "Mana'oi, has there been news of a ship? It's our sister ship, remember? A schooner, the *Fair American*?"

At the name of the ship, the villagers stiffen, but Young is oblivious.

Mana'oi responds with a smile, "Oh, Bo'sun John, no moku. Only when you came last with Kapene Med-caff."

Young explains, "Remember, we came through in spring on way from America to China. We have two ships and we traded here in Kailua Kona. There was a second ship. Smaller."

Mana'oi nods. "Ae, yes Bo'sun John. We trade. Ships go Canton."

Young switches in and out of Hawaiian as he becomes confused and uses more gestures. "You say you have not seen the *Fair American*, the smaller moku, since then? No people here talk of seeing a ship, a moku, since last moon? That ships' captain is Kapene Metcalfe's son, Keiki-kane, we cannot find moku in any of the bays here."

"No moku, Bo'sun John, no ship." Mana'oi' offers Young to enter his hut.

Wakana and Makena, Kamehameha's spies, watch from a distance. Mana'oi glances to them and back to Young as he disappears through the door.

Inside, woodcarvings hang on every side of the hut. Young forgets his mission. "Mana'oi, marvelous! You do all this? How very fine. Truly."

"Bo'sun John, you not see." He holds up a pouch. "I make much carvings like you show me game on ship."

Young pulls out of his pouch scrimshaw pieces of whalebones and shark's teeth he's crafted, along with necklaces and tiny boxes. "These are some I worked on during this China voyage."

"Nani. Much nani. Ah, no – English say *pretty*?"

Gentle laughter of women drifts from the back of the hut.

"That is right, *pretty* is a great word, Mana'oi'."

Mana'oi scowls at the women's laughter. "We go soon to my eating hut."

He opens a wooden box. "This I make when you go Canton, to give if you come back." He lifts out chess pieces made of monkey pod. They are carved as Hawaiian royalty and commoners. "You be chest warrior. But, I make these from Ali'i kings Hawaii."

Young handles the pieces with awe. Mana'oi hands him a bishop. It resembles a Hawaiian priest, a kahuna. "Mana'oi, you have been practicing this game?"

"Chest be like Hawaii game Ko-na-ne. See? King, Kahuna, Warrior, Commoner."

"We say *Pawn* for a commoner," Young offers.

Mana'oi repeats, "*Pawn.*"

"I have never seen such work, Mana'oi. Magnificent."

Mana'oi points to an exquisitely carved king. "This Kamehameha, Ali'i king this Island."

Young picks up a piece. "Ah…Another king instead of a Queen. What king this?"

Mana'oi's eyes narrow. "This Ka-he-kili, king

O-wha-who, Mowee, Ka-wa-ie, Molokai, Lanai. Very much power, always make war!"

Young changes the subject. "A grand gift – yes – priests, commoners, like knights and pawns. You make this sailor very happy. Many hours Aloha with this. Mahalo, Mana-oi, thank you. Maik-e – good friend."

Mana'oi offers his hand. "We go to eating hut."

Much later, moonbeams bounce on the shore of the bay. Waves slap. Several men sneak on the other side of the bay. A dog trots through the village.

The silvery back of a dolphin breaks the surface about a mile from the shore, near a tiny vessel. The canoe bears Isaac Davis. It bounces from wave to wave. There is no movement inside. The dolphin breaches and disappears.

In his friends hut, Young sleeps. Across the room in the shadows, Mana'oi crawls toward him, in great effort. A moment later, Mana'oi's hand covers John's mouth. He jumps awake in fear.

Mana'oi holds him down. "Bo'sun John. No speak. All dead. *Fair Amer- i–can*, all dead." Young stares at him, his eyes growing wide.

Mana'oi nods. He believes John understands and releases his grip, but his words like arrows dive into John's flesh as he whispers, "John, you live, you go now. Wiki-wiki anone. Danger." He gives John a small cudgel and points outside. "Bo'sun John, no speak. Warriors come. I send chest to ship. Go!"

Young crawls to the other side of the hut led by Mana'oi, who gestures toward an escape.

"Bless you," Young whispers and slips into the night.

Mana'oi, his hut, and the village disappear into the dark. Clouds race and cover the moon. Young gets his bearings and creeps down the trail.

Back in his hut, Mana'oi stares at dark shadows on the carved chess set in the moonlight. The figures look evil, foreboding. He begins to sing very low, a chant for his friend.

I fly to thy shrine, O, Kane, Approachable One
Let my friend be secure in your care
Grant him passage through night
Kana-hoa-lani, watch him to safety.

12

Fortune's Fools

The next day, amid the thick, dark green hills north of Kona, a small band of warriors carry what appears to be a large animal tied on a long pole. As the party moves along the path, Makena spots something in the lagoon below. He shouts to Wakana "Looks like a canoe. Something in it. No village there. I see no one fishing."

Wakana squints to see the contents of the canoe. "We can take our rest down there and look into it."

Wakana and his men arrive through the palm trees onto the beach.

Makena runs ahead and pulls the canoe ashore.

He finds the body of a bleeding human and turns it over. "A foreigner."

"Where are they all coming from?" Wakana takes a closer look. "Maybe from the other ship?" Warriors crowd around. The body is pulled out onto the sand. It is Davis.

Wakana studies the man. "He breathes. We'll take him along with the other one to the king. Prepare a sled."

At dawn the next day, Metcalf's Brigantine, the *Eleanora* sits in the bay, five miles south, still at Kealakekua. No natives are on shore. Metcalf comes to the rail as two sailors return in a dinghy.

Hastings hollers, "No sign of him, sir. An old man said he's up in the mountains with a woman."

Old Metcalfe glares toward the hills. "Damnation. Another bloody liar. Sound a cannon for him. But, I will not wait long. We must catch the tide."

Hastings is concerned. "But, Sir?"

Metcalfe stares him down. "I'd like to go and find the bastard and flog him but he's costing us time. We must look for the *Fair American.* They seem to be lost. We'll come back in a day or two. Rig out the steering sail booms."

On a mountain path with their prisoners in the Kohala highlands, Wakana, Makena, and their warriors sing as they go. One warrior plays an eerie tune on a mouth harp. A distant sound of a cannon booms.

Davis, on a hand-held sled begins to regain consciousness. He studies the figure on the pole in front of him. It begins to look like a human.

Young, barely distinguishable is wrapped in ropes and cloths, knocked unconscious some miles back in Kona, his mind lost in a sleeping brew.

Davis' struggles to speak, "Good God…"

A guard on watch at a narrow pass sees warriors, and yells to those further up, "Wakana with foreigners. Open the way!"

Pu'ukaloa Village, the home of King Kamehameha in the Kohala Highlands on the Island of Hawaii appears as the pass opens.

From Davis' blurred view, rows of neatly thatched huts dot the landscape as it opens to a wide valley. Fierce ten-foot carved wooden idols stand guard in front of the massive Heiau. Children, pigs, and dogs run and play. Old men round them up and keep them back as the warriors arrive with the two white men. A crowd begins to form.

A group of women tending a garden look up. Kaoana, a royal young chiefess of exquisite beauty, gently gives orders to other women to not stare at the group like idiots. She is unnaturally tall and muscular. Despite the rules, she puts down her work and watches the warriors pass with their strange cargo.

Young, dangles from the pole dazed. He can barely scan the view from upside-down.

Davis is conscious, but in horrible pain.

Kaoana, overcome with curiosity, joins the women to stare.

The party approaches the main temple, which sports three levels of rock, a sacred hut on each level.

Several priests watch the foreigners go by. They are attired in bright crimson and yellow, flowing, decorated robes. One whispers, "What does this mean?"

He is hushed by others. Kahuna Lani, the leading priest, steps out of his hut. He is massive, at least three hundred pounds, in his sixties, a strong-faced man with wise eyes, many colored necklaces and a yellow feather headpiece.

Kahuna Lani's eyes widen. "What is this? Two? We expected only one oysterman."

Wakana justifies, "We found another above Kailua. He must have been from the ship of the dead. Perhaps he will be useful to the king or will die."

Makena points to Young. "That one is not sick. Just angry. We gave him sleeping tea, but he will wake soon."

Kahuna Lani raises his hand. "The king will return at dawn. They are kapu. No one is to speak to them."

In the background, warriors cut Young off the pole. Kindly old women gently lift Davis from the sled. Priests order them away. Young stands and his gag is taken off. He's awake and enraged. He wants to run, but sees Davis carried into a hut and lurches forward. Warriors stop him. He staggers, hands still tied. "Let me talk to that man. Why have you brought us here? We are sailors in Her Majesty's – we are friends. Ho'alohaloha [I am friendly] Please – Ho'alohaloha!"

Wakana defers to the Kahuna, "What's he saying?"

Kahuna Lani snaps back, "Gibberish. Do not talk to them."

Young persuades the Kahuna. "I must get back to my ship. Moku. Moku. I have done no harm. Are we prisoners? For God's sake. Would someone tell me why we are -"

Young grabs Wakana, trying to get his attention.

Kahuna Lani decks Young, who lands like a sack of flour in the dust. "There. You rest now."

He orders Wakana. "You must not tell the King I hit this being. He wants them treated well. Go. Take him in."

Wakana and Makena watch the priests drag Young into the hut, then leave. They go, surrounded by commoners questioning them.

13

Purification

The next day, through a thick fog of steam in Kahuna Lani's purifying hut, John Young's naked body is curled up near a rock wall.

Through another cloud of grey steam, across the hut, Isaac Davis, also naked, begins to come to. He tries to focus, moaning in agony. "My God - what is this?"

A voice meets his through the fog, "Can't help there, I'm afraid."

Davis shakes his head. "Hello?" He crawls toward the voice, barely able to move from pain.

Young reaches through thick mist to find Davis. "Who are you? English?"

Davis' voice cracks, "Seaman, Isaac Davis. Welsh. Mariner, the *Fair American*, out of Boston."

First a hand, then Young emerges through the steam, whispering. "Quiet. Guards outside. All on the *Fair American* are dead. All dead, save you, apparently. I am very sorry, mate."

Davis studies him. "Dead. It is no surprise, sir. I saw many die. You are Mr. Young, the Bo'sun from the *Eleanora*?"

"Yes, if I can get back to it, I might still be." Young rubs his head.

Davis gets closer. "Are they trying to steam us to death?"

"Damned if I can figure." Young sees Davis' head. "Those are bad gashes, Lad."

"From cudgels. Yours not pretty either, mate."

Young rubs his wounded arms from the ropes used to tie him to the pole. "Bloody savages. What happened to you, Mister Davis?"

Davis clears his head. "We put in at North Kona. We couldn't find the *Eleanora*. We knew old Captain Metcalfe had told us to meet at Kealakekua Bay. But, we came in at Kirowah and were becalmed shortly after. The next day, canoes of natives arrive. They were so friendly. No weapons, all smiling - said they were taking us to water. I was carrying a water barrel. I remember thinking there was something strange. I even had thought to take another pistol but, I had to carry a barrel. We were led up a high cliff near a temple. The chief was smiling. Come to think, they all had the most kindly smiles. So, when suddenly they were attacking us from all sides, so many, it was impossible to fight."

A wound reopens on Davis' head and he wipes blood off his face. "Vicious warriors with clubs. I saw young Metcalfe go down first. I was at the end of the line. I dropped my barrel and ran. I thought perhaps I could get back to the ship to get my musket. I don't know about the others."

Davis' eyes connect with Young's. It sinks in. "So, yes. They are dead. All dead…" A deep sadness begins to roll through him, but he refuses to allow it. "I tried to swim to the schooner to warn Billings. But, I saw him go down as I was grabbed from behind. It was a massacre." His head droops. "Evil, murdering bastards. And why? These creatures haven't the least human feeling. Where did they find you? What happened to the *Eleanora*?"

"We were waiting for you at Kealakekua Bay. There was confusion about the *Fair American*. Our man on watch, Peters, disappeared and was killed, apparently just for the metal in the dingy he was in. The Captain went insane. The next day Metcalfe killed many in that village, and we set sail for Kona Bay in hopes the schooner might be there. I asked to go ashore to get information from a native friend who told me in secret about your ship and helped me escape. But, as I left the village, someone thumped me good. All went black." He rubs his neck and leans close to Davis. "Can you walk?"

Before Davis can answer, a cover is thrown off the opening of the hut. Priests enter with Kahuna Lani and grab the naked men. They are carried shouting and fighting out of the steam. Young and Davis, sure of impending death, yell all the way to a pond, where they are tossed in.

Kahuna Lani turns to another priest. "Strange creatures. Good. Now, they will be purified, at least."

The sailors surface. Young can't swim and is terrified. Gasping, he calls to Davis, "What are these demented animals trying to do?"

Davis stares in wonder at the Kahunas who gesture to attendants with trays of fruit. "Ha! I think it's a bath, mate. You won't drown. See how shallow it is? " He winces with pain. "This salt water might be good for my gashes." He angles his mouth away from the view of the priests, using a dark tone, "Do you know much of this language Mister Young?"

Young stands in a few feet of water, feeling rather stupid, but relieved. "Some. Can't think of any at the moment."

Davis leans into him and speaks quickly, "If we can get clothes, can we make it to the ship?"

Young looks to the Kahuna. "I was about to propose that when we were interrupted."

Davis whispers, "Perhaps we should accommodate them, throw them off the scent."

The priests beckon them out of the water. They comply with fake happy grins and a few bows.

Young whispers to Davis as he leaves the water. "Wait 'til sundown." He waves to the Kahunas. "Mahalo. Ma-ha-lo, gents!"

Davis joins in, "Yes. Lovely pond. Lovely." He bows.

The priests stare back, watching every move. "How very odd, these oystermen," Kahuna Lani opines to a priest.

Young and Davis offer more bows – the priests return a dubious bow, each sizing up the others in this charade.

Kahuna Lani offers a kindly nod to the white men while observing to his comrade, "They don't look very smart to me."

Davis nods warmly at Kahuna Lani and says to Young, "These blokes are big. But they look slow-witted." He gives the other priest a toothy grin. "Bet you know what happened to my mates, you bloody, savage brute."

The priest is somewhat confused. Kahuna Lani gestures toward a hut. "We must endeavor to treat these oyster ones with respect even though the gods have told us they are beings-without-souls. The king will advise us." The priests gesture and a phalanx of warriors escorts the mariners down the lane.

14

Ku-makani, Against the Wind

The sky is a magnificent magenta as wind whips palms near a group of huts. Several maidens laugh leaving a meeting. Paloa, a royal woman of eighteen, stands out among them as the most delicate, beautiful, and intelligent. Another royal Ali'i girl says to her, "…and I hear one of them is spirited and truly handsome."

Paloa wheels on her. "None of that. They are kapu. We must avoid them."

The king's conch trumpets the end of day, and workers come in from gardens and fields, singing, drenched in sweat.

Inside a supply hut near the temple, two large

warriors with spears guard the sailors as they sit playing a game. Young has his clothes back on. Davis is in his pants. Their hands are tied. They are depressed but determined. They watch the guards play Konane, a game like checkers, but played on a flat rock. The game gets serious as one guard takes out an apparently precious carved idol and puts it up for collateral. The other guard studies it and nods.

Davis tries to get comfortable, adjusting the bandages on his injuries. "If they would oblige us at least with some information."

"Perhaps it's better. Bad news can wait." Young adopts a cheerful attitude. "I have an idea. I'm going to assume they can't understand us, so I'm going to share my plan to you, but going to look at them so they won't think we are plotting." He looks straight at one of the guards. "So, do you think you could get loose and take this bloke here to your left?"

The guard looks at Young and smiles. He returns to the game.

Priests enter bearing wooden bowls of food. They put them down and untie Young and Davis who pounce on the food. The priest addresses the guards, "They eat like animals. Do they seem comfortable? The king wants them happy."

The head priest speaks in Hawaiian to the sailors, slowly as if to idiots, "The king comes to see you at dawn. He will explain all." He sees they do not understand, but tries again, "Kamehameha, Ali'i Kane. Wana'ao. King Kamehameha –" He gives up. "Tie them up when they're finished."

Young, while ravenously eating, looks to Davis. "Something about a king. I have heard that name."

An hour later, drums beat, a signal for evening rituals. In the hut, Davis and Young study a drowsy guard. They watch the other guard tossing Young's gold watch in his hands and the prize carving he won in the game.

The sailors have spent many minutes undoing ties on their hands. They wait until the other guard drops his eyelids.

"Now!" Young leaps up. He grabs a guard.

At the same time, Davis, weak from loss of blood, grabs a coconut bowl and slams it across the head of the other guard, knocking him out. As quietly as possible, they tie and gag the guards, then smear food drippings and dirt on their faces and bodies to make their skin look as dark as the natives.

"Mister Young – your hair."

Young rubs some of the paste in his sandy hair. He smiles at Davis. "You make a good savage."

Davis, not amused, picks up a spear and looks out. "Follow me, sir. I believe this side is safer."

"Right. Go." They scurry out down the backside of the temple huts and jump off a rock platform into the bushes, unseen. Behind the temple, a large group of warriors pass. The white men look much like village men in the dark. They dart across the trail behind them into brush at the edge of the village.

Night has fallen and there is just enough moonlight for Davis and Young to leap through a difficult hillside. They slump down near a cliff, staring up at the stars, breathless, pointing to navigational friends to guide them. The moon glitters on the sea below the trail.

Davis is first to assess their position, "I think Kealakekua is that way. South, sir."

"You're the captain here, I was up-side down all the way."

"Yes. How beastly. This way then." They scurry down the path. In the shadows, with their spears, they look like warriors on a savage hunt.

At dawn, the early birds gather in the trees, chattering. The two men move slowly past a sleeping village. Young steps on some dry leaves. A man looks out his hut in their direction. Young freezes. Davis pulls him into the brush. Davis freezes too and studies the hut for further activity. Seeing none, they move through the undergrowth as sun washes the night sky in a fanfare of reds and oranges. Birds swoop and sail over tops of majestic green precipices and ride the wind down slopes to the shore.

After many hours, Davis and Young lie down in a clearing and fall into exhausted sleep. Young jumps up after a moment, a vision of salvation on his face. He blinks and parts branches near him. The view of the bay reveals the *Eleanora*, at full sail, moving up the coast.

He jostles Davis. "There she is, Isaac. That's her!"

Davis jolts awake, sees the ship, and jumps up. "Hurry. This way." Isaac races downhill, Young running after, tossing the spears as they go. They leap through brush to make it to a point of land before the wind takes the ship further out to sea. Last reserves of energy and panic overtake them as they run.

Davis calls back, "We can swim out if they can't hear us from the point!"

Young sputters. "Blast man - I can't swim."

"I'll carry you!"

A peninsula of land can be seen just beyond the ship. Gasping for air, they scamper down the last slope toward it.

Young sees huts to the right of them, then natives in the fields. He looks at the ship "It's impossible." He shakes his head. "It won't do mate. Look." In a rage he grabs Davis. "What do you think you are you doing? We're no match for that wind. They are simply too far. And what will those men do if they see us? If we don't make the ship, it's sharks or spears, Lad!"

The *Eleanora* moves farther out to sea, beyond their reach.

Davis stares in horror at the retreating ship. "We will die here," he whispers.

Young brings a hammer down on his heart and takes a deep breath. He looks into the firmament for an answer. "A bit soon for that. If we can get to Kealakekua, I have a friend who might help us."

Davis stares out to sea. "I have not seen my wife in two years."

Young slaps his shoulder. "You never will if those warrior gents get wind of us. This way, mate."

Davis focuses. "Sir, we'd better take that path."

"Call me John. I've no rank, now. Just John."

"As you wish." After a last glance to the ship, they move deeper into the brush.

Aloha

More hours pass in a fog of silent rage and despair. Struggles with lava ledges and undergrowth have filled their dark, greasy savage faces with rivulets of sweat. Now they only look like dirty white men.

Davis moves slower, depressed and needing rest.

The sun is at her most crushing heat as Young begins to crawl over boulders. He pulls vines out of the way. A wild boar charges them from the bush, with a demonic battle-cry. Young is nearly gored, but leaps out of the way just in time. Davis, next on the warpath of the pig, dodges as the hairy beast careens past him and disappears as fast as he had appeared. It is a brief, harrowing reminder of the kind of world which now engulfs them. They slump, gasping.

Young sighs. "Too bad, he would have made such good eating."

Davis nods, winking, "That is what he thought about us."

The day wanes, as the men press southward to Kealakekua. Each is lost in a maze of regrets, failed plans and broken dreams. Memories of youth in the British Isles, family, and friends burn into their hearts. Future plans are smashed in the reality of being left behind. Lost in these feelings, the men move as if sleepwalking.

The bay and surrounding mountains roll out before them, a panorama of endless tropical landscape. However, hunger and thirst crowd even the most painful thoughts. Having eaten only bananas some hours earlier, their minds sink into confusion. Scratched, bruised, bleeding and sweating, they stop near the edge of a precipice. They hear a man laughing.

They turn to see a huge Hawaiian man stepping onto the trail, his massive frame silhouetted in the afternoon sunglow. His voice booms, "Wel-come. Aloha. My guests!"

They freeze like rabbits. The deep rumble of the man's laugh and wild amusement in his face present a rather demented, almost comic vision to the hopeless souls. Their eyes bug out at the sight, which brings even more laughter from the man.

King Kamehameha moves to them, arms outstretched. A bright red feather cape adorns his seven-foot height, revealing a beautiful sash and bright red loincloth. His physical presence is fierce, like a grand panther standing upright, muscles rippling, gleaming and tight in the half-light, but when he speaks, his velvet voice is mesmerizing. "Fear no! Well-come. See, I speak the Eng-lish."

Warriors leap in from everywhere. The King bubbles with joy again to see the great surprise on the faces of the white men confronted by so many warriors all at once from nowhere. He is like a child with new toys. But, within a second, he is dead serious, looking straight into their eyes.

"I am Kamehameha, king of Kona, Hamakua, Kohala, Kau, Servant and keeper of war god

Ku-Ka-ili-moku."

Young manages a weak warm look and extends a hand to shake, but thinks better of it. "I am Bo'sun, John Young, sir, English. On the *Eleanora*, out of Boston – Your Highness."

Overwhelmed by the creature before him, Davis stammers, "Seaman Isaac Davis from Wales, sir…" It's too much for him. He collapses in a faint.

Young tries to hold up his new friend.

The king is shocked to see his guests in such bad shape. His hand goes up in habitual command. He shouts in Hawaiian, "Lamakua. Refreshment! They are bleeding and starved."

In a nearby hut, Mana'oi and slaves bring platters of food. The mariners, having prepared for no less than death, watch in awe as servants move to make them comfortable on mats.

Kamehameha continues his prepared speech, "I wish you well-come to Havaee."

Davis focuses on the strange personage before him.

Young tries to swallow whatever food he can shove in his mouth.

Servants bring wet cloths and wipe blood from their bodies. Two Ali'i Chiefs enter. The first has cold eyes, in sharp contrast to Kamehameha's. He is Kiana, a fit and powerful warrior, who studies the prisoners like a restrained tiger. His handsome looks hide a dark interior. His body is adorned with whale carvings, rows of shells. A gold European watch hangs prominently around his neck.

To Kiana's side is Mapala, tattooed from head to foot, with no apparent intelligence. He is immense and adds to the mystery for the captives.

Kamehameha continues, "This Chief Kiana, half-brother to king for Kau-wai. He sail with English Moku pe-a many moons. He greet you. This Mapala, a chief this island much greet, too."

Having exhausted his English for the moment, Kamehameha gestures to an adjutant who moves in. He's forty, dressed above the waist in Hawaiian tapa cloth, but wears English trousers and shoes. Lamakua is a tall, thin man with tender eyes, and an aura of gentleness. He is clearly a diplomat.

"I am Lamakua. I sailed on the ship, *Hope*, with a Captain named Ingram. He taught me your tongue and much information about your King George as well as people of the British Islands."

This civility and near perfection of his English are beyond any understanding for Davis and Young, who are speechless at the unexpected, incongruous gentility.

Young stares. "That is very…it is a pleasure to meet you, sir."

Davis, in total exhaustion, mumbles, then dissolves into hoots of laughter.

Kamehameha is amazed at this insanity.

Davis apologizes, "Forgive me. I am… I must seem…" He cackles, wipes his eyes. "I am not quite myself," he sputters as Young, dubious, holds him up.

Kamehameha beams. He believes this to be a wonderful first meeting. He is anxious to get on with his agenda. "Lamakua teach me Eng-lish. You most wel-come." He becomes serious. "Feelings much sorry for men of dead ship." He gestures. "You eat now?"

Young is amazed at the mention of the dead sailors and looks to Davis. But, hunger drives him. "Eat? Yes, sir, I am hungry." He nudges Davis who is passing out again. "Isaac. Eat."

The king is dismayed as Young props up Davis. "He is very tired from traveling, and has many wounds your highness."

Kamehameha orders pillows brought. Davis slumps over as soon as Young lets go of him. The king is concerned for a moment then laughs. "Yes! He rest. Good." He watches Young like a tender mother watching an adorable child. "You eat good."

Young is not sure how to take the king. Their eyes connect at a deep level for just a moment, leaving both men confused, but neither can look away. All in the hut watch the king and the white man.

Young remembers a Hawaiian word, "Mahalo."

Kamehameha remembers an English word, "Wel-come."

16

Royal Caravan

The next day, the small Kona village is in a tempest to prepare for the king's return to his village in the north. Drums announce Kamehameha's entrance into the courtyard. Commoners assemble and prostrate themselves for the monarch passing by.

In a hut chosen for the prisoners, Young sleeps. Mana'oi approaches him, clearing his throat. Young jumps awake, in a nightmare of the events of the day before.

Mana'oi holds him. "Friend…"

Young, surprised to see him, tries to shake off sleep. "Mana'oi… last night. Who was that man?"

"Much good king. Ali'i King Kamehameha. Ka-may-ha-may-ha."

Young tries it out, "Ka-may-ha-may-ha."

Mana'oi is relieved. "King this island. Will be king all islands!"

Davis comes staggering into the hut, hands tied, and rages, "These savages are taking us back to that very same village where we escaped. This Lama-koo says we are 'obliged to go.' Obliged? Ha! We're his bloody prisoners. That is what we are. Savage bastards."

Young looks at him, too weak to be angry. "Miraculous what a bit of rest will do. Morning, Isaac." He stands. "Yes, we are his prisoners..."

Davis blinks. "You're just going to take it?"

Young takes a breath and launches in, "This king says he will protect us. God knows why. Maybe we're in the right camp. Maybe not. But, I am grateful he found us first before the other king could kill us."

Davis growls. "I'd rather take chances by myself. 'Other' king?"

Young assesses his wound. "Really? Perhaps you can escape again and find a cave to hide in? But, how will you know when a ship is coming? And who can you trust here? This king did not massacre our mates, someone else did."

"You trust the word of that savage chief?"

Young chuckles. "He said when he arrived at his village and found us gone, he put a *Kapoo* - a special protection on us. His runners passed the word down the coast. We were like animals hiding in the bush and all the time they could not touch us or *they* would have been killed." He guffaws at the irony. "So, why kill us now?"

"I am sure we'll give them a dozen reasons before the week is out."

"I would say we're more likely to stay alive with this man, lunatic that he seems to be, than without him. At least until a vessel arrives."

Lamakua and Kiana enter. Kiana studies them, filled with suspicion.

Davis doesn't like Kiana on sight. "We're coming. You need not drag us for God's sake."

Lamakua nods to Kiana to back off. "My friends, we must begin. It is a day's journey to Pukaloa."

Davis bristles. "We are quite aware of that. We just came from there."

They move out of the hut.

Kamehameha arrives, impressive in a long tapa cape and feather helmet. The commoners prostrate themselves. Davis is appalled by this tide of human subservience.

Kamehameha, nervous about his morning speech to his *guests*, positions himself to speak. When he does, it is well-rehearsed, but clumsy, "Good Mor...ning, to my – guests – Kohn Yohhng!"

Young, very impressed, nods and offers a look of acceptance.

Responding to this tiny semblance of friendship, Kamehameha explodes in joy, "...and to Akake Davis!"

Isaac stomps forward, making no effort to hide his rage. "I am *Isaac. Seaman Isaac William Davis*, who wants to go home to his wife in Wales, who watched savages like you murder innocent men for no reason, who is not impressed with your pomp and your grand manners because I am your bloody prisoner, *not* your guest. *Guest?* Bloody Hell. Ha!" He raises his hands in disgust.

Kamehameha's warriors lunge for him with spears. John cannot move.

Davis lowers his hands. "Alright. Alright."

Kiana's eyes flash, hoping for the opportunity to kill Davis. A tense moment passes as Kamehameha allows Davis to squirm. He wonders how to handle these men. A moment later, he orders the warriors to back off, then pins Davis with his stare. He is losing patience. "You are..." He whispers to Lamakua, who whispers back. He continues in a deep, fierce voice, "...my es--teeme *guessssssss*. No prisoner. We go. *Now*."

Davis shoots a look to Young who shrugs and glances to Lamakua.

Davis snears. " '*Esteemed guests*'. Bloody hell."

Kamehameha shifts his body and all common-ers hit the ground again as he moves out of the clearing. Lamakua follows Kamehameha out first, then Davis, Young and the retinue.

When the royal party has passed a safe distance, Mana'oi lifts his head from the ground slightly. Young glances back. They share a moment of fellowship and cautious relief.

17

Kiapolo Council

In a hut in the Eastern Highlands, several chiefs and kahunas argue. Slaves fan them. Keoua, Kamehameha's cousin, and one of his many enemies, makes an impassioned plea to the group, "We must strike now. *Now,* my brothers."

The first chief shakes his head. "No. We will wait. We will win when Kahekili attacks from Maui. These men mean nothing."

Another chief slams down his fist. "If the white men are swayed by Kamehameha, many more whites will come perhaps to help him. Then, Kamehameha would have an advantage. This is our chance. Now is the time."

Keawe, a wizened, more venerable chief, raises his hand. "It is better Kamehameha's fury be on Kahekili than on us. Kahekili and his sons cannot protect us here on Hawaii. We are too far from Oahu. Kamehameha hovers on our border. We suffer still from his last war. We must make our peace with him until we are stronger."

Keoua raises his hand to challenge. "You know, uncle, how I respect you, but, I know Kamehameha and my cousin Kiana must not have these men. They will destroy us. Trust me, it is the best choice to act swiftly." Keoua beckons a warrior standing at the ready for orders. His words are clear and firm, "Disappear as soon as the white men are dead. Disguise yourselves. No one must ever know who did it."

The warrior bows and leaves. The chiefs nod in agreement.

On the Northern trail, the midday sun drenches the king's traveling party as the group of thirty wends their way up a narrow mountain pass. Young and Davis are in the middle of the warriors. Their hands are tied. Davis snarls. "By now, the *Eleanora's* caught a fine wind headed for the Americas."

"Best not think about it, lad."

"And what are you pondering in this heat?" The acid in Davis' voice is new to Young. He doesn't like it.

Young grins cynically. "I am dreaming of shepherd's pie, mate. Something I reserve for life's more difficult patches."

On a hillside above the northern road, a group of Keoua's most skilled warriors watch Kamehameha's party from above, restraining huge boulders with heavy ropes.

Down on the road, three scouts move ahead of Kamehameha, who is in conference with Lamakua. The scouts do not see Keoua's men.

Kamehameha laments, "But, when will my love return from Kauai? Why have we not heard a word?"

Lamakua chooses his words cautiously, "That is all Ka'ahumanu's messenger said, my king. 'By the full moon's tide, if there is wind." Kamehameha growls. "That is not good enough," "Lamakua. Why do the gods make some women to think so well? You see how clever she states that? It gives her free reign to come back whenever she chooses because she can always blame it on the wind."

"I have long since given up trying to understand them." He attempts to change the subject back to the white men. "My king, Kiana and I secured the ship of the dead ones near Keauhou and have posted guards on it as you commanded. We have hidden it under many branches in the lagoon there."

Kamehameha is saddened. "For one of my most trusted chiefs to dishonor me that way with the English, it was foolish and evil. Too many dead. He will be punished."

Lamakua sighs, stares out over the valley as they walk. "Of course. But, my king, perhaps the gods have spoken. If he had not done these things, the sailors would not be in your power now."

"True, but, if it was the will of the gods, something else could have brought them here." He gazes at the sky. "Wild clouds…a bad sign." He sees something odd in the rocks. "What's that up there?" He shades his eyes, but decides it's nothing.

The company moves forward into the narrow pass.

On the rock pass above, Keoua's lead man eyes the party moving below. He watches as Kamehameha passes under him. He waits for more men to make their way through the tight pass, then gives the signal in a low voice, "Ano. Ano."

Davis hears and then sees boulders fall from above. "Look John. Look up!"

As Young and Kamehameha's warriors look up, it is too late, the trap has sprung. Huge boulders careen down the mountain at brutal speed. The rocks land, crushing two of Kamehameha's men on the trail, cutting the party into two sections in the middle of the pass.

The king jumps up, catches hold of a vine and swings across the rock path, near the top of the boulders as they crash and settle. Dust and debris cloud his sight for a moment, but he sees the head of a spear as it flies toward him. He catches it mid-air and throws it at an enemy warrior, who howls in pain.

On the other side of the boulders, Kamehameha's men who were cut off with Davis and Young are quick to circle and protect the prisoners as best they can.

As a warrior unties the sailors' hands spears fly in from everywhere at once. One guard is hit near Young, then another. One flank is open. Davis and Young dodge spears, then pick them up to defend themselves. They are awkward, having no training, their courage is their only weapon. The four remaining guards close ranks to cover the sailors, but a spear hits Davis in the thigh. He screams and falls.

One of Kamehameha's men from the other side of the boulders climbs over a precipice and is killed by a spear. Lamakua and Kiana are also trapped on the other side. They climb up, but the rocks are too steep. The men defending Young and Davis lose ground. Another warrior goes down.

A spear hits Young in the back. He exhales in a scream and falls in the dirt.

One of the enemy glares at Davis raising his spear. As he pulls back to aim, he is struck in the chest. Davis looks to where the spear came from. With a shout from the top of the boulders, Kamehameha stands taunting the enemy. Many spears sail through the air at him all at once, but he dodges them with glee. Davis is stunned by Kamehameha's courage and skill. In a shocking instant, the savage maniac has become his savior. In quick strokes, Kamehameha grabs spears mid-air and sends them back into Keoua's remaining band. After a final volley, they retreat. Having bungled the job, Keoua's warriors race back up the slope.

Kamehameha throws a spear killing one more of the fleeing enemy, then comes to join Lamakua who has found a way over the crevice. He holds Young who cannot move.

Young stares to the sky, then closes his eyes. Warriors come to hold him down as Lamakua quickly and deftly pulls the spear out of his back. Young moans and loses consciousness.

Davis looks the other way, holding his leg above the knee, as blood gushes from the wound.

Other warriors of the king scream in agony as they die. Survivors take stock of the injured.

Kamehameha comes to Davis. He rips off a piece of his garment and forces it in Davis' mouth. The king positions his large hand on Isaac's thigh. Davis realizes the spear must be pulled out. Kamehameha forces him down. "Is good, Akake. Good."

Davis bites hard and closes his eyes. Kamehameha looks on with compassion and gestures for warriors to help hold Davis down. The king grits his teeth and grabs the spear protruding from Davis thigh. "Ahiiieeee!" The high, piercing cry coming from the king mixes with Davis' howls, all of which echo through the mountainside. Davis passes out.

Kamehameha takes the bloody spear and hurls it into the dirt. He looks to Lamakua, who holds Young. "So what do the gods mean by this? Tell me."

Lamakua has no answer.

18

Twilight Journey

Pu'uka-loa, Kamehameha's Village

The king's party is heralded by messengers who shout news of disaster through the village. As they enter with the dead and wounded, dogs bark, women weep, and men rush in from everywhere.

Kahuna Lani and other priests hurry from the temple. As Kamehameha's emblem bearer enters, he announces, "Our king approaches!" Commoners fall prostrate as Kamehameha sweeps into view. The weeping worsens as the group passes.

He bears Young on a makeshift sled. Davis, and other wounded are carried, or on foot. The gait of Kamehameha is slow. His tapa cape flows behind him as he walks to the priests.

The king speaks, his voice passionate. "A group of the enemy tried to kill the foreigners. I am sure Keoua sent them. Ten men gave their lives. Keoua and his vicious chiefs will pay dearly for this I promise you." He raises his hand for the priests to be dismissed.

He moves closer to Kahuna Lani. "Tend to the wounds of these white men and make them as comfortable as you can. Pray with all your strength for the gods to heal them. But, if they heal, do not let them trick you again and escape or I promise you, you will join your ancestors."

The venerable kahuna winces a bit. "It will be done, my king."

Kamehameha's face drains of energy. "I will be surprised if they live long enough to even try another escape. I must sleep."

Kahuna Lani bows. "Yes, my king. The gods send you rest."

The Kahuna and priests take Young and Davis to huts.

As Isaac is carried off, he locks eyes with Kamehameha. In spite of the cavernous depth of his hate, he registers the fact Kamehameha saved his life. It is a brief moment, but a seed of gratitude is perceived. The king attempts a hint of encouragement. Davis closes his eyes in pain, a vision of the king's face searing into his mind.

The King's Compound is quiet as a healing night passes. The dawn casts a strange, pulsing, red glow on Kamehameha's emblem, fixed to a pole next to his hut. Drums announce the day. Seabirds scream and fight overhead. The royal huts are adorned with bright red and brown colored mats, strings of perfect shells, and carved wooden plaques of sacred faces.

Kamehameha leaves his sleeping hut. He strides to the temple. As he enters the sacred area, he strips off his clothing and dives into the purification pool. He emerges, singing to an unseen god and heads for the inner temple. He meets a priest who hands him the carcass of a pig. He carries it to the altar as another priest lays down a beautiful tapa cloth. He places the pig on the altar, ignited by the first rays of the sun. The priests prostrate themselves as Kamehameha kneels down and chants,

Oh, god of the earth, be appeased by this offering.
Be kind to the ones injured. Heal their wounds...

Pardon our sins and faults of the heart...
Find favor in these foreigners and sew their
hearts to our cause.
Bring health to their bodies and the bodies of my
warriors until they have passed the age of walk-
ing. I worship You, O god of the earth...
and I now accept your will for these men...

He remains kneeling. The fire of the sun's rays
pour onto the altar. The light ignites the king's
eyes as if an unseen power fills him. He bows his
head again and drops to the floor.

A short time later, the king emerges from the
temple with Kahuna Lani, in hushed conversation.
Kamehameha leaves the temple and disappears
up the hill into the undergrowth.

A bright blue parrot squawks on the branch
of a hala tree, while a small brown boy feeds him
a banana. Young women gossip as they prepare
baskets of fruit.

Foundations for two new huts for the foreigners are being lashed together by village craftsmen.
Slaves bring fresh thatch for the roofs.

Dead warriors are carried past them in the
distance.

19

Rumors and Rules

A week has passed, and the village has tried a score of ways to get back to normal, but it is impossible with the bizarre white men in their midst. Facts laced with fiction fly through the groups of women and men with breakneck speed, necessitating updated revisions, which then spur new heights of gossip within hours of the last report.

In the course of the week, there have been such fictions as a tale that John Young had flown off his bed, circled the island on the back of a mother shark seen by moonlight and that Davis had chanted a mele prophecy that brought on an early birth of a child in the village. None of this had been witnessed by priests and warrior guards stationed around the huts day and night. But, rumors continued.

The only truth was that Davis had been singing a sea shanty in his delirium, and a child indeed was born early, which was merely a coincidence. But, the image of Young, sailing across the moon on a fish even made the king laugh.

However, the men of the village have strict orders to ignore all gossip while they guard the sailors, or they will be killed. And the king further issued an edict that only the most sensible women be allowed to nurse the mariners. All other women to be sent away.

Inside the healing hut today, a strange, oily, pungent, paste is being applied to Young's deeply wounded back.

A sweet-hearted, huge, elder woman, Nahena, scoops more paste from a wooden dish and rubs it in. Young winces and moans. She sings a cooing, haunting tune to him. He winces again, but less painfully. Several other elder women move in and out, each attempting a casual look at one or both of these oyster-skinned men, before being violently shooed out.

Davis watches two elder ladies trying to entertain him with their hands holding a string game.

He mumbles, "*Cat's Cradle*," as another elder woman attends his wound. He is a bad patient. "Eyow. My God, woman, are you digging for buried treasure or maybe this is punishment for not bowing to your savage king." Davis gives the formidable woman a manly shove but to his surprise she ignores him and forces a drink from a coconut shell down his throat.

Two other women enter and hold Davis as his words become slurred and he begins to pass out. One woman mutters to the other, "He's finally going to sleep. I gave him all I had."

Nahena studies Isaac Davis. "This one's wound, I believe, comes from a place deeper than flesh. It is his heart that hurts most. Let me sing to his pain." Nahena coos as she dabs Davis's thigh with a different paste. His eyes open and then go to half-mast as he watches her face. She sings a lovely, lilting melody. He takes in the velvet sounds and closes his eyes. Nahena continues to observe him as she speaks to the women, knowing Isaac can't understand her. "He has beautiful thighs, don't you think?" She hums.

Davis, resting easier, says, "That is better... thank you..." He sinks into the peace of her song. "Yes... thank you..."

The women like the sounds from Davis. They copy the tones. Nahena begins, "Etta--kank--ooo..."

Davis, eyes still closed, enunciates, "No. Th - Th - thank... thank... yoooo.

Nahena responds, "Kaaannk...ooooo." She laughs. "Kank ....oooo."

Across the hut, John Young's eyes slit open. He dryly adds, "Charming." He groans and goes back to sleep.

Other ladies join Nahena, making it a game, "Kaaannnk...oooo. Kaaank...ooo."

Outside the hut, Kaoana mingles among the guards. The elegant princess had seen the prisoners from her garden. She is joined by other young women trying to get a peek at the men. She uses her status to gain entrance and enters the hut alone. Once inside, she hurries to Young and hands him an orchid and flashes a quick mischievous grin.

Young's eyes pop open as she touches him.

Nahena is annoyed. "You above all you should know better, Kaoana. They are still kapu. Stay out."

Young, revived by Kaoana's beauty, lifts his head calling as she is ushered out. "Beautiful flower - thank you."

This brings a new round of louder *Kankoooo's* from the giggling women who feel they've garnered high marks in their English lesson.

Davis, waking, is not amused. "Good God, not again."

Nahena quiets the women. Young sinks back in pain.

OO

Hours later, a throng of priests arrive, scattering the young women outside. The elder women hurry out as the priests enter. Several slaves bring covered trays of pork and papaya.

When Lamakua enters, Young gets a clearer vision of him up close.

Davis, seeing the king's emissary, blinks awake and marshals his wits for a confrontation. Lamakua's kind spirit usually brings comfort to those around him, but in the painful condition the sailors are in, they can hardly bear the thought of one more message from the king.

Lamakua speaks with authority, "I have been sent by our king to say he is most sad you were attacked."

Davis unleashes his venom, "Oh, not as sorry as we are, mate. If the king had not taken us prisoner in the first place, then I would be far away on the sea by now."

Young gathers strength. "Isaac, let's have the apology before the flogging. Let the man finish. He's obviously on orders."

Davis retorts, "Certainly. So the 'king' is sad?"

Lamakua continues, "He is most sad. He surprise by enemy —"

Davis interrupts, "Enemy? And who might the 'enemy' be?"

"Kahekili, King of Maui, Oahu and Molokai," Lamakua explains. "Kahekili is enemy of this island. Your attackers sent from him. Kahekili will not win when war comes."

Davis sneers. "We shall be home in England by then."

Lamakua is silent.

Young struggles onto one elbow. "Please thank King Kamehameha for saving our lives, sir."

Lamakua decides to change the subject. "There is a ho'omana for you tonight."

Davis blinks. "A what?"

Lamakua pronounces, "Hoo-oo-ma-na ceremony for all wounded. Is *wounded*, correct word? You body have pain?"

Young tries to look less indignant. "Yes, much pain. What happens at this…ceremony?"

Lamakua explains. "We ask gods to heal wounds, bring peace, harvest. We give sacrifices."

Davis is dubious. "What? Human sacrifice?"

Lamakua searches for better words. "No - No, only pig and foods for god Kane. Beings only sacrifice when break kapu laws."

Young is relieved. "Good. You see, in our land, humans are never sacrificed. It is thought of as, well, not possible."

Davis snorts. "No, we don't sacrifice people to savage gods, Mister Lamakua."

"In Havaee only war god want sacrifice of the body. Other gods want for – many things." Lamakua feels he's in deep water and lowers his eyes. "My Eng-lish not good, is bad. I sorry."

Young's eyes reveal warmth. "Your English is the best I have heard from any native in the whole of this ocean, sir."

Lamakua's eyes twinkle. "This true?" A wave of kindness passes between them and the adjutant begins to relax. "You must not fear. My king believe gods protect you."

Davis chortles. "Protect us? Well, they could have arrived a bit sooner that day in the mountains."

Lamakua has had about enough of Davis. He crosses to leave. "The gods do their will, not care our likes. I go to my King." He locks eyes with Isaac. "It is my prayer you be well." He leaves.

Davis sulks. "Prison."

Young muses to himself. *A gentle emissary for such a fierce king.*

20

The Ceremony

On the edge of the village, elder ladies gossip while weaving baskets. From behind them in the gathering darkness, Kamehameha appears. They are surprised by him and fall to the ground. He walks by as they cower.

One woman looks to the other after it is safe. "He has been all day, praying on the mountain. We must tell the others we can begin the ceremony."

Paloa, the delicate royal princess of great beauty stares into the future. She is petite by comparison with other royal women, but there is a sweet dignity about her that is immediately visible and sets her apart. She is attended by slaves, who place wreaths of flowers on her head and wrists. The doe-eyed girl is oddly confident. She looks out her thatched window, continuing to envision where she will stand on the ceremonial grounds and when it is her turn to chant about the journey of her king.

She rises and the women retreat. She begins to recite her poem in a strong, clear voice. She moves her hands, her fingers ripple in the most delicate and graceful ways imaginable to the drumbeat in her mind. Each movement has a different word...

Evil night...my king will always
escape you. He will be wherever
you are not... Light surrounding him...
The wind singing to him...
His words rising in the night are like
Mists on the mountain and
Thunder rolling with the sea...

Out near the edge of the village, flames leap from torches into the night sky. Villagers sing and three warriors offer healing movement poems and hulas for the foreigners' recovery. Their prayers for "beings with no souls" create passionate movements with arms and hands flowing in rhythmic motions, creating stories of victories over enemies and sharing dreams as they appeal to the gods. The powerful beating of drums and many gourds create a stunning atmosphere of worship.

Among the crowds moving toward the ceremonial place, the crippled young boy, Opa, plays a primitive lute. He dances, awkwardly apart from the others, but with great feeling.

Guards are placed at the foreigner's hut, standing or sitting at their posts. They play games of chance and talk quietly.

Inside the hut of the *haoles,* or "*those with no souls*", the sailors are elevated into barely comfortable positions to watch the ceremony out the window of the hut. The firelight dances on their hopeless, stony faces.

Davis, accepting for a moment his fate and allowing a deep, long sigh, turns to Young. "A double portion of grog would do well tonight, eh?"

Young, watches the panoply of dancers, drummers, and villagers. He agrees, "Yes. I miss that grog. I don't miss old Metcalfe's snarling tongue, however."

Davis glances down at his wound covered in the poultice applied by the elder ladies. "Hope this potion they have rubbed into us doesn't render us gangrenous. It is painful way to die."

Young continues watching the ceremony. "Indeed. This is a veritable mystery. These natives are truly putting great efforts into our recovery, lad. There are a few malevolent fellows, I am sure, but not the people I have seen so far. All the prayers to their gods and good wishes seem sincere. I see it in their eyes when they walk by. I believe they all want us to live."

Davis considers. "You are correct. Perhaps we can be used as good bargaining with our king? I have been thinking for hours about it. Why, John? Who do they think we are? Surely, not gods. That myth was over long ago."

"Yes. They thought Cook was a god, until they saw him hemorrhaging."

Davis laughs. "And they certainly have seen everything our bodies do. They *know* we're very human. But, when those savages were sent to kill us in the mountains, Kamehameha's personal guards died protecting us. Why would any king be willing to lose such important men for the likes of us?"

Young looks at the guards. "My mind keeps turning on that. I do not know. Rather like the looks of these blighters now. I might even sleep."

Davis studies the guards with his cynical squint. "Keep one eye open. They could be in the service of the *other* king." He leans back and tries to move his leg. Painfully, he realizes his mistake, gives up, and closes his eyes.

Young notices Davis has fallen asleep. He becomes fascinated by the dancers as fever sweat runs down his face. The movements are sensuous, their hands, with fingers like leaves on branches in the wind, seem to speak strange, enchanting words. He yearns to know the hearts and secrets of such people. The long plaited hair of the men rolls across their backs as they circle and sway. The music is captivating, the drums mystical, their cadence hypnotic. The huge wooden idols loom up behind the dancers like Mana'oi's chess pieces. In the grip of his fever, they seem alive, moving, dangerous. The tune of an old hymn begins to course through his thoughts. Tears well in his eyes. He mumbles, his head nodding along with the heavy drumbeats "...*the watery deep I pass... Jesus in my view... and thru the howling wilderness... my way pursue...*"

21

Prophetic Squid

While another murky week passes for the sailors, with moments of delirium, moments of lucidity, many preparations move forward in the huts of the king.

In the sultry afternoon, Kamehameha's slaves hold up garments for his perusal. He screws up his face as he studies each cape, previewing how it might help him achieve his goal as an inspiration to his people.

A messenger runs into the courtyard, greets a chief and announces, "The country people have come. They have their gifts for the King."

The king throws down a cape, "I told you!

There will be no bringing of gifts until the *haoles* are able to receive them with me here. Why is it no one listens to the king?" He looks around to hurl something and decides against it. "Where was I?"

The slaves run to him with remaining capes. He flexes his fingers to control his rage.

Across the village, Young and Davis are tended by Nahena, cooing a now familiar tune to her patients. Young's wound is nearly healed. Davis' leg is massaged by a huge woman with hands like mallets. He is lying calm as the giantess sings her sweet song to him, "Lomi-lomi…lomi-lomi…"

Outside, priests' scatter children. "News!" Kahuna Lani yells as he lopes down the lane, disrupting a circle of women making leis. "Good news. Good news!" Lamakua joins him.

Young lifts his head. "He's full of pluck. What day is it?"

Davis is sleepy. "Don't know.…"

The Kahuna announces. "The gods give joy. The squid died *under* water. You will become well!" Lamakua adds with great pleasure, "Good day! You will see the king. You are more well."

"Squid?" Young mutters. Davis moans. Bearers enter and begin to load the confused white men on stretchers. Lamakua is counting on the sailors to come peacefully. "You will be walking now!"

Davis retorts, "A squid died in the water, so you drag us somewhere because of that?"

Lamakua encourages, "No. Only go to see king. You are going better!"

Davis bristles. "Getting, *getting* better. And we wish we could be going. *Going home.*"

Young chafes at being put on a stretcher, "I can walk, thank you. Tell them I can walk."

Kahuna Lani snaps in Hawaiian at the guards, "Take that away. He will go on his feet."

Davis gets up too quickly. "I can walk. Oh -- " He moans, falls back. "Damn. Damn." The ladies help him on the stretcher. "Bloody Hell. Damn. Lamakua, have they killed those murdering, mountain bastards yet?"

Lamakua looks curious, not able to translate. "Moun-tain bas-tards?"

Davis sputters with sarcasm. "Yes. Remember, the warriors who tried to kill us with gigantic boulders."

Lamakua smiles. "Ah, yes. A hunting party killed those and bring bodies to king. Chief Keoua who sent warriors, not same. Hard to find – hard to kill. We find Keoua soon."

The mariners leave the hut for the first time in weeks. The light hurts their eyes. To villagers waiting on the path, they look weak. Young staggers with dignity and Davis is carried along. Villagers press in to see the sailors pass. They sing and throw flowers. Two names are clear, "Aloha, Olohana! Aloha Akake!"

Young beckons Lamakua. "Who is *Olohana*?

Lamakua's hand sweeps the air. "You, sir. They know you are bo'sun of a ship. A moku pe-a. Much mana in this. *Olo-hana*. Come from you name bo'sun call 'Oll hands. Oll hands', *Olohana*."

Young finds it charming. "All hands. Yes. All hands."

Lamakua explains, "They mean honor for you."

Young chuckles. "Lamakua, I have often heard this word 'mana', what is its meaning?"

Lamakua translates, "Mana is power. Power from gods." He points to his heart.

Young considers this while hands of natives fall adoringly on him as he moves along. He is charmed by the love in their eyes.

He lifts his hand and smiles – the villagers cheer. "Lamakua, I was a Boatswain. I could have been a ship's captain. Now I am Kamehameha's prisoner."

Davis takes in the sea of sweet faces. "Hmm. John, *Olohana*, not bad. Better than *Akake*. What a wretched name. What a place. If it wasn't prison, it would be paradise."

In the courtyard of the king, Kamehameha sits, arrayed in an exquisite cape he chose for this special event. There is an undeniable air of destiny about him. He is buoyant, greeting various chiefs with his luminous smile as the sailors are brought in.

Kiana and others sit flanking Kamehameha. The white men are given seats of honor near the king.

Davis notices Kiana, the most supercilious of the inner circle. He makes no effort to hide his loathing of the sailors. It chills Davis' blood, but he is obliged to sit next to him.

Kamehameha rises and opens his arms. "Please to be welcome Olohana and Akake. How are feelings of you?" His voice has magical warmth when he chooses to use it. Today it is thick with special honey.

Young glances at Davis who declines to speak, so John gives his answer. "King Kamehameha, Mr. Isaac Davis and I want to say we are very grateful for the efforts of everyone in the village and all who have cared for us. But, we want to ask you…"

Unable to hold his tongue, Davis dives in, "You have protected us. Your men have died doing so. You have given us every comfort. Why are you doing this? Why keep us here?"

The king catches a word here and there. He speaks in broken English. Lamakua translates. "My people not see ships. Chief Kapene Kuke come Havaee. Much mana. Much fighting. My people take his life Kealakekua Bay. Many my people die also on that moon. Many seasons pass. Many wars my people fight. In all seasons since, war, always war. Blood like a river. I ask gods this killing never more." His eyes burn like coals.

He moves to Davis, aware he speaks to the lone survivor of the *Fair American*. "Akake, Kona Chief sacrifice white men in anger. I punish. I punish! I hide ship to one day give to one who own. I can do this. I cannot put breathing back into men. I cannot do this."

Davis steps forward. "King Kamehameha, your warriors saved me, you also saved me. I am in your debt. But, what good is the *Fair American* to me now if Mr. Young and I cannot sail her to get home? Why will you not let us go when we are healed?"

Lamakua translates.

Young is confused. "Respectfully, sir, why keep us here? What do you want from us?"

Kamehameha looks at both men with lightning in his eyes. "You teach me. I protect you."

Young is incredulous. "Teach you?"

Davis stutters. "Teach you what?

Kamehameha's excitement fills the hut. "Britain war. Weapons King George. Many fear the *haole men*, not Kamehameha! I learn Britain war. Burning sand. All weapons. I see much harvest for my people. Win war. Kill Kahekili. Make peace, make ships. Much aloha for all my people."

The sailors are stunned. Lamakua watches carefully. The king senses their panic. His voice becomes like a mellow, deep, drum, "Since before my grandfathers, always war. My heart with pain for my people. I like dance with little ones, fish in sweet wind, watch day come and go with no blood. I long peace, Olohana. My war god, Ku-Ka-ili-moku. He say *Now*. Must be strong more than Kahekili. Say *get red-mouth gun. Learn Britain ways – fight, shoot burning sand. Kill Kahekili!*"

He repeats this last in Hawaiian over and over. His chiefs leap in heartfelt cheers. The king wipes tears and then cocks his head jauntily. "Yes. Why to trust Kamehameha? Why, Olohana? Akake?" He thrusts his hand to his heart and pounds his chest. "I prove true – prove good king. I, Kamehameha rule all Havaee in peace."

Davis speaks with foreboding, "Sir, you want us to teach you about war…so you can have peace?"

Kamehameha stands his ground. "Only way, Akake, Olohana, only way!"

Young joins in, "I believe the *red-mouthed gun* would be a cannon, Isaac." He looks at Lamakua. "Can-non. Boom…?"

Kamehameha shouts with joy, "Boom. Boom! Can-non, yes."

Young's eyes lock with Kamehameha's. He straightens up to impress the king with his resolve. "I will help you, Kamehameha, I will help you *only* until a ship comes to take me back to England, to my home, my family, my people, my work. Do you understand?" His eyes match the passion of the king. "Lamakua, tell him."

Lamakua begins to translate in Hawaiian, and a rapid outrage fires through the assembly.

Kiana implores the king in Hawaiian. "You see? He says it. He says he will leave on the first ship to England. They will betray you! They are beings with no souls – I lived with men like them on a ship for months. I saw their cold eyes. I know what they do."

Kamehameha spits back at Kiana, "You see nothing. Be quiet, you fool. I will never let them go." He grabs hold of Young's arm. Young stiffens, but doesn't move. "Olohana, I cannot trust you not tell English King what is ship of dead. This bring death to my people. English come, kill my people. Olohana, speak. Living better than death for you, yes? Living?"

Young speaks the horror he fears. "If we try to leave, we will be killed? We would never tell King George – we would not even get near the King George. You need not worry --"

Kamehameha grabs a vial of sand. "To protect my people, I kill this many like you." He pours the sand onto the ground.

Davis jumps up from his stretcher. "You barbaric, monster –"

Young grabs Davis. "Isaac, listen to me. Captain Clerke laid waste to Kealakekua after Cook's death. The king cannot risk another such retaliation from England. He was there that day. You understand? I see it now. I do not like it, but I understand what is happening here. They cannot afford to let us tell the British what we have seen and what we know."

Davis resists. "They should have thought of that before they massacred my shipmates!"

Young stares him down. "And what about Metcalfe's massacre at Olowalu? Did he think? Have we no barbarians in Britain? Do we not have our own monsters as well? We're alive, Isaac, don't press it. We must wait for better times."

Kamehameha separates them. "I give you huts, food. You teach my warriors." He loses any ability to think in English, demands in Hawaiian, "Tell them. Tell them."

Lamakua is a frightening presence as he echoes the king's edict, "You choose death or choose life here – on Hawaii. You must choose, now!" This is a side of him the sailors have not seen. They are overwhelmed.

Kamehameha is wild, enraged. "I protect my people. I protect you. You stay or die."

"Death to them!" Kiana rushes to attack, but is restrained by warriors.

All are hushed.

Young hangs his head, breathing heavy, then lifts his eyes to meet Kamehameha's. "I choose life. I stay."

Davis turns away.

Young sets his teeth and looks to Davis. "Sorry, mate. At least it looks like I will have a go at killing the blokes who ordered us to be killed." Another moment. "Isaac – life or death?"

Davis stares at the sand floor. "And if these savages don't win the first battle, are *we* then sacrificed?"

Young smiles ironically. "If the enemy wins, yes, I expect so. As well as all the men in this hut."

Davis shakes his head. "There's no help for it – a bloody flogging either way. We had better be damn good teachers, John. I know nothing of war. But, don't tell him that."

Kamehameha and the chiefs are confused, sensing conflict in the sailors. Finally, Davis reluctantly nods to Young. It begins a lifetime bargain written on two hearts, sealed in one shared glance.

Young declares, "Mister Davis agrees. He will teach your warriors, with me."

Lamakua remains calm, but can barely contain his pleasure. He speaks in Hawaiian to the king, "They agree to train your men for war."

Kamehameha leaps into the air, seven feet of glistening sinews like an enrapt dolphin breeching in some attempt at flight – a startling sight for all. "Aieee!"

This sparks reaction among the chiefs who speak all at once in delight. Kiana watches with disgust.

Kamehameha claps his hands. "Mahalo – Mahalo. You choose well, my friends."

"Hardly a choice, sir," Young murmurs.

Kamehameha embraces Young, who recoils, still aching from his injuries. The king jumps back and orders in Hawaiian, "These wounds! Don't touch these men. Let them rest!" Rattan chairs are brought and the sailors sit, despondent.

Kamehameha is too happy to notice. He gestures, "My friends, gifts from best village,

Kiholo." Lamakua signals a slave who shouts to waiting servants. The crippled boy, Opa, enters, playing a tune on his pipe. The melody floats into his sea of hopelessness and has a calming effect.

Behind Opa, villagers burst through the entrance of the hut, prostrating themselves before the king as they shove gifts towards him with downcast faces, hoping for a good word. He orders the natives to give their wares to the sailors.

Davis and Young are astonished as villagers crowd in with many fine crafts. Before them are placed colorful woven cords, exquisite tapa cloth, breadfruit, beautifully carved wooden bowls, trays and neck decorations. They watch this unexpected display in dubious curiosity. Elder ladies who had cared for them, appear with sparkling eyes, carrying magenta and yellow flower leis, singing as they lay them over the heads of the mariners.

As the procession continues, Davis takes off some of his garlands and looks to the king. "King Kamehameha, thank you for the gifts, your people are very kind, but I must know – you say the ship of the dead has been hidden by your warriors, taken somewhere. Where is the ship, *Fair American?*"

The king and Lamakua confer in whispers. The king pronounces, "I take you, when you well.

Ship safe, Akake. All safe." Kamehameha places a garland of ti leaves around Davis's neck. Davis is embarrassed. "You need not do that."

Kamehameha does the same to Young, who studies the king. "You are generous, sir, but, as this training commences, I will need servants to help teach your men. I need one named Mana'oi from Kealakekua. He is essential for my work."

Kamehameha mumbles to Lamakua. Kiana rejects the idea. Lamakua turns to Young, "This man you speak of is only Commoner. You will have servants and kahuna. No need for that man."

Young bluffs his way forward, "I need him. I need Mana'oi from Kona or I do not teach."

Lamakua translates. Kiana demands Young be punished. Kamehameha puts a hand on Kiana's arm. He backs off. The king smiles. "You shall have, Olohana."

Young goes for the next rung. "I want for him a hut. No, wait - *Huts* and food. Yes, huts, food and anything Mana'oi needs, yes?"

Lamakua's translation brings another round of huffing and puffing among the chiefs. Young stands his ground.

The king winks. "Olohana know his power. You see, Kamehameha good king."

Young nods. "Ma-halo, Kamehameha. Thank

you." The bargain takes shape. Kiana sulks near the entrance. Mapala, Kiana's trusting friend, joins him like a dog follows his master.

Young instructs Davis. "Isaac, *mahalo* means *Thank You.* I am sure you have no use for that word yet." Davis nods. "Right, mate. We know that is the favorite of the old women healers. But, perhaps they could also learn the word *please* from our language as well?" Young lets this pass.

The crippled boy, Opa, plays another tune, filling the hut with music. He dances as best he can. Davis and Young are impressed with the boy's effort. More gifts are placed in front of the sailors. It's obvious bribery, but, there's a kindness in it that cannot be denied.

Kamehameha beams as his vision of future peace grows and swirls round him, ascending like a great hawk taking flight.

22

Dreams

Three weeks have passed. A waterfall pours into a turquoise lagoon.

On the shore, Isaac, nearly healed, plays an old English tune on Opa's native lute. Opa is carving another lute for himself on a mat at a short distance. Now and again, Opa watches Davis as a worshipper studies a hero.

John sits against a palm tree and hums as he braids a length of rope. The two sailors are tan, more composed and on the verge of robust health.

A guard unit of warriors, laugh and talk as they build a canoe nearby. They barely watch the white men.

Four young women, including Kaoana, approach from rocky cliffs above. They pretend disinterest in the white men, but watch them often, giggle and make the men and their guards increasingly restless. They dive off the ledge of the waterfall into the lagoon.

Young decides to ignore them. He puts his head back and rests on a palm. "I dreamt I was at sea... I was not in a ship... I was just...floating."

Davis scans the area around him, aware Opa can't understand him. "John, if the opportunity arises, I'll take my chances. Will you come?"

Young closes his eyes. "Hmm. It's hard to know what to do. He's either astoundingly pure in spirit, or vilely conniving and never to be trusted."

Davis stops playing. "Kamehameha?"

Young hums. "Yes."

Davis continues strumming, but studies Opa to make sure he cannot understand their discussion. "The savage chief who killed our mates wore the most good-natured smile just before the slaughter. I even remember thinking, *What kindly people these are.* I will never make that mistake again."

One of the most seductive of the women catches Davis' glance. She poses for him from her perch above the water. Davis is mesmerized, but looks away.

Young notices the woman looking at Davis. "You've a right to your distrust, but, there are far worse jailers than Kamehameha."

Davis puts down the lute. "Speaking of behavior, I have been thinking about ours. Remember what we heard happened on the *Bounty*? Those men went insane in these islands. They were weak-willed and unable to resist temptation. When the kapu between us and the females is lifted, we would do well to be puritans, avoiding trouble with the men and scandals at home."

Young chortles. "Home. Look, Lad, the better I feel, the lovelier they look. I am sorry, but in spite of all I know of these island people, or *savages*, as you like to call them, they have a charm that is... beyond description. Your suggestion seems a bit—"

Davis cuts in curtly, "You're widowed and free. I understand. I just think it deeply unwise, and against morality."

Young, his head resting back on his folded arms, studies his friend. "Have you been faithful to your wife?"

Davis blinks. "My vows were sacred, yes." He feels Young's trenchant gaze. "However...it has not been so for her."

Young, cautious, gently moves to the next question, "Are you sure of this? What I mean is, one can be wrong. Do you know of this infidelity without any doubt?"

Davis stares at the sand. "Yes, she has betrayed me."

Young is astounded. "Then why the bloody hell do you want to go back to her? You think she is mending her ways? My God, man."

Davis, deeply hurt, gets up to leave. He changes his mind, turns around and defies Young. "There is a thing called honor. It is all I have. But, of course you well-bred chaps perhaps have no need of such things."

Young jumps up. "Now, what? Are you lecturing me?"

Davis brims with rage. "I've eaten dirt from every high born fool on land and sea. I've worked hard to build a life with integrity and honor. And I'm not going to throw it away indulging myself with a village of savages. I'll leave that to the likes of you, Mister Young."

"You cheeky bastard." John rears back and leaps for Davis.

Isaac swings a right hook. "No man calls me —"

Young tries to block him, but Davis keeps coming, clipping him again as they roll into the sand, landing as many punches as strength will allow.

Opa, his eyes like saucers, grabs his lute and yells at the sailors in Hawaiian, "Stop. Stop. No!"

The women jump out of the water to watch. They cannot believe the sailors are fighting instead of flirting with them. Guards come over the dunes, shouting and waving spears.

Growling and spitting epithets, the mariners wrestle as Kahuna Lani, Lamakua, and several priests approach from the other side of the slope.

Opa sees them and calls out to Davis, "Akake. Kahuna Lani. Lamakua!"

Kahuna Lani sails into the glade, robes billowing in the wind, like a rigged-out, wind-bloated brigantine. His eyes bug at the sight of his valuable charges attempting to kill each other in a storm of sand, fists, and blood.

Guards arrive at the scene. "Olohana! Akake!"

Young takes a final blow from Davis as he gets up, brushing off sand.

Davis whirls around to see the assembled natives as he wipes blood from his nose and stands, gasping and spent.

Lamakua, ever the diplomat, makes a clever response, "Good. Wrestling makes strong. You must both compete in the ceremony games when we—"

Davis, panting, cuts him off, "Oh, yes, we are

just dandy, having the time of our lives, in this Godforsaken place."

Lamakua's rejoinder is even more cheerful, "You make practice for to teach warriors?

Young guffaws. "Yes, just planning our strategy for training." He walks away to get his gear together.

Davis sees Opa holding the precious lute shaking with fear. He grabs it and stalks off. "Thank you, Opa."

Kahuna Lani follows Young, speaking in Hawaiian, "The turnstone bird has gone from the nest. He is gone. It is time to go."

"Lamakua, what's he babbling about now?" Young demands.

Lamakua hurries to keep up. "The gods say you may travel. The King makes ready. Come."

Davis mumbles, "That bloody bird must have flown. At least now I can see my ship."

Young confronts Lamakua, "We are his slaves. That is clear. So, when must we depart?"

Lamakua sighs. "At dawn."

Young grabs his work and heads back to the village.

Davis, sheepish, catches up to Young with Opa close behind. He rubs his head in remorse. His burly, handsome features and sky-blue eyes try to connect with Young. "Sorry, mate... I should not have said all that. I didn't mean to."

Young offers a cautious hand. "Already forgotten. It was my fault. My fault all the way."

The priests follow at a safe distance. The guards, embarrassed and tense, run to keep up as the group moves through the underbrush.

Opa proclaims in his best new English, "I go to ship. I serve you, Akake."

Davis commands, "No, ho'okapu. Forbidden, Opa. You guard village from Kahekili. You stay." But Opa follows him, trying to persuade him.

The women, forgotten by the men in the chaos, stand near the waterfall and talk, disappointed the white men are leaving. However, the royal princess, Kaoana, stares in the direction of John Young, happy to have simply been near him. She watches him until he is out of sight.

23

Ship of the Dead

A turnstone bird arcs majestically, flying down the coast of the island of Hawaii as his feathers of shimmering red, flare across the horizon. Tall towers of billowing clouds rise to magnificent heights. The afternoon sun has gone behind clouds, darkening the road as king Kamehameha leads his procession down a steep slope.

The retinue includes Young, Davis, Kiana, lower chiefs and two younger kahunas sent to be spiritual advisors on the journey to the ill-fated schooner, hidden in a cove.

Many thoughts about the sacrificed sailors by natives from their islands make the warriors on the trail quiet and pensive. They consider the consequences of the vicious slaughter on the future of the people in their kingdom. The first stop is the village nearest the slaughter.

Davis, anxious to see his ship, still has a slight limp, favoring the bad leg, which was brutally broken by a native's cudgel six weeks earlier.

Young moves to the king, looking at his spear. "How long would it take to learn to throw one of these? You call it a *po-lu-lu*?"

Kamehameha hands him the spear. "Polulu. Good. I teach. Ha! *I teach you*, Olohana"

Hearing this, Davis moves up to listen. Kamehameha gestures for Young to hold up the spear. Young holds it, surprised at its heaviness, then hands it to Davis, who stares at the weapon, assessing its power.

A call from a messenger breaks the moment, "The village of Kamee'eamoku, Kona Chief!"

The king's party enters a lane of huts. At first sight of Kamehameha, villagers weep and prostrate themselves before him as he moves toward the hut of the disgraced Chief. A spirit of terror consumes them – they hardly breathe even after the king has passed by, for fear he will punish them for the crimes of their chief.

In front of the chief's hut, a kahuna kneels and announces, "The king approaches."

There is an odd lack of retinue at the chief's hut with none of the usual court members of such a village to guard it. Silence hangs in the air.

Kamehameha stops. All in attendance stop. He looks directly at the hut. A voice rolls out of him like thunder, "Kame'eamoku. Come out or die."

After a moment, a low, painful moan emanates from the hut. The Kona Chief, Kame'eamoku appears. He trembles, holds onto the palm fronds supporting his doorframe. The once arrogant chief is a broken man.

Davis is amazed to view such a sea-change. He is not even sure it is the same man. The chief who warmly greeted his ship and led the massacre of his shipmates was so confident and powerful that it is only when Isaac sees the tattooed shark upon the chief's breast he is certain it is the same man. The chief recognizes Davis at the same moment and, in horror, turns to escape.

Kamehameha's warriors hold him. In rapid-fire Hawaiian, the king verbally pummels the chief, who falls to his knees, weeping, barely able to support himself. "You say you suffered at the hands of whites? But, is this a reason to *kill any* whites that arrive upon our shores? Did you send word to me? Did you *ask my permission* to attack those men? They were innocent, wanting only water. *Water*, do you hear me? You have disgraced our people." His huge hand comes down in a stinging blow that knocks the kneeling chief to the ground.

Kame'eamoku lies screaming as if his heart would break. He then looks to Kiana for support. Kiana offers only a cold stare.

The king points to Davis. "This man has hard words against you. If English hear, they will come. Many of our people will die because of you. Should you live? Answer me. Should you live? Speak."

Kame'eamoku crawls, moaning, groveling toward Kamehameha's feet. "What must I do? Please, forgive me. Your heart is a stone. What must I do, my king?"

Kamehameha looks at the weeping chief and lifts his hand determinedly, as a preface to an edict, "You and your people will tend the land in Puako until you prove true. As many years as it takes you will tend the land there. If you betray me again, you die."

Kame'eamoku is relieved to not hear a sentence of death. He drops back to the ground. He can barely speak, "As you wish… I am grateful, my king." He continues prostrating himself before Kamehameha.

Young whispers to Davis, "If this is a show they are consummate thespians. I believe it. He seems truly repentant."

Kamehameha leaves with Davis, Young and his retinue following. The king is visibly shaken by his own rage.

That afternoon, further down the coast above a cove, the company wends their way to the hiding place. The long, human ribbon, led by the king in his striking yellow cape, his standard bearer carrying his colors of yellow and red tapa cloth rippling in the breeze, stops on a ridge where the cove can now be seen.

Davis approaches the king, as he stares into the cove. "I don't see it. The cove is empty."

Kamehameha looks sidelong at Davis with a fiery glint. "You have no belief for me, Akake. You wait." Kamehameha picks up his pace, enjoying this special surprise, in hopes the day's events will win him at least a bit of warmth in the cold hearts of his white prisoners. As the king leads down the slope, he shouts commands. Drummers in the retinue begin to pound an intense beat. The group arrives on a slope near the beach. The king raises his hand. Drums cease.

"Now. See Fair Moku for my sailors. Bring ship! Akake. Olohana. See!"

Palm branches and foliage move like the forest of Dunsinane in Shakespeare's Scottish play. The cove comes alive with motion. The prow of the *Fair American* emerges as local villagers, swimming their hearts out, tow it into view.

Running to the shore, Kamehameha pronounces, "Akake, See. Far Meri-kan." His tone reveals this is somewhat of a game for him and the local villagers.

Davis only stares solemnly at the ship, remembering the slaughter.

The king notices Davis' suffering and orders his people to be respectful. "Stop smiling you idiots," he demands in Hawaiian. "This being is very sad for his friends who are dead from this ship. Look sad."

The natives quickly do their best to look sad.

Davis moves closer to the shore. As he does so, he realizes he is now grateful to see the ship, any ship. *There may be a way home after all.*

Young takes in all of this with quiet irony, knowing this vessel to be only one more possession, like himself, under the power of the quixotic and mercurial king.

The schooner, Fair American

24

The Strategy

Hours pass in a flurry of activity near the shore and on the *Fair American,* as canoes are tied around the ship, supervised by Young.

Up the beach, Mana'oi and his wife, Nakui, appear, escorted by king's men.

Young hurries to embrace the old carver. "Mana'oi. Aloha. Aloha, Nakui."

Mana'oi's eyes are red from weeping. He arrives at Young's side and bows repeatedly clutching at Young's clothing. "Olohana. You honor me. I never forget. Gods bring you joy."

Young prevents Mana'oi from bowing again.

"No, no, you are my only Hawaiian friends here, Mana'oi. You and your ladywife. Come, see the ship." He puts his arm around Mana'oi's shoulder, escorting him to the others.

The chiefs are horrified to see the white mariner so friendly and warm to a simple craftsman, who in their eyes is one cut above a slave or two cuts above a kauva, one of their *untouchables*.

But, Kamehameha has watched this moment from a distance and is encouraged to see Young's happiness. He hopes it will bring great results in how he teaches the army.

In the lower cabin of the *Fair American*, Davis searches through what is left of his gear. He glances around to make sure he is not being watched. He pulls a piece of siding out of the hull connected to his bunk. He slides it out and lifts out a beautiful dulcimer. Next, he takes a volume of Shakespeare and a Bible. He stuffs them in a sack, and heads on deck.

Kamehameha's graceful fingers embrace the rigging with love as he studies it. He sees Davis come up from below and tries to charm information out of him. He takes a casual stance. "Akake, you see how King George make ship?" He jumps up and down, testing the deck. "Is strong. War canoe strong. Moku Fair Mari-ka, more strong."

Davis decides to engage. "The British king, George, chooses men from his kingdom to build his ships. I do not think King George could actually build one himself. Special men in my land make ships. Moku. I can only sail them, sir. I cannot make them." Adding a wry grin. "If that is what you are asking."

Kamehameha's dark eyes sparkle as he holds the helm with reverence. "My people one day make ships. Strong ships, mahi moku, Akake."

Davis reluctantly admires Kamehameha's confidence. He finds himself drawn to something deep in the king. "If you will it, sir, I believe your people will make them."

Kamehameha runs his hand across a well-carved railing with awe. "The name of the wood?"

Kiana, from a distance, watches Davis and the king. When they look away from him, he steals a handful of nails from a container and hides them in his clothing.

Moments later, the king's massive war canoe bearing a score of warriors, enters the bay, the warriors' paddles slicing the water at a rapid pace, speeding them round the point. Lamakua stands in the prow. The King and all his men on the shore hail the arrival of the war canoe with whoops and shouts.

Young and Davis move swiftly with the mainsail and rigging of the *Fair American*, giving orders as best they can to the warriors who must learn how to sail the schooner with them. The two vessels in the bay present a strange tableau. A new spirit of courage wells up in the hearts of Kamehameha's warriors as they see their king's war vessel join forces with a white man's ship. The king has promised his chiefs new and better weapons and it seems the gods are placing them into his hands. Hopes of finally winning against Kahekili are raised up along with the huge sails.

In camp, after the sun has retreated and fires burn, the men eat, talk and laugh. Davis sits in a spot by himself, reading his Bible. He glances at the king. Young, nearby, talks with Mana'oi. Kamehameha councils with his men around the largest fire in the center of the camp.

Davis shuts the book and ambles over to Young. After a short exchange, they both walk to the edge of the fire, near Kamehameha, perched on a rock. All eyes turn to them, as their presence is interrupting the king's story.

Davis clears his throat. "You, sir, want us to improve your army. But, Kamehameha, we know nothing of your army. Or anything about how you fight your battles here."

Young nods. "How have you been fighting wars in these islands? What happens first? We cannot help you if we do not know the weapons and strategy you use now."

Lamakua translates. A cat-like smile spreads across Kamehameha's face. He calls for slaves with torches. He offers places for Young and Davis next to him. The dancing firelight bounces on their faces as they glance around the circle and are accepted by the other men. The hearts of all in attendance are aware, despite any thoughts of hate for the whites, they are being woven together as a part of something larger than themselves.

Kamehameha launches in, "This good, Akake, Olohana. I show you."

He points to Lamakua. "Battle kahuna, teacher, so too his father."

"Kamehameha make Kahe k-I'i, war plan. Lamakua, say how *to fight*." He whispers in Hawaiian, "What is English for *regiments*?" Lamakua scratches his head. "I don't know. Try *'groups of men.'*"

Kamehameha says to Young, "I give names groups of men – who fight."

Young attempts to help. "In English, sir, we call them, *regiments*. Groups of men in battle, fighting. Re-gee-ment." The king and warriors mumble the word.

Kamehameha winks. "Mahalo, Olohana, I name the le-gee-men." He gestures for the men to come closer. The men crowd in. Kamehameha draws symbols with a stick in the sand. His confidence swells as he calls out the names with great panache, "Huna-lewa."

Lamakua translates, "Huna-lewa, first body. Strong, quick, fight with short spears.

Kamehameha draws another symbol. "Huna-pa'a... Wa'a-kaua."

Davis moves close and pronounces awkwardly, "Huna-p-a-a...Wa-a-ka-wa?

The warriors chortle and sputter at Davis's mispronunciation. Kamehameha frowns and they stop. "Akake. Is good you speak Hawaiian. Huna-pa-a good. This be Huna-leewa." He draws another symbol.

"I am trying to understand the weapons you use," says Young. "They come after Hoona-leewa? From the sides?"

Lamakua clarifies, "Yes - These groups, many men, all short spears and clubs."

The design in the sand is now a series of lines, arcs and arrows, which Kamehameha connects. "Pulu-kaua... Papa-kaua. Group close to king..."

Lamakua instructs, "These carry Po-lulus, very long spears."

Kamehameha draws a large oval around all the groups.

Lamakua continues, "At first, these groups move like one group, men very tight...like coconut, with King inside."

Davis raises his eyebrows at Young, who smiles in agreement. "This is quite efficient, actually. I mean the king in the coconut is good strategy, sir.

"Where would the king put men with muskets?" Young interrupts to Lamakua. "Kanaka, muss-ket? *Burning sand?*"

Kamehameha stops Lamakua from translating. "I see! Where to go *mussketi?*"

Lamakua smiles. "My king, your English is improving."

Davis points to different symbols. "I see your strategy so far, but, we must have a plan for re-loading when in battle. Perhaps here."

Kamehameha stares into the firelight, catches a vision, and looks back to Davis. He points to a rounded symbol near the front of the first body of men. "Here. Muss-kets." He looks to Lamakua. "This good?"

All consider the king's plan.

"Yes," Lamakua considers. "The king plans well. Mr. Young, you train Huna-lewa warriors first with the muskets. This will surprise the enemy and they will run. There is time for second row to re-load.

"Alright, we'll train Ho-oona-loowa first," John declares.

Davis, correcting Young, tries out Hawaiian words, "John, it's Huna-leeeewa, Huna-leeeeewa, I believe."

Kamehameha tosses his head back, chuckling at Davis. "Maika'i, friend Akake. Maika'i." He slaps Lamakua on the shoulder, who then laughs, allowing the other chiefs to join the king's amusement. Caught in the moment, Young and Davis succumb to the frivolity. The king stands, followed by all in the circle. They laugh and throw cheers into the night sky. A strange brotherhood is taking shape.

Across the cove, Kahekili's spy observes the flames from the war camp leaping in the dark. He hears the laughter of the men float across the water. Twigs snap beneath his feet as he retreats into the underbrush.

25

House of Bones

On the island of Oahu, frothy waves roll in from the point across the long, wide bay. A large crater looms in the background. At a mid-point on the shore, a massive, decorated hut stands like a sentinel on the harbor side of the beach.

To a lowly fisherman sent from Kamehameha to spy on Oahu, it has the appearance of simply a large royal hut from a distance. Standard bearers and fierce warriors guard the front, holding King Kahekili's emblem, a huge, ominous, shark.

But as the cautious fisherman, blending in as a merchant selling wares, takes a closer look, the structure of the hut has a ghoulish aspect. The colors of its sides have an eerie texture that do not become clear until they are much closer, and his eye discerns the horror of the configuration of hundreds of human thigh bones, ribs and shin-bones, all lashed together, decorated with dried skulls.

The fisherman spy disappears into the crowd as a group of richly dressed chiefs approach. One man has the respect of all the others and walks in front. He is a swaggering man in his late fifties, massive and imposing. His cold gaze ironically has the indifference of a shark. His face is riddled with tattoos and scars. He is Kahekili, King and overlord of the islands of Oahu, Maui, Lani, and Molokai. He is on his way into his house of human bones to discuss, yet again, the necessity of putting down the renegade king of the island of Hawaii, Kamehameha.

The fisherman tries to observe what he can of the council and circles to the side behind the guards.

Once in the hut, Kahekili takes his place on a throne, also decorated with parts of skulls and lined with glistening teeth. In attendance are his sons, Kalani-Kupule, Kapahili and many other chiefs, including Keoua and Kiwalo, from a remote part of the island of Hawaii.

Kahekili addresses the assembly. His eyes come to rest on the chiefs from the island of Hawaii. "You are sure you were not seen in your travels?"

Keoua reassures the king in a deep bow. "We came in disguise, Kahekili, my king. No one knows we are here. I, and my people give undying service to you.

Kiwalo nods. "Kahekili, we commit our armies to you for victory over Kamehameha. He is dangerous to our people. An evil spirit has consumed him. He and his followers must be destroyed."

Kahekili looks each man in the eye then focuses on them with contempt. "I hear your allegiance. But, Kamehameha has new weapons and the white men's strategy to help him. We agreed we must get these weapons from them. You failed to kill the oyster-men when you had the chance."

The impending doom for these two Hawaiian comrades is clear and all other chiefs in the hut look away, not offering support, wishing not to draw attention, knowing their bones could be the next to line the walls.

Instead, Kahekili, speaks with charm, "Worry not. The white men make no difference. Not to us. Let Kamehameha amuse himself with these toys. We have much greater manpower to crush them. Now listen to my son, Kalani-Kupule."

A gawky, but brutal young man, with a rippled scar on his right temple, stands up facing the nervous chiefs. "There are many more of us than all his armies. Kamehameha will be destroyed, I assure you. The old sorcerer on Lanai prophesied the Kona chief, Kame'eamoku, who killed the haoles on the white sailor's ship, will soon join us with a large army. Another prophecy reveals spirits will kill Kamehameha even before the first battle. So, you see, we will not likely even need to meet him on the field."

Those assembled raise their hands in a cheer of joy.

Kahekili, hearing this, serenely watches their relieved faces. The barbarous king takes the focus again, holding his hand up. "Other chiefs are unhappy with Kamehameha as well. The clever and trusted Kiana for one, a mighty warrior with many followers, is joining us. So you see, lovely children, fear has no place in our hearts. Come to the temple, we offer our sacrifices."

26

The Brotherhood

Two days later, in a bay near Pu'ukaloa, birds circle at the edge of the village. Opa throws stones at birds as he waits for his king and Davis to return. He hears drums and singing on the sea. He squints to see better. His eyes grow large as the *Fair American* rounds the point at full sail accompanied by a large number of warriors paddling, singing and shouting as they accompany the ship. The song is louder. Opa runs across the slope. As quickly as a lame boy can, he leaps over rocks and hollers, "Haole mahi moku!"

Kamehameha's war canoe leads the procession. But, the king is not in his canoe. He is at the helm of the schooner, holding it and singing with his warriors. A standard bearer slave near him holds high the banner with Kamehameha's colors. The deity, Ku-Ka-ili-moku, his long rows of sharp pointed teeth and stark staring eyes, is also held aloft, creating a powerful response from the crowd onshore. Guards announce the return of the king with large conch shells. People charge in from every direction.

Ka'a-humanu, Kamehameha's favorite woman, hurries out of his hut to meet a messenger. At the news of the king's arrival, she screams and picks up the messenger for a moment, swinging him in the air. She kisses the horrified man and drops him, almost gently, as she races to a ridge near the hill overlooking the bay, shouting in delight when she sees the two vessels enter the harbor. She floats down the slope toward the bay, her tapa cape catching the wind.

On the shore, dozens of men and women jump in canoes. Others swim to the vessels.

Young orders his warriors to drop the mainsail. His "All hands" can be heard across the water.

Davis is in the rigging for the first time in months and feels healthy again. He helps his new native sailors with tasks on the *Fair American*, and shouts orders to drop anchor in the bay.

Kamehameha, the clear victor, offers a wide gesture from the helm. He did not steal this vessel, it came to him, one might say, straight from the gods, and he has managed to hide it so far even from King Kahekili. He throws off his cape, leaping toward the water and twisting in the air like a flying fish, dives into the sea and re-surfaces in full stroke to his breathless sweetheart. Ka'ahumanu, impatient, dives in and swims toward her lover.

On the other side of the schooner, Young, caught up in duties as "captain-bo'sun," prepares to get in a dinghy. He claps the shoulders of his new mates. "Well done, lads. Maika'i."

The warriors in his care are beaming with pride at the encouragement, even though they can't understand a word he says. Other warriors receive him in the dinghy with cheers as they head for shore.

Kamehameha sees Ka'a-humanu swimming towards him and decides to surprise her. He looks mischievous as he dives deep enough to swim under her voluminous body. She cannot see him. She circles, curious at his disappearance. She howls with delight as his large hands caress her thighs. His head pops up and his arms embrace her.

As Young jumps on shore, he is engulfed by an adoring horde of young women bearing flower leis, the force of which knocks him flat in the water. He comes up sputtering, but, decides to release himself into their midst, letting go of concern about the kapu. He sees Davis in the crowd at a short distance. "Hey, mate, look!"

A buxom maiden sees Davis and says in Hawaiian, "Oh, there's the other one. How beautiful he is." She dives in, swimming to him.

Another girl screams to her friends, "Look at his muscles!"

Davis, too shy to handle this, jumps out of his canoe and swims back to the ship. Having started too late, he's soon also submerged in a gaggle of women who nearly drown him.

Young, in the midst of ladies, calls, "Isaac. No escape for you!"

Kamehameha and Ka'ahumanu emerge on the shore. He sweeps her into his arms, nuzzling her, the way Hawaiians kiss. "You should have seen me, Ka'a. I was holding the wheel. I was guiding that English ship. Olohana is teaching me. You must come with me next time."

Ka'ahumanu seductively holds his chin in her formidable hand. "You are the cleverest man on sea or land, my king. I have always known this."

Kamehameha winks. "Ah, yes, yes, I know that too, but I always rather hear it from your lips, my wild love. Welcome home. Come meet my new friends."

They laugh, seeing Young and Davis buried in women pulling at their clothes.

A host of priests subdue the girls as the white mariners, dripping with water and flowers, leave the shore to escape.

The priests hold the women at bay. "Leave off. Give them rest. Go prepare for the games."

Davis and Young scramble up the beach. Young still chortles from all the attention, Davis limps from ill-fitting shoes and his old wounds.

Once inside Young's hut, Davis, unlaces soggy shoes. Young, also wet, lies on his cot.

Davis tosses a shoe. "John, I am trying. But, it is more than one can endure. These ridiculous laws, their eating rules and *kapus*, the utterly bizarre customs, language, the nakedness, the filth, Lord. And those *women*."

Young rolls over, chuckling. "They were just glad to finally see us close up. They prayed so diligently the gods would heal us. The kapu is over. And we are alive. Let's enjoy the fact."

Davis snorts. "Every aspect of these females is so unlike our women. They have no sense of… sense of …"

Young sits up with a friendly warning. "I tell you,

truly, they mean no harm, my friend." He pauses. "Isaac...do you not miss the touch of a woman?"

Davis is appalled. "Just any woman? No. Mine? Yes. And certainly not twenty-five all at once - and some bigger than me!" He rips a shoelace. "These blasted shoes are too small."

"But, didn't they go to great lengths to find you shoes? Not many shoes around these islands. And your shredded feet from lava rocks needed more protection to heal. They are trying to take good care of you."

"That is very amusing. Yes, just keep smiling that asinine grin, John. There won't be a happy end to all this foolishness, mark my words."

"Asinine, hmm...one of your fancy words."

Davis pulls off his other shoe, tosses it out the window onto a rock ledge. It bounces back and almost hits him. He stumbles out of the hut in a huff. After a moment, he whirls back into the hut, grabbing the other shoe. "God help me, John, I'm beginning to respect this savage king. If we don't get away from these islands we will become barbarians, just like them." He stumbles out and disappears down the path. He throws the other shoe into the brush.

Young gazes after him, musing, wondering if Davis is right.

Storming into his hut, Davis stubs his toe and curses.

Opa runs in proudly, having retrieved Davis' shoes. "Kahuna Akake. Shooz."

Davis curses again and yanks the shoes from the youth and tosses them out the window. "No. Leave them." He sees the boy's crestfallen look. "Opa, too small. Pipipi, Mahalo, Opa. I thank you, but I must learn to go barefoot. These damned islands."

Opa gives Davis a quizzical smile and runs out down the path. He makes sure Davis is not watching him and ducks down the slope where the shoes landed. He picks them up and puts one on his good foot, then stands up, walks, gestures like Davis. He throws the other shoe down and exclaims like Davis, "Damn - Damn Shooz!"

Young watches Opa from his hut, amused at the sight of him pretending to be Davis. He takes a musket and starts to clean it when Mana'oi appears at his door with a box in his hands. "Aloha Mana'oi. Please, come in."

As he enters, Mana'oi looks around, checking every detail of the newly-made hut. "Olohana, your hut is maika'i for you? Is sat-is-fact-ion ?"

Young is quick to respond, "Oh, yes. Maika'i, my friend. Sit down."

Mana'oi relaxes.

"And what about supplies I had the king send to you? Maika'i? Is your hut is good?"

Mana'oi struggles to speak. The old craftsman is deeply humbled and begins to weep. "Maika'i, Master Olohana. Maika'i loa."

Young puts his hand on Mana'oi's shoulder. He holds out his hand to shake. "Call me only 'John'. You are my ho-aloha, friend. We will work together, Mana'oi." Young recognizes the box under Mana'oi's arm. "Ah, the chess set? Mahalo!"

Mana'oi, elated, puts the box down. He blurts out a grand idea burning in his mind, "Olohana, you teach Kamehameha game. Yes?"

For the first time since his capture, Young allows a deep laugh, sparked by a sense of irony. He tumbles into his hammock as the amusement subsides, taking with it much of the suffering of the last weeks. "Mana'oi, a pawn like me teaching this king chess? What a bizarre idea…" Sadness overtakes him. "In truth, I am his slave."

Mana'oi looks confused.

Young reaches for the musket he is cleaning, one from the *Fair American*. "Have a look. Muss-ket…" He aims it. "See? Boom. You understand?"

Mana'oi takes it gingerly, aware of the death it can bring. "Muss-ket…where burning sand go?"

"Powder. Gunpowder". It has none in it right now. But, with powder, here, and a small ball like this, goes here." He demonstrates. "In the hands of Kamehameha's warriors, it will change these islands forever. You will be a part of that. Do you want this fight with King Kahekili?"

"Yes. Must win."

27

War Games

At the king's ceremonial grounds, two weeks later, the people of Pu'uka-loa village gather for the most magnificent harvest celebration in many seasons. The warriors are nervous as they practice their competition fights with spears clashing, drums beating, and wild shouts of mock battles heard from all over the festival grounds. The sound is deafening, but exhilarating. Other teams of warriors prepare to compete to throw spears, box, share drum skills or practice the martial art of Lua.

At a safe distance, children play their own versions of the war games. They pummel each other with great veracity and fun, their shouts and squeals adding to the general chaos.

On the outer grounds, kahunas and chiefs mingle with jugglers, musicians and dancers. The women, wander among them and parade their most beautiful tapa gowns and leis. The elderly sit and watch, commenting on this one and that one, noting who is looking better this year and who is not.

Everyone in attendance senses they are a part of a growing kingdom, an island beginning to be called by his people, "the land of Kamehameha the Great". The Commoners talk in the privacy of their huts of the wisdom and power of their king. They too, finally believe his armies can overcome Kahekili in the coming war. They share stories about Kamehameha's exploits and his kindness to the lowest of the common people, the slaves and even the kauva. These tales have become inflated over the years, which has given him more power and mystery than he has rightly earned for himself. However, there is much truth in the stories.

Aside from a good harvest and preparing for war, Kamehameha's court and villagers have gathered to thank the gods for healing the white men who have brought weapons and new knowledge to help them.

A messenger announces the king's procession into the festivities. Hundreds fall to the ground as the king, then high chiefs, then kahunas, followed by Young and Davis and other luminaries enter the ceremonial grounds. Kamehameha, becomes an impresario, making a show of ushering Young and Davis into honored seats next to himself.

Lamakua, Kiana, Kahuna Lani, and other Chiefs and Chiefesses sit higher than the Commoners. Mana'oi and his woman, Nakui, enter and sit with the artisans. Most carry or wear articles they have carved or made.

The Princess Kaoana sits with other royals near Young and watches him intently.

Ka'a-humanu and other wives and courtesans sit in an area on the same level as the king. Ka'a-humanu tosses a sidelong glance of approval and curiosity toward Young and Davis. Her magical eyes reveal her rare quickness of mind.

This look from her is not lost on Young. "Isaac, I must say, that Ka'a-humanu, has the king's heart. She is his favorite. You see there, she is the one with the little dog."

Davis whispers, "I see. By the way, am I wrong, or haven't we been eating dog?"

Young replies to Davis with a wink, "Maybe. But not *that* dog."

Ka'a-humanu offers a wave in the direction of Young and Davis, but they realize it is a wave intended for Kamehameha, who is just beyond them. He returns it with a tender gaze. She blushes.

A conch blows. A hush falls over the crowd as they realize something of great import is toward. Paloa, the young poetess, enters, wearing a sarong decked with layers of ferns. Drummers move to accompany her. She sings and moves in exquisite grace, her arms languidly waving like a breeze embracing palm fronds. Her hands and fingers take the entire audience into her enchanting world, her eyes exude a curious wisdom and strength.

Davis and Young are aware of the important stories and history told at these events and gently tap Lamakua for translation.

Lamakua whispers the tale her movements tell, "She sings a *mele*."

Young nods. "Mele. A story…yes?"

Yes… *Long, long ago, ago prophets say The*
Great One will be ruler of all our island peoples.
To win the wars he will lead the bravest,
strongest, warriors with words like flames.
These men will possess…hearts of fire…eyes like
hawks…courage like the sea.
They will join him in victory over all enemies.

The Great One…
Kamehameha, Kamehameha, Kamehameha."

Young speaks sotto voce, "King George could use more of this, mate."

Davis, in spite of himself, is impressed by Paloa and her final graceful pose. Resounding cheers rise as she leads a line of dancers into a circle before disappearing into the night.

"I have not seen this young woman Paloa before. Why is that?" Davis proffers.

"She's been here all the time I expect."

Davis catches Young's amusement and downplays his interest with an acid retort, "I only mention she has an obvious fine intelligence."

Young smiles. "And is intensely beautiful."

Kamehameha has caught some of their conversation. He smiles and puts a hand on Davis' shoulder. "Paloa father say want Paloa learn English. You teach, Akake?"

Davis, awkward, tries to jump ship. "Oh, Kamehameha, your highness, I hardly speak English myself. John's the one with proper schooling, sir. He could teach her far better than I."

"You are too humble, lad. And I'm not the Shakespeare worshipper. That distinction goes to Isaac, sir." Young's having fun now, even feeling gregarious, making Davis squirm. "Use those books off the ship. Would make easy teaching"

Kamehameha offers, "You worship Snakes-beer, Akake? Olohana, I ask who you worship. You say *gods*, yes?"

"I said I worship God. One God."

Kamehameha is confused. "Snakes-beer…what god he?

Davis sputters. "It is Shhhakes…Shhakespeare. He was only a man. He wrote very fine words, sir. But, he was not a god. Only a great man."

Kamehameha is relentless. "Akake, you teach Eng-lish Paloa. And teach your word-god-man Snakesbeer."

The reluctant mariner grits his teeth. The king's manner is a mix of child-like whim and purring panther, which Davis is unable to thwart. "Lord, sir. I'll try my best."

Kamehameha claps his hands. "This very good!"

The dancers come to a resounding finish and hurry off the ceremonial stage.

Warriors charge in for the fight competition. They are huge, prepared, tattooed and wear bright colored headbands and loincloths.

Kamehameha stands. All are quiet. Lamakua translates to the sailors as the king speaks.

"My people, our time of peace is ended. Harvest is done, our offerings given. We now have our games and prepare for war. Surely as the moon is full, Kahekili and his sons seek death for us. But, they will not succeed." The assembly goes mad with cheers. He silences them.

"My god, Ku-Ka-ili-moku, the greatest god of war, has sent friends to help us. Olohana and Akake."

Young and Davis, embarrassed, wave and smile as the crowd gives them an ovation.

Kamehameha pronounces, "My warriors! You must learn from these men. Submit to their teaching. With your courage and the power from their red-mouth guns, we will win. And now, games!" Kamehameha signals a herald who blows a conch. A long arching sound. The groups of men toss insults at each other as they run onto the field.

One group sports Kamehameha's colors on their backs, the other has Kahekili's colors. The "War" begins as those playing "Kahekili's men" heartily engage the king's men. Shouts, cat-calls are exchanged and spears clang. Whoops from villagers rise and fall as the two sides slam each other. Kahekili's men begin to "die". The crowd's roar escalates to a fever pitch. Men drop all over the field.

Davis and Young are astonished at the bizarre sight. Davis rubs his chin. "Are they injured? Is this in earnest?"

Lamakua clarifies, "No, Akake. When man knocked down, he only *play* dead. See? No blood. Is Game." Lamakua jumps up cheering his side. "Kill him! Aha!"

The crowd goes into a frenzy as the leader of Kahekili's group is "killed." Another conch is blown, and boys run onto the field counting "dead" men. As a "dead" man is counted, he gets up, good-naturedly brushes himself off, bows to the cheering crowd and leaves. The boys call numbers to the scorekeeper, Kahuna Lani. A conch is blown again. There's a hush.

Kahuna Lani, his robes rippling in the breeze, ascends the platform. He holds up the banner of Kiana, and announces, "Lanakila. The winner is... Kiana's Warriors!"

The various teams are shocked and shout out mixed reactions, some needing to be restrained. Kiana's faction joins in a hooting cheer and gloat over the other teams.

Young asks Lamakua, "What's wrong? Why are they angry?"

"Kiana's men win. Some people angry they lose...lose, how to say? Not win. Many beads and kala–much – *value* is a word?"

Young howls with glee. "Isaac! They are bloody gamblers. I should have guessed." He slaps Davis on the back. "We might as well be on the docks in England, mate."

The crowd is policed by priests. New teams enter the field as drums pound. This time boxing matches are launched. The crowd, forgetting losses, cheer for their new favorites. A quick exchange of beads and ornaments are bet.

Kiana appears and whispers to Lamakua, who asks Kamehameha. The king nods.

Lamakua comes to Young, embarrassed. "The Ali'i from Kauai, Chief Kiana, has brought a black stone to you, this mean Kiana challenge you. Olohana, will you fight him?"

"Lamakua, I'm a peace-loving sailor, not a wrestler. No, I do not accept this challenge. I no fight Ali'i Kiana."

Lamakua and Kamehameha look from Young to Davis. "Tell Chief Kiana, I also decline. That means *no*." Lamakua goes to Kiana and translates.

Kiana in Hawaiian exclaims to his cronies, "Worthless white men…cowards. Ha!"

Kamehameha gives Kiana a hard look, but gives Davis a smile. "One day I bet on you, Akake. Your mana strong."

"I fear you would lose, sir. I suppose I am stronger than some, but I still choose a musket or a blade when I fight."

Kamehameha goes to Kiana, and speaks harshly in Hawaiian, "You are behaving like a boy. Wait until you get onto their training field, you will likely be the coward."

The crowd cheers. Kamehameha looks. Two huge men have squared off on the center of the field. The conch blows. The men circle and grapple each other, back and forth in a clutch. One of the men puts his foot at a strategic angle and flips the loser, who hits the ground in a cloud of dust.

The sounds of terrified screaming sail over the celebration as several priests drag a man and woman toward Kamehameha. Everything stops.

The crowd turns to watch the king. Words are exchanged with Kahuna Lani and his liege. The king raises his hand. Drums begin again and games continue as if nothing happened. Kamehameha moves quickly toward the temple with Kahuna Lani. The two prisoners are dragged after them.

Young questions Lamakua, "What offense did those two people commit?"

Avoiding him, Lamakua replies, "They broke kapu, Olohana. They broke law."

Davis peers through the audience as the couple are taken roughly into the temple. "Which law did they break?"

"Eating of food."

"Eating?"

Lamakua bristles, "Woman and man in same hut. This is kapu."

Davis is appalled. "I have heard of this ridiculous law. But, surely the king will show mercy."

Lamakua snaps, "I not know this show *mer-cee*. They must die or gods punish our people."

"What? *Die for sharing food?* It is barbaric. I have seen strange customs in many lands, but, this? This is not—"

Lamakua cuts him off, "It is kapu!"

Davis gets up and heads in the direction of the temple.

Young leaps up. "Where're you going?"

Davis ignores him.

Young rushes after him. The crowd turns to watch. Lamakua follows Young.

Davis' rage is growing by the second. "Killed? Murdered? For eating together, John? My God, man, we cannot be a part of this madness. I cannot stand by. I cannot."

Young grabs his arm. "Don't interfere. Perhaps, when we have been here longer, we can—"

Davis stomps down the path.

"Isaac, it's their law. Don't interfere."

"Have you no conscience? Are you going to do nothing and let these savages take innocent lives for nothing?"

Part of the crowd has left the arena and begun placing bets on Davis and Young.

Young grabs Davis again, this time his hand tightly on Davis' arm. "Isaac, listen to me. Are you ready to die for those two people, those *savages* as you call them? I am not. I must respect the customs here until I can influence the king. And they'll kill us both if you try to stop them. Calm yourself, man. We are being watched."

Davis shoves Young. "Leave off. I must at least plead for them. I'm not a barbarian."

The boxers also stop fighting and watch Young and Davis.

Young presses his case, "Listen, these laws are ancient. Those two knew the law and broke it anyway. They made a choice. Tell me what good will be done if we die protesting."

Davis shakes free. "Perhaps nothing, but, I must try."

Young follows Davis trailed by dozens of villagers, combatants and revelers. "Isaac, we must both stay alive. What good are we dead?"

"I cannot watch this."

"Then don't." Young lunges, punching Davis squarely on the jaw. Davis drops to the ground, out cold. The crowd roars thinking this is a part of the entertainment. Bets are paid.

Lamakua hangs his head, knowing he has lost control of his prisoners.

The crowd shouts for Young and places a wreath on his head. He yanks it off and throws it away. The people are confused. Davis shakes himself and rises.

Kamehameha, returns from the execution, sees Davis, and assumes they were boxing. Commoners hit the ground, prostrating. "Olohana. I not see. Fight again. I make wager!"

"Sir, did you just kill those two people?" Young demands.

Kamehameha is relieved. "It is so. Yes, all is good now."

Davis turns to leave, but wheels around to the king. "No, Kamehameha, not good. Evil. Your laws are evil. Do you hear me? La-wehala La-wehala. Tell him, Lamakua."

The Hawaiians hear their word for evil and are shocked that it is spoken against their king. Several chiefs, all speak at once, moving to protect him. Lamakua restrains them.

Young cuts in, facing Kamehameha. "What he means, sir, is only…"

Davis cannot see any danger, only feels outrage. "Have you no idea what you have just done? Those hapless creatures were only eating? How could any gods think that two people…"

Young steps in. "Isaac, stop—"

Kamehameha's expression turns fierce. An icy cold tone takes over. "Do not speak. Our gods not your gods."

Davis bridles. "Sir, how well I know that. Your people need our wisdom and our God far, far more than they need to be taught our ways of war."

Kamehameha's bodyguards keep Davis from getting any closer.

Young intervenes. "Sir, he doesn't know what he's saying."

Kamehameha grabs Davis and holds his shirt tight to his throat. "No speak against our gods. I offer you life. I give huts. Food. Protect from Kahekili. Obey me or die, Akake."

Davis backs down. He starts to leave, then steps back toward the king. The guards stiffen.

He is careful to be calm. "Sir, I am your prisoner. Yes. You hold my life. Yes. But, I am not a prisoner of your gods. And I never will be. But, you are. You and all your people are imprisoned by gigantic ignorance." He walks down the path to his hut.

The guards move in. Kamehameha holds up his hand. "Let him go."

Young takes a breath. "Sir, we are grateful for your kindness. Please forgive Isaac, he meant no harm to your people. There is much he does not understand about your laws. Goodnight." He leaves.

The crowd is silent and frightened. The priests confer.

Kahuna Lani leans in to have Kamehameha's ear. "My king, these men are dangerous. Perhaps, if you would consider doing without their war teachings?"

Kamehameha turns from him and studies the sailors heading back to their huts. He considers for a long moment. "Watch them. If they try to leave, you must kill them. But, hear me, I do not wish for it. Go." He lifts his hands to the crowd and forces a smile, then laughs. "Where is the wrestling match? Let's see who is going to win. There must always be a winner, my people." He laughs.

The people move back into their seats. The next boxing match begins.

However, the king's face has become a mask behind which his heart is deeply conflicted.

28

Training Field

The same men, who fought brilliantly in war games three days before, sit in neat rows, awkwardly holding muskets along with others holding training "muskets" carved out of bamboo, all feeling foolish.

Kiana, in the front, chafes in the tutelage of white men. There is an even greater tension between Kamehameha, Young, and Davis. The king covers it well, standing at a distance, posing for his troops with a real musket. Young uses his most military demeanor to keep control of the situation and run interference between Davis and the king.

Young addresses the warriors. As he speaks, Lamakua translates, "The King will demonstrate how to hold and point your musket. Watch very carefully. As you know it is a deadly weapon." Young signals the king.

Kamehameha takes his musket and points it at Davis with a mischievous look in his eye. Davis stares back at the king, undaunted. The king chuckles and points the gun at his warriors who get nervous and duck. He points to one of them. "He to be Kahekili". The man comes up, terrified. The king aims and pretends to pull the trigger saying, "Boom!"

The warrior stares at the king, wide-eyed. The king points down and the warrior dives to the ground doing his best to play *dead*.

Kamehameha raises the musket. He points to a man in the front row. "He be Kalani-Kupule." He "shoots" again. The next man drops.

Awed response ripples through the warriors. The *dead* man jumps up and brushes himself off. The group cheers.

Young gestures for quiet. Lamakua translates. "As the king has just shown us, these weapons are very dangerous. A few of you have seen what they do when loaded with *burning sand*. We call it *gunpowder*. Mr. Davis will demonstrate."

Davis takes his loaded musket and tosses a coconut into the air, a little too close to the king. He shoots with live ammunition. "*Boom!*" The coconut is blown to bits.

Kamehameha jumps in fear, along with the warriors. "Maika'i. Very good. Yes, good." While he sees terror in the eyes of his men, the king slaps Davis on the back. Davis doesn't respond.

Young regains control. "Thank you! Now, just as you have always trained with a spear, you must train now with a musket. Respect its mana. Akake and I will show you with the king's musket, how to clean and load it quickly. Loa wiki. Remember, to shoot is easy. Clean and load, not easy. It will take much practice to clean and load fast, but you will know in time. Watch carefully…"

The sailors demonstrate – Young with the king's musket and Davis with his. The king comes in close. Young cleans the barrel with a swiftness gained only from years of experience. Davis does the same. The two work together and speak as they act, "Clean barrel, load ball, aim, fire." The shots explode in a resounding "*boom.*" They shatter the pristine landscape around them. Kiana looks concerned he might be in over his head. A group of villagers has gathered on the perimeter, ducking every time they shoot.

Weeks later, a young boy, held high in the arms of Kamehameha, is focused intensely on his older brother holding a musket out on the training field. The boy can hardly breathe as he watches the warrior aim at the "target", a coconut, held by another warrior twenty yards away. Other children and chiefs sit with them, hypnotized by the training exercises. Beads of sweat course down the face of the young warrior.

John Young orders, "Fire!" The coconut is tossed up, the warrior pulls down on the target and squeezes the trigger – boom! No one breathes. The coconut blasts into bits.

With lightning speed, the warrior cleans the barrel, re-loads, and stands at attention. The warriors go wild. Young is impressed. The crowd is jubilant.

Davis readies rows of warriors in a training exercise.

"Holo-mua," Kamehameha shouts praises from a rock above. He has never been happier. The troops below him are in rows, with every part of their minds and hearts marshalled to fight in a new way.

Young and Davis, exhausted and sweaty take the rest of the warriors through the drill with no ammunition. They've been at it for many days. "Ready, First line," shouts Young. The first line pretends to aim and fire, acting as one unit, shouting, "Boom!"

Davis commands, "Second line." The first line kneels in place, "cleans and loads", the second line "shoots." Second line warriors shout, "Boom!"

"First line," orders Young. The second line kneels, "cleans and loads" next shot as first line shouts. "Boom!" This is done with astounding efficiency, following which Young calls out, "Hold Fire! Yes. Excellent. Maika'i!"

Davis is surprised at what he is seeing. "Yes, lads – well done!"

Young turns back to the rows of warriors, who now feel powerful, having mastered the drill. "At ease men." He stares at the warriors, still at attention, like rows of statues. "Maika'i hana. Strong. No more today. Aloha! Go!"

Kamehameha raises his hands to the warriors, "Mahalo nui loa. He'e nalu!" The men then fall out, hooting with joy, disperse and run wildly toward the shore.

The king hurries down from his rock to intercept the sailors. "My friends. You teach good." He walks with them toward the beach. The king's massive hands land on the shoulders of the two white men. "My people will see peace because you give them teaching. Better morning come soon." the king's gait is so fast, he begins to circle back around the sailors, enjoying their company like a brilliant child enchanted with new pets. He stops mid-step, concerned. "Akake... Olohana... Your hearts resting now? How is your feelings? I want you have joy. Ko Hawaii nei. Much aloha."

Young is polite. "Everything is as well as it can be, sir."

Trying to be civil, Davis adds, "Your men are good students."

"Wait." Kamehameha stops and stares at the two men. One of his most useful gifts is sensing deep feelings in humans around him. Being able to see pockets of molten lava in minds and hearts of others has been a boon to him all his life, so he is disappointed to see these white men have yet to understand the good fortune they have stumbled onto with him on his journey of great conquest. He confronts Davis. "Do not have hate for Kamehameha, Akake. The gods punish me if I stop all kapu of my people. They must obey."

Being true British islanders, and not given to the emotions so rich in Hawaiians, the mariners stare at the hulking figure before them, still remembering the murder of innocent people weeks before. In this moment the king becomes aware he has allowed his personal desire for their friendship to overshadow his goals for using these men. He has overstepped his kingly bounds and is no longer looking for mere obedience from these slaves. He feels anger stirring as he longs for a warm look or word from them in spite of the fact he has been taught they have no souls.

The eyes of both men make it clear to him the warmth is not there. Losing patience, the king explodes, "No. I not talk to you. You only Commoners. If I talk King George, he know my heart. He see Kamehameha friend. Much mana King George. Ho-aloha."

A twinkle pops in Young's eye. He tries not to look at Davis, who is suppressing a laugh.

The king's rage swells. "Is laughing? Is laugh to me?"

Young holds up his hands. "Sir, No. You are completely correct."

Davis dives in, "Yes. It is a true thing, sir. Our king would certainly agree with you, Kamehameha. It matters not what we think about anything. We are only workmen, prisoners, sailors – we are your slaves. Why do you care what we think or feel?"

The king sees the truth but, chooses to move beyond. "No, Akake, is matter to me. You good warriors. Much good mana. King need good men to be friend to follow where he go, or he go alone."

Mercurial man that he is, he becomes jovial again. He scurries ahead of them, fairly dancing down the lane. "Now *I* to teach you. Come follow, you *Blokes*!"

They come to a bend in the trail. A massive beach stretches before them with turquoise waves breaking six or seven feet high.

Many warriors shout as they catch the best waves and maneuver long wooden boards on froth and curl. The rest of the training warriors, laugh and jostle each other as they head for the shore and dive in.

Crashing through the waves they toss the boards into the sea and leap on them. Soon they are careening down the curl.

The white men are stunned as the warriors show brief dominance over the willful surf, each man in his own wild dance to balance his board as the wave carries him toward the shore.

Young shoots a look to Davis. "So this is where they all go when they disappear from the training field? I hope to God he doesn't expect to get me out there. Madness."

The king has grabbed a board brought to him by a servant and carries it toward the surf. He calls back to the sailors, "Akake. Olohana. I teach. Come!"

Caught in a manly web, they reluctantly take off their shirts. Young, very dubious, puts his shirt on a rock and places his watch on top of it. "You go, Isaac. Tell him I will just observe first. I loathe all these wretched water games. I wasn't made to swim."

The warriors laugh and yell to the white men to join them. It is a challenge these mariners must at least attempt or suffer grief from their native students.

Davis decides he would like to learn this sport and runs to the surf, looking back to Young. "Come on, John. It's their most harmless activity."

"Sharks are not harmless, mate," Young shouts. "You go!"

Kamehameha offers his board to Isaac. Pressed into service by noblesse oblige, Davis bravely attempts to get on the board. He immediately loses balance and slides off. Kamehameha's men howl with glee. Davis laughs too and gives the board back to the king, who leaps on and shows off his amazing skill. He takes several waves and is able to dip far down the wave and slide back up. He spins away just at the moment when he has had the best of its curl. He embraces the sea with his awareness of her many powers. Davis watches from the shallows and is impressed. John watches from the shore, only his feet in the surf, determined to bail out on this.

Back in the lagoon, the rock where Young and Davis's shirts are draped, is visited by a beautiful hand. The hand grabs Young's watch. It disappears.

At the urging of the king's men, Davis tries a bit more to stay on the board for a brief ride as warriors cheer him on. Cautious, he rises to stand as a wave carries him aloft, able to balance, only to lose it and be dumped into the sea in an embarrassing cartwheel. The warriors hoot and holler, but Davis is still under the water.

Young watches from the shore, concerned for Davis. The king searches for him. He finally appears, his head bobs out of a wave. He roars with laughter, his strong, burly arms stroking through the current like a fish. Young swallows hard and waves.

The warriors jostle Davis and laugh as he shoves the king's board back to him through the waves. The king and Isaac continue to enjoy this brief, wild, respite, leaving behind all thoughts of gun barrels, targets, burning sand, spears, death, anger and the many perils of impending war.

Musing from the shore, Young takes a deep

breath as his eyes drift up to the exquisite horizon. "*Will I ever see England again?*"

29

Watch and Book

I n Young's hut that evening, John and Isaac clean muskets, both men lost in the silence of their thoughts. Finally, Young looks up. "The king was in a jolly mood today."

Davis snorts. "Got visions of victory now."

"Yes. Lamakua told me he sleeps with his musket."

"Truly? He's like a child. A gigantic, petulant, all-powerful, brilliant baby. How do you restrain yourself, John? I am always one step from destruction with him."

"Perhaps I'm a coward."

Davis retorts, "Not likely, mate."

Young stops his task. "My father said, 'The test of a man's mettle comes always by surprise.' Now I know what he meant. I wonder how he would have behaved in my place."

Isaac studies Young. "I've been meaning to thank you for saving my life. They would have killed me that night."

Young chuckles, puts his musket down, looking for his watch. "You think I was saving your life? Don't fool yourself. I was only trying to save mine."

"You're a humble man. I know what you did. I thank the Almighty for you."

Young looks out the hut window, and speaks from a deep place, "Don't ever let me stop you from doing your conscience again."

"Our two fates are in the same cup, my friend. I don't wish to bring you greater suffering." He gets up and stares into the night.

"We're aboard a very strange ship, sir."

Young sighs. "Aye."

"Let's hope this captain doesn't run us on the rocks." The moment renders them both mute.

Young moves away. He searches his bunk. Abruptly, he throws down his shirt and looks in the direction of the beach. "I remember. I carefully put it on my shirt. These damned thieves!"

"What is it?"

"My watch. Someone has stolen it. They will *kill* you for fishing on a holy day, but think nothing of stealing one blind." He storms out. "Hide my musket. I'm going to complain."

The next morning, the Pu'ukaloa temple area is crowded with people in the normal commerce of a day. Boys chase girls as old women carry tapa roots from the countryside. In a corner of the courtyard a crowd stands near Young, Lamakua, and others listening to an announcement. In the group, is Kaoana, looking very calm.

Kahuna Lani, in Hawaiian, chastises the villagers roundly, "...and the king is very disappointed someone would take this piece of metal from Olohana that speaks to him and tells him what to do. He does not demand punishment, but if whoever has borrowed it, will be very kind to bring it to him quickly. This very day. Thank you."

Hearing this, Young is amused at the tyranny of his watch. *Perhaps time should not have such power over me. It certainly has no meaning for these people. They are not bound by it in any way.*

Across the village in Davis' hut, Isaac is in his hammock, composing a tune on his dulcimer.

Opa is enthralled nearby harmonizing with his native lute. The melody is sweet and brings them both solace. They are in another world when a voice is heard outside.

Malama, a higher chief, gets Davis' attention. "Aloha Kahuna Akake…"

Annoyed, Davis puts down his instrument and raises his tapa curtain. He suddenly remembers his promise to the king. "Ah, yes, English lesson, welcome."

Paloa, moves into the hut, her languid movements fill the atmosphere with a sweetness as she covers her nervous anticipation. She has come for her first English lesson chaperoned by her grandfather, a wizened, elder gentleman. He waits for her, sitting on a stool outside the hut. Davis ushers Opa out. Opa, stubborn, sits near John Young's hut.

Down the lane, Kaoana arrives looking for Young and, not seeing him, comes to Opa. She asks where Young is and when he will be back. Opa points toward the temple. She leaves.

Inside Davis' hut, Paloa looks with expectant eyes, as they sit. She has many suitors, and is not attracted to Davis. She sees him only as she has been schooled, as one of those strange creatures with ghostly skin and no soul. But, she is obedient and wanting to please her family, who have chosen this study of English.

Davis resents this encounter. He attempts politeness. "Pa-loa. A fine name. Well, we will begin lesson with this." He searches through his book. "Ah, this is a great story. Do you know, Paloa, what I mean… *story*?"

She looks at him and has no idea.

He ignores a flash of attraction for her. Clutching his old friend, the volume of Shakespeare, he gains confidence. "Well, trust me, this is a truly great play. '*The Tempest.*' The Storm. Uh. *Ino*"? He uses gestures to the sky as if pounding rain.

Paloa, concerned, gets up and looks outside for signs of a storm. Seeing the beautiful day looks at Davis as if to say, "Are you crazy?"

Davis sees this in her eyes. "No." He points to pages in the book. "In story… ino. It is a mele written by mister Wil-li-am Shakes-peare."

Paloa, as if discovering gold responds, "Mele? Ino? Ah…" She implies a storm with graceful gestures, a type of sign language.

Isaac is thrilled. "Yes. You see the story – the mele – begins on a ship, a moku, in a storm, Ino… listen."

He reads, "*Master, Bo'sun. Bo'sun, cried the men*" – like Olohana – *Here master. What cheer?*

Master, Speak to the mariners! Fall to't yarely, or we run aground!" He looks up and realizes Paloa is lost. "You see, they are in trouble in the storm... But, I see – you do not see."

Isaac is in trouble. He looks at Paloa, a dawning awareness that she is truly exquisitely beautiful, which paralyzes him. He points to the book. "This is book... Buh-Buh-BuuuuuuuuK. Many, many mele." He taps on the book.

Now she giggles and holds out her hand. He hands her the book. She looks at the book, touches it and runs her long, lovely fingers over its cover. She tries out the word, "Buuuuk... Mele Buuuuuk?"

Davis is astonished to have made headway. "Maika'i Pa-loa. Mele *Book*."

Paloa repeats, 'Mele Buuk.'

Easy, Book of Meles. Sure. He feels better. He looks up and sees her huge, intense eyes studying him. He is lost, fathoms deep. "So the ship you see, is caught up in the storm and the men are marooned... marooned... on an enchanted... island."

30

Golden Cave

Out on the pathway near the highest cliffs, the late afternoon sun catches the side of the mountain, scorching it. As Kaoana walks on a narrow trail on the cliff, she notices Ka'ahumanu in the distance moving fast away from the beach. She sees Kiana approach Ka'ahumanu. They do not see her watching.

Ka'ahumanu speaks to Kiana for a moment. He laughs and speaks to her. She shoves him hard and continues on her way. He stares after her, sullen.

Kaoana turns quickly, so as not to be seen by them, and hurries down the slope to the temple grounds.

In the blacksmith hut under a banyan tree, a slave hammers hot metals. Young, who has been overseeing workers with Mana'oi, looks at the butt end of his musket with awe. On the musket handle *OLOHANA YOUNG, BO'SUN* is exquisitely carved.

"How very kind of you, Mana'oi. Thank you. It is beautiful."

He looks at the slave who has just polished the handle. "And this shine. Very good. Maika'I. Mahalo. Thank you."

The Kauva slave acts as if John had not spoken to him. Young is confused.

Mana'oi raises his hand. "No speak. Olohana, he Kauwa *Cow-va.*"

"Why not? He is doing good work. He did a fine job."

Mana'oi moves further away and Young follows. "Olohana, Kauva, never speak, no Kauva speak. Slave. Only work."

Young senses from Mana'oi's abhorrence of this man, that he is an outcast of some kind.

"I saw a moon-shaped scar on his head. Do all Kauva have that?"

"All. Mark Kauva.

"Why are they so? How did it begin?

"I know not. Kauva all my days." Mana-oi changes the subject. "I pray gods bring you much power with musket, Olohana. Let us see in sun." He goes to the entrance.

He sees a woman approaching. Mana'oi, suddenly aware he will be in the presence of an Ali'i princess, prostrates himself and scuttles away.

Young calls out, "No, wait, Mana'oi,"

Young is suddenly alone with the young woman, "May we be of service?"

Kaoana feels awkward. She calls to Mana'oi to serve her. He returns to them, with head bowed. "Tell Olohana I know who took his metal friend. I will show him where it is if he will go with me in secret. Only in secret. Tell him and then leave us and tell no one."

Mana'oi turns to John, eyes averted. "Olohana, this be Ali'i Kaoana. She is daughter of Kamehameha brother. He lives in Ka'u. She say she take you to your watch. I go now."

Young sees Mana'oi hurry off. He extends his right hand toward Kaoana. She nods and extends her hand. It is a gesture becoming somewhat accepted among Hawaiians, after seeing haoles like to use it to greet people. They shake hands.

Young is formal in his introduction, "A pleasure to have your acquaintance, Miss Ka-o-ana."

She is shy, all her bravery abandoning her as she stares at him, weak and frozen.

Young leans in. "My *uwakī?* You say you take me to my watch, my *uwakī?*"

She smiles and moves down the path, looking back to make sure he is following. Young follows. Up around a curve Mana'oi turns back to look to see where John and the princess are going. He feels guilty for looking, but cannot stop himself.

A half hour later, the sky is turning a deep, pulsing, fuchsia. Young, baffled, follows Kaoana along the shore. Seabirds call and circle them. He remembers the warm smile she gave him that day in the healing hut. He has wondered about her. They walk in silence.

She gestures toward the sky. "Akala."

Young guesses from her expression that she is referring to the beauty of the sky. "Yes… lovely sky."

They walk further. Young is nervous. "I don't like secrets, Miss Kaoana. This not good. I could get into a load of trouble with your people. Are *you engaged?* You don't understand do you? You… Kaoana – Pa'a 'oe? You engaged?"

Kaoana shakes her head *no*, then giggles.

Young, horrified she may have mistook this question for a proposal, tries to back out of any misunderstanding, "Not that I meant that I, I mean I didn't mean – Lord, Kaoana, are you sure this is about my watch? My Uwaki? Mea makamea? My treasure?" He stoops down and draws the shape of the watch in the sand.

She snickers again and leads him into some rocks. Over a rise, Young sees a hidden lagoon, encircled by boulders, with gentle waves washing into it. The sunset's reds and pinks create an enchanting view. As they cross around the lagoon, Kaoana sees a fish move in the water. In a flash, she throws her small dagger and spears it. A perfect shot. Young is stunned, and even more concerned.

She retrieves the fish and hands it to him. "Makana, *gift*."

Young staggers a little, holding the fish gingerly. "Oh, Mahalo. That was – very quick Princess. Maika'i. You just happen to have that daggar? Hm… and you are well-trained, I see."

Kaoana gestures for him to sit. He does. In swift movements she lifts up a rock and pulls out a calabash, opens the top and takes out Young's gold timepiece. He grins and takes the watch. He is beginning to catch on.

"Kaoana… did you take this?"

She pretends not to understand. She takes out a carved comb from the calabash. He takes the comb, confused. She takes it and to his surprise combs his hair. He is unable to move. She giggles. Young is sure now of his 'thievery theory'.

"This is for me? This comb? No'o? *Mine?*"

Kaoana nods. "Ae. *Yes.*"

She puts her hand to his face and then puts the comb through his hair again. As the comb is moved through each inch of his skull, a molten heat moves through Young's body, which he fights hard to resist. He fears retribution from her relatives if he touches her. But, his heart is truly charmed by her sweetness.

"Kaoana, how very kind. You are... dear God, what is the word for it? You are very beautiful. Nani'oe *beautiful.*"

The princess looks him straight in the eye. "Olohana... Kipona aloha... Olohana... *I love you, deeply...*"

She leans forward, closes her eyes and rubs her nose across his cheek. He has heard about this way of kissing but never tried it. He closes his eyes and follows her lead. He returns the gesture with his nose, trying to give and receive the affection. But, he cannot keep himself from gently lifting her chin.

"Blast. Forgive me. I must..." He kisses her lips. She opens her eyes feeling this new, unexpected sensation. A voice floats on the wind. Kaoana hears it and holds him tight. Down the beach, Opa runs, hollers in every direction, "Kahuna Olohana.

Kahuna Olohana!"

Young puts a hand on her shoulder. "A'ohe alia. *No, wait.* I must go." He kisses her once more and hurries away.

Young appears on the shore from around the rocks as Opa runs to him. "Kahuna Olohana! Akake say come. Wiki-wiki."

Opa and Young enter Kamehameha's storehouse. Mana'oi keeps Opa out.

Kamehameha, Davis, Lamakua and other chiefs search through boxes from the ship.

"What is this about? I couldn't understand Opa."

Davis rages, "We've been looking all over for you. Someone leaked water into the saltpeter. Some of the boxes are wet. We've opened all of them. Some of the powder might be useless. It was not rain, they were carefully covered. This is sabotage, John."

Young sits, rubs his head. "Someone who knows about gunpowder...?"

The king looks at Young. "Olohana, can fix? Can shoot mussket?"

Davis shakes his head. "Once wet, drying it out properly will be hard – it clumps up – there is a traitor – or a group of traitors trying to harm your military," Lamakua translates to the king.

Kamehameha pounds his fist on a box. "I will kill the traitors." He calls to several chiefs. "Find out what you can. Question everyone!"

Lamakua encourages the king. "We will ask the gods for a ship to buy more powder."

Young posits. "We still have the cannon ammunition. Lamakua, ask Kamehameha, could there be from his inner circle of chiefs, someone – or men – that wish him harm?"

Lamakua translates. A sardonic look overtakes the king's face. "Olohana, traitors like storm. Never far off. Come away."

The group walks out into the growing darkness, despondent and confused.

Davis whispers to Young. "We had better find out who did this."

"It could be coming from anywhere. He is loved, but the ones who hate him, do so with deadly devotion."

The horizon is filled with black clouds exploding with lightning. They cross the temple grounds as pounding rain overtakes them. The wooden images now look like so many giant guardians. Their stoic, obsidian eyes in the lightning flashes challenge the power of the thundering tempest.

31

When Kings Go Forth

March, 1790

Weeks later, torches burn around Kamehameha's inner courtyard. The king, Young, Davis, Lamakua, Mapala several other chiefs, chiefesses, several servants and Opa, laugh and recreate themselves. The atmosphere is one of great camaraderie.

Kamehameha and Young are at a table, playing chess. The king wears one of Young's English shirts, re-sewn and made to fit his massive frame. Young sports some of the king's neck ornaments and no shirt. They create a delightfully incongruous picture.

At a distance, Opa plays Davis' dulcimer.

Ka'ahumanu and Kaoana make necklaces of shells, talking and teasing while keeping an eye on the chess game. One of Kamehameha's infant sons sleeps on the lap of Old Nahena.

The king makes a move. Young is astonished by the bad choice. "Sir, that would put your king in danger." The king gives him one of his sly looks. "Puh, puh." Young shrugs and studies the board. In a flash, he sees the wisdom of the king's move and is impressed. "Oh, I see. Well, sir. Looks like I'm in a lot of trouble..." Kamehameha claps his hands like a happy child. "Check! Aha. I win. I sorry. We have game like this, Olohana. *Konane.* I teach you one day." Young looks for a way to get out of check. Drums beat in the distance.

In a corner, Davis reads out loud to Paloa, Lamakua, Mana'oi and Nakui. Paloa has become smitten with Davis, but he is using all his strength not to fall for her. He reads with great reverence...

Be not afeared... The isle is full of noises, sounds and sweet airs that give delight and hurt not. Sometimes a thousand twangling instruments will hum about my ears, and sometime voices

*that if I then waked after a long sleep, will make
me sleep again—*

Lamakua interrupts, "Forgive me, Kahuna
Akake..."

"Yes?"

"I am giving much ear to your story, but, you say
this written by one of wisest men of your Britain?"

Davis grins. "Yes, William Shakespeare."

"But the mischief man, Cali-ban and others be
like many I know in Havaee. You always say Britain
people not like us. This not true?"

Issac chuckles. "Of course...we have much
mischief makers and many evildoers, too. So, I
suppose there's good and evil in every land."

Lamakua nods in agreement.

"*So...then in dreaming, the clouds methought would
open and show riches ready to drop upon me...*" He
glances up and sees all the faces focused on him.
Humbled by their adoration, the kidnapped mariner, slave to King Kamehameha, Welsh lover of
poetry, man-on-brink-of-passion, holds his book
closer to the torch, allows the goodness of living to
fill his soul for at least this brief moment. He reads.

Wind billows the flames in the courtyard as all
in this unlikely community proceed in what could
be called the most pleasant of times.

In a cave on the coast of Maui, fire licks the bottom of a large cauldron. Someone is chanting. A hand takes a utensil and pulls a nasty-looking mass out of a boiling pot. The entrails of an animal are nearby. The mass from the pot is wrapped and given slowly to other hands belonging to an elderly Kauva. The slave leaves the hut.

The sorcerer sits down and continues the chant. He is a wizened old man with a moon-shaped scar on his forehead. As he chants, he looks across the room and nods to someone sitting in the corner. It is Chief Kiana of Kauai, who has come on an important secret mission from the island of Hawaii.

Outside, a full moon floats. The Kauva slave moves down a path. An owl, perched on a nearby branch stares at him, hoots and flutters into darkness.

32

The Unexpected

It is a hot afternoon on the Pu'ukaloa training field two weeks later. A conch blows. Roughly a hundred men are in training exercises, split in two groups and wearing different colors to identify what side they are on. A sham battle begins.

Kamehameha, from on a rock throne on the sideline, watches as Kiana and Davis lead regiments against Lamakua and Young. John and Isaac, now dark and tanned, are becoming more proficient at throwing spears.

The two groups fight with hearty discipline. Squadrons with small fake cannon hurry into position shouting *Boom!* at appropriate moments. Behind them, regiments with muskets shout *Boom!* appear comic, but are deadly serious. After these, come men with spears.

Kamehameha cheers for both sides, having the time of his life. He warns Young, "Olohana – Behind you!" Young "spears" the guy on his flank and salutes the king. The king cheers. 'Ae. Good!" He puts his hand on his neck where a boil protrudes from his upper shoulder. It looks ugly.

Lamakua and Young win the round, earning a roar from the crowd. The sun commences its downward path on the edge of the training area as Davis and Young, very dirty, with bloody nicks and cuts brushed off, shake hands with other leaders of the battle.

Kiana, a sore loser, drives a spear into the trunk of a young palm. The group breaks up with laughter and as much male joshing – as much as can now be enjoyed by both cultures.

Young's eyes dart behind them. He slaps a few more shoulders and hurries off. As he rounds a cluster of trees, Mana'oi runs up behind him, out of breath. "Olohana, may I speak to you?"

Young chortles and keeps moving, "Mana'oi, too bad you were on the wrong side today! Good fight, eh?"

Mana'oi doubles his speed to keep up with Young. "I must speak to you."

Young stops and puts a hand on Mana'oi's shoulder. "Not now. How about after sunset? At my hut. Yes?"

Mana'oi is disappointed. "Then I will come at burning of torches, Olohana."

Young runs, taking off the colored tapa he was wearing for battle. He races into a sugar cane field, his eyes darting here and there as if looking for a treasure.

Kaoana's dark, silky head pops up, giggling. Young dives for her through the sugar cane. She squeals with delight, like a child caught in a game of hide and seek. Young embraces her and gushes with pride, "Lanakila, Kaoana. *We won!*" He kisses her, his longer hair, dark tan, and trail of recent tattoos down his back reveals a final transformation into a Hawaiian warrior. After another kiss, they jump up and run through the field, down the slope, toward their secret cove.

In the munitions hut on the far side of the village, Davis and Lamakua watch slaves put muskets in racks. Lamakua is concerned. "We must have many guards to keep safe good gunpowder."

"Yes. But, we can trade for more if a ship comes. A messenger spoke to the king of a "nui moku" coming. That's a large ship, isn't it?"

"I not know ship coming. Perhaps talk of Kahekili's spies on Maui. They pretend to be fishermen."

Suddenly, there are voices outside. Kamehameha and Ka'ahumanu, talk angrily behind the hut. Lamakua and Davis dismiss the slaves, knowing they should not be hearing it.

Outside the hut, Kamehameha holds Ka'ahumanu by the shoulders. "You think me a fool?"

Ka'ahumanu weeps. "I told you, it's all lies. Let me go."

"He's been your partner at the games, I've seen the smile you give him, why shouldn't I believe it?"

"You trust everyone before me! Yet, I am the truest friend you have. They are lying. And you are wrong to believe them."

Inside, Lamakua and Davis are caught. It is too late to leave.

Davis mouths to Lamakua, "Who is he talking about?"

Lamakua, reluctant, draws a name in the sand, "Kiana."

Davis is not surprised to hear Kiana is making trouble with Ka'ahumanu. The sound of weeping fades as they move down the path.

Isaac whispers to Lamakua. "Kiana is a very ambitious man."

"It is so. But, he is royal and has won many battles for Kamehameha." Lamakua shakes his head in sadness.

"Your ways are strange. The king has fifteen wives, why is he upset if this one is unfaithful?"

"Ka'ahumanu only one he love. Real love many time confuse mind, yes? Even mind of king..." He pauses. "Akake, no love confuse with your people?"

Davis stares at him, nailed. "Lamakua, you possess much wisdom. Yes, many people of my country are confused in love as well. And I am the most confused man on earth."

Lamakua studies him. "You, Akake?"

Davis smirks. "Yes. So, do not listen to me. I am crazy. Hewa Hewa."

꩜

Several miles away, in a hut on a hillside, a crippled man followed by two men, pulls a sled of sweet potatoes toward a cave. A closer look reveals Kiana, in disguise. The coastline sunset spews scarlet across the evening horizon. Kiana disappears into the rocks.

In the cave, Kiana and two chiefs, Pohaku, and Limalana, plot over a tiny fire, tended by a slave.

Kiana's voice rises, "But, no – you don't see? Without Kamehameha, the army will not stand. Kahekili will win."

"If the sorcerer's work fails? What then?" asks Pohaku.

Kiana is confident. "A few days and he will die. I assure you. He has been taking the poison for over a week." Kiana rises. "Be careful. Return by the backside of the hill. Both of you. Go."

On a grassy area near the edge of the sheer Kohala cliffs, two lovers roll slowly, passionately. It is the king and Ka'ahumanu, now on the other side of their argument. They have both succumbed to the depths of their passion and have exhausted themselves in making love. Still breathing hard, they move into a comfortable position to watch the sunset's flames competing with theirs. She nuzzles in, feeling safe and blissful.

Kamehameha, is confident and in awe of her once more. "Kahu, you are all women to me. I see now the gods have made you from parts of themselves – the blinding red of Kane-wahi-lani's sky is your love, the blue of Huli-koa's sea is your voice, and these windswept mountains…" He caresses her breasts. "…you received these from Ka-haku, for yours are shaped like Mauna Loa herself…"

She is amused, enjoying the image. "Ahhhhhh…"

His fingers course through her hair. "Even the waterfalls of Waipio Valley do not shine like this."

Ka'ahumanu is overcome. "My king, you flatter me too much… too much."

He buries his head in her arms. "No, my queen, I promise you, this is true. I can have any woman, but I want you because you are far above all the rest."

She notices the boil on his neck as she caresses him. "My Love, what is this affliction?"

He is not ready to give up his pleasure. "Nothing – just my jealousy seeping out, like puss. Only a boil of some kind." He pauses. "Yes, only my foolish mistrust – my arrogance bursting out. Kahuna Lani is treating it…"

She decides to let it go. "Look, my hero, the red goddess is not happy with only part of the sky, she wants all of it. That is how my heart burns for you. I want only you, all of you – and all your secrets, too."

Kamehameha chuckles. "All of me worth having, you have, sweet girl." He sweeps her into his arms. She throws her concern to the wind, and yields to him again.

Back in the village, Davis, in his hut, works on an English lesson for Paloa. Opa fashions a spear for Davis. Young appears in the doorway of the hut, his hair ripples in the wind.

Davis looks up. "Ah, John. Mana'oi is after you. I told him to come round later."

Young blinks. "I quite forgot. Did you see the sunset? Most brilliant and pleasing tonight." He continues sheepishly. "Isaac, I would like to have a talk with you, alone."

Davis glances at Opa. "That's a good lad." Davis gestures. "Kala mai'ia'u. Excuse me, sorry. Opa – Kaumaha." Opa leaves.

Young ponders. "I have been in conference with myself. I believe it's time for me to marry again."

Davis stares at him and looks down at his Bible. "Really. I was just writing Paloa's lesson. It's from Proverbs: 'The way of a fool is right in his own eyes, but he that harkens unto counsel is wise.' "

Young is vexed. "No. I'm not looking for counsel, Isaac. I'm looking for a best man. Perhaps the king and her father won't see me as the choice for a royal niece. But, I am going to ask him."

"What? "... see you as the right choice for Kaoana"? Well, I'm afraid I don't. I thought royal sons had already placed offers for the young widow."

"None have won her heart, Isaac."

Davis stays calm, but his words cut deep, "And where do you plan to live?"

"She will go home with me. That is, if we ever can return." An urge overtakes him. "Isaac, my wife died years ago. I thought there could never be anyone. My heart was a stone. A cave. Maybe a chasm. I never thought anyone could enter there or make me... want to be back into the light. Kaoana is not a savage."

"Is it not "savage" she can be killed for even entering your "eating hut"? Is it wise to marry a woman from such a place and expect that if some way you can get home she could ever be able to fit in there?"

"Wait," Young demands. "I hope to effect some changes here. Over time I could, for God's sake, I need your help not a lecture."

Mana'oi appears in the entrance desperate. "Olohana, Akake, forgive me, I am heavy with a burden and nowhere to put it!" Young whirls on him, agitated. "Mana'oi, what is it?"

Mana'oi struggles. "I fear for the king, for his life."

"Fear? How, Mana'oi What is it?"

The old man speaks in panic, "From evil person who..." He tries to translate, "Evil -- la'au make...'awa. Awa. Kill. I fear he die!"

Davis takes a guess, "Poison, Mana'oi? Poison?" Davis grabs his chest to indicate a physical description.

"Yes. Awa. Poison."

"Trying to poison him?" Young takes him by the shoulders. "Why haven't you told anyone?"

Mana'oi looks around to make sure no one overhears. "Guilty one could be Ali'i. I not accuse Ali'i, they kill me – and my Nakui – my family. I only trust you."

33

Night of Owls

Young and Davis approach the entrance of Kamehameha's huts. His personal warriors are guarding. The sailors come closer. The guards are very cautious about this strange visitation of white men in the middle of the night.

The first guard jumps to attention. "Kapu… kihi o ka po. *Sacred Place.* Kapu. Kapu!"

Young and Davis keep coming. Dogs wake and bark. Several other guards come running.

John holds up his hands. "Palekana malu. *No danger.* Oleluho'ouna 'ia Kamehameha *We have message for the king.*"

One man, who has begun to trust the mariners,

decides to wake the king. Against the shouts of the other guards, he runs into the king's hut. Already awakened and curious, Kamehameha emerges. From nearby, Kiana, Lamakua, and Mapala come out to see what's happening. The king holds up his arms to silence the guards. John steps forward.

"What is it, my friends?"

"Sir, we have reason to feel you may be in danger." Young glances toward the others. "But we cannot talk here. Please, would you come to my hut?"

Kamehameha is cautious, but something in the eyes of the sailors speaks to him. "You hut, Olohana? Why?"

Young persuades. "Sir, I understand your question. But, you see – this is secret for you to hear only, mea huna. If you trust Olohana, if you trust Akake, please, come." Young musters courage, turns and walks back down the slope.

Kamehameha looks at them sternly and gestures to his guards. Two warriors come with him as he follows the white men. Kiana watches them go, concerned.

Shortly after, they enter Young's hut. Davis brings out the medical bag from the *Fair American*. Young gets out of earshot of the guards outside. "Sir, we have been told from one who loves you, but fears for his life, someone plans to kill you. Perhaps in food or in some other way."

Davis lowers his voice, "La 'au make, Kamehameha." He grabs his throat with both hands. "Poison. La'au make."

"Ana ana? Who say? Who is?"

Young is careful. "He is a loyal Commoner who heard it from a merchant he trusts. The fisherman heard it up in the Highlands at Mauna Loa."

The king begins to get the drift.

Davis looks over the king's exposed flesh. "Sir, do you have an open wound on you somewhere? A sore? A boil? Ma'I palapu. He said you might have a boil."

Kamehameha turns his back and lifts his hair, revealing the sore covered with a strange paste.

Davis studies the infection. "This could be how they try to kill you, sir. Do you trust me to examine this?"

Because of the position on his neck, he cannot view the sore himself. He rubs near it. "I have pain for it all this day."

Davis opens the bag, takes out several vials. "John, would you lift that lamp? What is that paste?"

The king shrugs. "Kahuna Lani put on. Make good."

Davis considers. "Perhaps it's the paste that has the poison. Who you say put this on?"

Kamehameha speaks defensively, "Kahuna Lani heal Kamehameha many years. Is true."

Davis assures him, "I see. Yes. But where does Kahuna Lani get this paste? Ho'opipili, Kamehameha? Who makes this healing paste for Kahuna Lani? Where does he get it? What if it is poison? Ana ana?"

Kamehameha measures his words, "If ana ana – someone die. Not Kamehameha." He looks at the bag. "Britannee la au – medi-cine, is fix?"

Davis shakes up a bottle in preparation. "Sir, this will not hurt you. It has healed many sailors from boils. May I wash off that paste and begin with this? I hope it is not too late."

"Do Britannee medi-cine, Akake."

"You trust me?"

"Akake no win from death of Kamehameha. My enemy gain much I die. You fix."

Davis and the king share a knowing look. "Sir, sit here." The king does so. Davis takes the top of the vial. "John, can you use that water to clean it? And hand me that cloth. I'm going to lance this."

Later, as Young and Davis toss in their cots. A torch burns in the temple. Kahuna Lani sweats profusely under Kamehameha's gaze in the flickering flame. The king wears a cape, concealing Davis' bandages.

Kahuna Lani begs, "Then, I prepared the first part of the remedy. But, I had to send for the herbs to make the second part."

The king's eyes bore into him. "Where did you send? By whom? When?"

The elder kahuna takes a deep breath, tries to remember exactly how it happened. "My king, Limalana, said he would see to it. Then later, one of Pohaku's men brought it to me. Send me to Pele's fires if I lie."

"Where are they? I haven't seen them these two days. That is strange, is it not?"

"Limalana went to visit his father in the hills near Mauna Loa. Pohaku, I do not know."

The King contemplates. "The mountains. Wherever he went, he will be on his way back, for the council in three days. It may be my imagination. But, I have been dizzy today. My mind has been foggy. I have a fever. Do not tell anyone. Give me your word?"

Kahuna Lani's sincerity is impressive. "My king, I pray it was not poison. I pray the gods protect you. I would never do anything to hurt you!" The kahuna falls to his knees, sobbing.

The king rises. "Tell no one anything about this until I speak to you again. Go."

"Yes, my king."

Kamehameha leaves. He gazes at the night sky, sweat pouring down his face from the high fever. An owl suddenly lands in a tree nearby. He stares at it for a long moment, wipes the sweat from his face and heads toward his hut. A moment later, he changes his mind, turns and heads into the brush, the opposite direction.

Ka'ahumanu wakes with a start in the king's hut. She doesn't see Kamehameha. Nahena sits nearby. "Where is he?" She begins to get up.

Nahena hushes her. "Gone to the temple, my lady. Sleep."

Ka'ahumanu slowly lies back, staring out at clouds racing across the moon.

Hours later, in a mountain pass a mile away, a shadowy figure moves down the path in the moonlight. On the hillside is a cave. Flickering from inside, flames whip shadows on trees. A kauva slave leaves the cave with trash. As he steps down the path he is yanked off his feet and dragged into the bushes.

A few moments later, Kamehameha emerges from the underbrush adjusting the garb of the kauva. He enters the cave.

In the cave, the fire illuminates Pohaku and Limalana in conference, sharing a meal. The slave appears in the darkness behind them.

Pohaku realizes his plate is empty. "Bring more meat."

The slave nods and prepares more meat.

Limalana takes a drink. "He is a friend of Kahekili's. Kamehameha has never suspected him."

A hand slides the dish near Pohaku and retreats subserviently.

"Clean the other fish," Pohaku orders.

The slave mumbles a reply and slinks back into darkness.

Pohaku contemplates. "Yes. It is surprising how blind some men can be."

"True, and it is very hard to know who you can trust."

Pohaku straightens up, listens, then relaxes. "When Kamehameha is dead, I'll likely have two or three districts all my own. I won't be blind. I'll watch everyone…"

The slave listens.

Limalana pokes at the last of the fire. "You think Keawe will join us?"

Pohaku tosses a rind onto a flame. "No. I do not trust him. He seems too loyal to Kamehameha. Some men you can never figure. He's a fool."

Suddenly they hear the sound of feet on the path outside. The chiefs jump. Limalana grabs his spear. "What's that?"

Pohaku pulls a knife and joins him going to the mouth of the cave. They look into the night. A strange breeze is blowing. They scan the landscape, seeing nothing. They look up, as an owl takes off from a branch.

Limalana guffaws. "Only an owl. Come back in."

As they reenter cave, down the slope behind them, out of their hearing, darts the covered figure of a slave. The wind lifts up his dirty coverings, revealing Kamehameha's distinctive profile and flashing eye. But, once safe, he slows down, taking part of the garment to wipe the fever sweat pouring from him. His face is tense, vulnerable, revealing deep pain of betrayal. He nearly falls from exhaustion, but stumbles down the trail.

34

A Cold Dish

Three days later, drums beat announcing the war council. Chiefs and chiefesses are assembled waiting for the king. Young, Davis, and Lamakua sit together. Everyone is anxious and worried.

"Why the assembly?' asks Davis.

"They didn't say exactly. Only that he wanted to see both of us sitting near the front. I assume he's alive and this is not the directive from someone who has taken over the compound. No one seems to know anything. Just a lot of rumors."

"I didn't sleep. How 'bout you, mate?"

"Not well at all. If he dies, our lives will be in

the hands of madmen." A conch is blown signaling the council commencement.

Limalana and Pohaku enter with others and sit, cautiously looking around. Another conch trumpets the entrance of the king.

Kamehameha enters, looking fit. All prostrate themselves. The white men bow. He is dressed magnificently in his ceremonial yellow and red-feathered cape, crowned with his bright feather helmet. He looks every inch a brave leader again.

The sailors are relieved, and awed to see him looking so powerful, a man so recently deathly ill. He raises his hand for quiet and sits. He gestures for his subjects to sit.

The king addresses the crowd with a pleasant tone. In his eloquent Hawaiian, he speaks. "Today, the wind blows calm and sweet, leaving the darkness behind. I am heavy in heart to tell you this truth. To have the sweetness of lasting peace it seems we must prepare for a night of war. Today, the stones returned from the journey to Kahekili and his sons. As you know, if he had chosen the white stone our time of peace would come sooner. But, he chose the black stone of war."

The crowd rustles with concern. Kamehameha adds passionately, "We have lived in the mouth of the Thunderer of Death long enough. It is time to send Kahekili into the night forever."

All cheer and raise hands to him, Limalana and Pohaku looking as eager as the rest.

Kamehameha gestures for quiet. "We will continue our war games until the new moon when Kahekili and his sons will meet us on Maui. Now, I am sorry to inform you of a great loss. Two of our chiefs, who once had been such loyal friends, Limalana and Pohaku, in whom I had placed much trust, sadly have left us."

Pohaku in panic of hope, raises his hand to get the king's attention. "We are here, my Ali'i!"

Limalana joins his comrade. "Yes, we are here, my king!" They wave their hands to get his attention.

Kamehameha ignores them and continues as the group stirs. Young and Davis exchange glances.

The king speaks as if the two traitor chiefs were not there, "Yes, two men in whom I had great trust. They were found to be plotting my death – by sorcery – by poison."

Shock jolts the assembly. Everyone freezes. The king adds, "But, as you see, they did not succeed. They are dead."

Limalana and Pohaku try to escape. The king's warriors cut them down with spears.

Young and Davis are aghast at the swiftness of this justice. Kiana looks to the king, not sure of his safety.

Kamehameha continues without a look to Kiana, "As I said, they have paid the price of their treachery and I mourn their loss."

After the bodies are dragged out of the area, he gestures toward the sailors. "Olohana and Akake were loyal to warn me. I am very grateful to them, and I hope you will also be grateful to them for they have many reasons to hate me and have decided I am their friend. This is true friendship indeed. May their god and Ku-Ka-ili-moku reward them for their courage and kindness." He claps his hands. "Now, good news. A ship comes. Our fishermen have seen one coming from Otahete. We will welcome it and trade."

The assembly, quick to adapt, responds with chatter. Young and Davis, still reeling from the killings, take in the news.

The king proceeds, "We will purchase what weapons and ammunition is possible. Our finest crafts and hogs will be needed to trade. Bring your best to the shore. I will return soon. Pray this ship will sell us powder for our weapons."

After Kamehameha leaves, the priests begin

to chant. Drums pound. Warriors escort Young and Davis toward the king's hut. Along the path to Kamehameha's compound, Kiana slips away and blends into the crowd. John and Isaac, under heavy guard, follow Lamakua.

A short time after, Kamehameha, Lamakua, Young, and Davis sit alone in a waiting area in the king's hut. Davis watches as the ceremonial headdress is taken off. Kamehameha, in private shows some strain and weakness from the fever, lifts his hair and shows his wound to Davis. Talking in broken English, he seems the opposite of the god-like man who had just spoken to his people. "Sailor's medicine good for a king. My heart embrace for you. I learn word, *embrace*, from Lamakua. Good?" He becomes very serious. "Akake, Olohana – I am sorry to ask you. Lamakua, you tell them…"

They see the sweat now upon his brow, and the exhaustion.

Lamakua, in his best diplomatic fashion tries to soften the blow. "The king is much sorry to put you under guard, because a ship comes. He know you want to go. He need weapons. He want promise. You help trade, not escape. They must not know of the *Fair American*. Men hide it in back in the lagoon."

A moment passes while the mariners consider. Young steps forward, seeing a way to seize the moment and ask for Kaoana to be his wife. "Kamehameha, when you brought me here, my heart was in England. Every day for months my heart only thought of my life as a sailor and how to escape and get back to my country. Now, I can say to you, my heart is here – in Havaee. You have my promise. I will not escape. I have a good reason to stay."

Isaac Davis looks at the king. "I will not tell the Captain what happened to my ship. I will help you trade. You have my word, Kamehameha. I hope that is good enough."

When Lamakua finishes translating, Kamehameha gets up and takes them in his arms. The king wipes more sweat from his face. "Is good for Kamehameha, my friends. Good for my people."

35

The Lucia,
Kawaihae Bay, Hawaii

By afternoon, the king, his guards and caravan head through thick undergrowth to Kawaihae Bay. In the blazing sunlight, the gentle waves of the bay look like sheets of diamonds spreading out to the sea beyond. The ship has dropped anchor and prepares for trading.

Lamakua, Young, and Davis arrive on shore with the king. Many canoes filled with villagers and their goods wait for orders near the beach. The king and his retinue launch his large double-hulled canoe through the water to the brigantine, the *Lucia*, with a full crew standing near the starboard side.

The Captain, Ruiz Alonso Sandoval, stands near the Jacob's ladder, peering through his scope. He turns to his first mate. "Looks like the king himself. And there are two white men. Surrounded by warriors. That is strange. Perhaps deserters. There are more and more these days."

The king's craft arrives alongside. Young climbs the ladder. Kamehameha and Lamakua follow, then Davis. Several warriors come to watch for trouble. Sandoval shakes hands with Young.

Sandoval's voice has the warm tone of Spaniards, "Buenos dias, Senor, I am Captain Ruiz Alonso Sandoval, from España."

Young smiles. "Sir, I am Bo'sun John Hemmings, the *Providence* out of New Bedford, but I hail from England. This is King Kamehameha. The king of this island."

The king, looking very genteel, shakes hands with Sandoval.

"This is the king's regent, Chief Lamakua, and a shipmate, seaman Isaac Smythe."

There are greetings all around. Sandoval, still congenial, ventures, "Odd to see white men in these waters without ships."

Young doesn't blink. "Oh, we were left here, sir, to do geological surveys by our captain on the *Eleanora*. We shall be picked up on their way back from other islands. Where are you headed?"

"Nootka Sound. Fur-trading. I see you have a great load of quite needed trade for us there, Mister Hemmings."

Young is startled to hear himself spoken to in a different name. "Oh, yes, King Kamehameha, wishes to trade many goods for what stores you might have in muskets, powder and shot."

Sandoval is surprised. "Weapons? What need has he for weapons and powder, Mister Hemmings?"

Kamehameha, impatient, interrupts, "Kapene, please help peaceful king of Havaee. Kahekili, evil Maui king, bring war to my people."

Davis decides to help. "These people are at great risk from the Maui king, Captain. He speaks the truth. There is danger and they only wish to defend themselves."

Kamehameha retains a sense of calm. "Need power of musket to protect my people."

Sandoval is still cautious. "And you would not use this power on foreigners?"

Davis responds, "Only if attacked first. You can understand defending one's land, sir."

Young adds, "We can vouch for the king. He fights only for peace. We have been treated most fairly by him."

Sandoval is convinced, for the moment. "Come to my cabin. We will discuss terms." He leads them below decks.

Young looks about the ship as they go. "I don't suppose you'd have any spare cannon or swivel guns?"

Sandoval scoffs, "Cannon? Is that not excessive?"

"These people are in grave danger. And therefore so are Mister Smythe and myself. Perhaps you should see what we have to trade…"

Davis looks longingly at the ship's rigging as they go below. Kamehameha watches him. The warriors watch everyone.

That evening drums are pounding a proud beat to welcome the trading party back to Pu'ukaloa village. Davis and Young oversee the unloading of muskets and ammunition into supply huts under heavy guard. Kiana examines the guns. Young, very relieved, lifts a load of saltpeter and lays it carefully under a tarp. "Well, 'Smythe,' I'd say Captain Sandoval was quite generous after all. We will give those Maui boys a surprise, eh?"

Davis stares at him, sad. "John, you shouldn't have had to trade all your carvings. And the exquisite chess set Mana'oi gave you. That captain's a thief."

"The king's happy. Perhaps it will purchase my bride."

Past the guards, various girls watch them, from a distance, giggling. Paloa stands with them, hoping Davis will look at her.

Young notices her. "Someone's waiting for you, Isaac."

Davis is embarrassed at the attention. "She is truly a good student."

Young sports a broad grin. "And she truly enjoys her teacher."

"She's very young, John. Are we done here?"

Kiana strides up, pretending fellowship, aware of the power Young and Davis now have with the king. "These good. Is good, yes, Olohana?"

"As good as Spain can make, Kiana."

Kiana grins. "We win. We win – yes?"

Davis nods. "Anything you say, Prince."

Young watches Kiana leave. "I don't like that bloke.

Young agrees. "Aye… a bit sudden with his affability, eh?"

36

The Message

A messenger prostrates himself before Kahekili's quarters on Maui. "I must see the king!" Guards let him through. Fearfully, he proceeds to the throne of Kahekili, who sits looking through a small telescope out to sea. "My Ali'i. I am sorry to report. I came as soon as I could. Pohaku and LimaLana have been sacrificed for sorcery."

Kahekili rises in a rage. "What? You lie. Traitor!" He grabs a spear from his bodyguard and stabs the messenger, who slumps to the ground. His bodyguards jump to his side. Others come running. The bodyguard shouts to the group, "He attempted to kill the king. He was possessed of a spirit!"

Kahekili sits back in an icy stare. "Send to Kaenae before the end of this night. The village and kauwa sorcerer must be destroyed. He has failed to bring down Kamehameha. Burn their huts. Send their bones to Oahu." He jumps up. "Lawakua, we must strike quickly and make it a surprise. Send word to Hana Bay. Your swiftest runner. Tell them be ready on the third dawn. Without fail. Tell them we leave for Kahului on the second dawn. Go."

In Isaac Davis' hut, Paloa sits next to Davis, reading from the Bible. She has no comprehension of the meanings of the words.

Paloa continues, "… The eyes of the—"

Isaac helps. "Lord."

"Rord… are in every place… "

"Good, Paloa. Next is, "Beholding the evil… '"

"Be-holding the e-vil and the… good."

"That was excellent, Paloa!"

She looks up, noticing he has stopped. Davis says softly, "I'm going to miss you… " She is confused. He takes her face in his hands. "It's alright, I don't want you to understand what I'm saying. Paloa… " He aches to kiss her, but doesn't. He releases her and hands her the Bible. "You have a beautiful soul… Keep this to remember me. You will be a good wife one day." He gets up. "Lesson over. Goodnight, Paloa. Aloha ahi ahi."

"Aloha ahi ahi, good-night, kahuna Akake. Mahalo." Her hands lift to his face briefly as she sports her new language perfectly, "Thank you. Mister Davis."

Davis, charmed by this last effort, aches to touch her.

She turns to go. He watches her. She turns back, takes his face in her hands, and kisses him sweetly. When she leaves he stares after her, struggling. He goes to his desk, takes a pen, and scratches words on a dried piece of tapa.

John – fear not – I will keep the secret forever… forgive me for putting you at risk, but I believe your loyalty has now proven to the king that you will not betray him. Ever. Besides, he needs you too much for his war. Forgive me. God be with you. Isaac.

At the ceremonial field, a celebration is forming. Villagers joyful from the good trading, dance or play games. A group of children celebrate. Opa, who has never fit in, argues with a playmate. Davis, passing by sees the altercation.

One young boy is tough and big, grabs a toy carved spear from Opa. "It's mine. I won it." Opa won't budge. The other boy pulls harder. "You idiot. Let go." Opa, in spite of his weak leg has strong arms. He grabs the boy and takes him down, punching him when he hits the dirt. He cannot stop punching. "I'll kill you!"

Davis moves in, roughly picks him up and shakes him. "Uoki. *Stop it.* Come with me you bully." He drags Opa away as the other child tries to recover. The other children run away. He drags the struggling Opa to a spot nearby and sits him down. Opa is humiliated to have been carried out of the fight. Isaac, aware of the short time he has left, tries to do some good. "You must stop this. Why do you keep attacking your mates?"

"I hate them."

"Why?"

Opa weeps. "They say gods hate me."

"Why would the gods hate you?"

"They give me this leg."

Davis thinks quickly. "But, you have the gift of music. If the gods hated you, why would they give you such a gift? You must not believe them."

Opa wipes tears with the back of his hand. "Yes. They hupo. Stupid. I better."

"No." Isaac takes his time. "No, Opa, my friend, no, none of us is born better than any other. We all have different gifts. You must learn to return good for evil. You know *hala*? Forgive? A hard thing, yes, but if you forgive, it will make you a great, strong warrior one day." He hands him the toy spear.

Opa sobs. "I play war, they laugh… my leg. I not be warrior."

Davis is moved by Opa's pain, but needs to make his escape. He holds him, not knowing what to say. "You must see. It is they who are deformed. Inside."

Opa looks up.

"Listen. You see, your leg is shaped badly, but their hearts are shaped badly like your leg. However, your heart is whole and strong, see? Their hearts more sick than your leg. Much more. So, you must feel sorry for them."

Opa seems to understand even if he's not ready to agree.

Davis holds him at arm's length and looks him in the eye. "You are good. Maika'i and very brave – koa. And you will forget their laughter as you play your music." He gets up. "Now, I must sleep. Goodnight."

Opa, better again, gets up, "You come to fires? All dancing. I play for you."

"I must sleep. You go… Play and enjoy."

"I will play for them! Mahalo."

"Yes!" Isaac watches him hop back to the celebration using the spear to steady himself. He creates the image of Opa in his mind for a keepsake. He heads for his hut, watching his guards gamble. They hardly notice him. Villagers dance in the distance around the fires. He goes unnoticed. Once in his hut, Davis creates a mock body in his hammock. Dressed in dark clothing, he rubs paste on himself, and blows out the lamp. He lifts up a flap in the back of his hut. No guards are near. He slips out. From there, he darts into the undergrowth.

One of the guards gets up, laughing, and heads for Davis' hut. Another man joins him. They take a torch and lift it at the door. Thinking Davis asleep, they return to their game.

◗◖

Deep in the forest on the west side of the island, the sound of heavy breathing and pounding feet disturbs sleeping birds, who ruffle feathers and move briefly as a man runs past them.

The man, a dark form, running through the forest trail, leaps and jumps over brush as if chased by furies. It is Wakana. He emerges from the brush and runs into the sleeping Pu'ukaloa village, waking dogs and light sleepers. Wending his way through rows of huts, the swift spy arrives at Kamehameha's gate. Dozing guards jump awake, raising spears.

"Who's there?" one calls as he is nearly knocked down by Wakana.

"The king. Tell the king – Kahekili War canoes from Maui coming! Go!" He leans over trying to get his breath back. Horrified, the guards run to tell the chief minister. Wakana slumps into the surrounding dark. He looks up to the gods for help and weeps for fear of the coming attack.

Kamehameha is sleeping in his private hut. One of his guards comes to the door. "My king, my king…"

The king moves out of his cot, yanking himself from sleep. "What is it?" He senses danger. "Kahekili? Is he coming?"

The guard sinks to the floor, fearing the king's reaction. "Yes, my king, he means to surprise you."

Kamehameha grabs his gear. "Well, he has. But, we will still win. Get up, you fool, and follow me. We must wake all the others." They hurry out.

On the shore of Kawaihae Bay, in the waning dark, birds trill their first wake up call, while the night sky begins its retreat in the glow of dawn. Barely recognizable, the Santa Lucia rests in the calm bay. Rustling in the trees flushes out birds, followed by Isaac Davis, arriving on the beach, exhausted from his escape from Pu'ukaloa. He grabs an empty canoe sitting on the shore and shoves it in the water.

On the *Santa Lucia* a short time after, a guard spots Davis.

Gaperos, a Spanish sailor, hails men on watch, "Man off starboard." Others lift lanterns to see. Davis calls as he hears their excited reports, "Ahoy *Santa Lucia*! Mister Smythe for Captain Sandoval. Sailor seeks admittance!"

Dubious, but willing, they throw the ladder, having met him earlier.

Fontane, the Bo'sun, leans over the rail to help him up. "Take my hand, mate."

Davis crawls up and lands on the deck, looking behind him across the bay. "I may be followed, how soon do you sail, sir, may I be so bold to ask?"

Fontane is happy to see him. "The captain was waiting for you, ya sluggard."

Sandoval strides up from below. He shakes Isaac's hand. "Mister Smythe. Welcome aboard. I'm glad to help. I was confused by that note you slipped me on your visit. You were kidnapped on a Portuguese ship in China and then what were the circumstances that followed?"

Davis affects a congenial tone, "It's a long tale, sir. I only wish to return to America with you. I am most deeply obliged to you and I will make an able seaman, I warrant you. My goal is Wales."

Sandoval, satisfied for now, offers a cautious grin. "You will earn your passage, you can be sure. Make preparations, Mr. Fontane."

Fontane signals, "All hands. Prepare to weigh anchor."

As the sailors shout rigging calls, Davis breathes more freely, his hopes rising with the sails. Sandoval passes by. "Get a rest, Smythe. Go below and get some grog from Mister Bissel."

Davis is escorted by a sailor. He looks back to the beach as he steps below deck. The shore is empty.

❦

Pu' ukaloa village is alive with activity, everyone pours their panic into tasks. In the king's huts, a meeting of Kamehameha's most trusted warriors is in session. The king, Lamakua, and Kahuna Lani sit facing five messengers standing in front of them.

Kamehameha's voice goes like an arrow into each man, "… and you, Pau Ahi, go as far south as Keokeo. Tell all the warriors in the villages on your route they must meet us in Mahukona by the second dawn. Send all other people to Cities of Refuge. Put wings on your feet, my brothers." He stands, they salute him, and rush out. Kamehameha sits in stunned silence, taking a moment to collect himself.

Lamakua moves to his side. "Shall I wake Olohana and Akake?"

Kamehaneha realizes despite all the training the kidnapped mariners have given his warriors, it is likely not enough for what lies ahead. His vision of using new weapons and a different kind of warfare is about to be tested. "Yes, and send for Kiana."

From another side of the hut comes Kahuna Lani. "My king, I will prepare the priests."

Kamehameha stands. "Ku-Ka-ili-moku is a hungry god, my brother. We must feed to him Kahekili and his entire evil army. This time we must go all the way to the Iao Valley or we will not succeed. We meet in the temple at dawn."

On the *Santa Lucia*, South of Kawaihae, top sails are going up. In the galley, Davis sits with Fontane, revived by the grog. Davis feels the effect of good Spanish rum coursing through his veins. "A good draft, Mister Bissell. Are we going south around the island first?"

Fontane scoffs, "A curious one ya are. Aye, Smythe, going south. We'll pick up more water and pigs at Kiholo, then round the end of the island for the Americas." I must be back to the rigging. Come up when you've put something on your stomach besides rum."

Davis laughs. "Aye, sir. I will be up." He grabs some hard biscuit.

Fontane ascends then cackles to Davis. "Ye must have some good tales of these savages for us, especially those females." He leaves. Bissell goes from the galley to the captain's quarters. Davis sits alone, hearing Fontane's derisive words ripple round his brain. He is caught off-guard, realizing he does not share the insulting sentiments. He no longer thinks of the Hawaiians as savages, he just wants to get home. The ship creaks and moans.

37

Chameleon

Young's eyes snap open as he hears cries outside his hut. Men run by shouting orders. He sits up and is pulled into the chaos before truly awake.

Lamakua calls at his entrance in terror, gasping for breath. "Olohana!" He slumps in relief to see Young staring at him.

"I heard shouting...what is it?" Young grabs clothes.

Lamakua grabs Young and embraces him. "Olohana. I thought you gone, too."

Young snaps to attention. "Gone? What?"

"Akake gone to ship of Spaniard. Gone."

"Impossible. I just saw him tonight." Young dashes out. Lamakua follows him. Drums beat as hard as Young's heart as he enters Davis' hut. "Issac?" He stops, sees the empty cot and mass of cloth Davis had rigged. Sounds of women screaming reach his ears, while his mind is seized with dread. Davis' volume of Shakespeare is on the table and he thinks it impossible Isaac would leave it behind. He grabs the book, finding the letter inside. He reads the note then sees a post-script

And John, I leave this Shakespeare to you and my Bible for Paloa, in hopes some good may come from them for these people.

He stares in disbelief. A conch blows repeating the call to arms.

Lamakua enters with guards. "Olohana, come to the king with us."

"Yes," Young nods. "Wait." Next to the Shakespeare is Davis' lute with a note - *For Opa.* He picks up the letter.

The guards are impatient.

Young faces Lamakua squarely. "You must believe me, sir. I knew nothing of this. Do you believe me? I knew nothing."

The guards surround Young. Lamakua reassures him. "I believe you. Come to the king. There is much to do. Kahekili sends his army in surprise."

Young misses a step. "Kahekili? Attack? We are not ready!"

⚭

In Kiholo Bay, South of Pu'Ukaloa, day is dawning. The Santa Lucia at full sail, heads down the coast.

On the deck of the swift galleon, Captain Sandoval looks through his scope for the best route into the small bay. He sees something strange. Fontane is nearby. He watches sailors work on the mainsail.

Davis, on deck, helps with the rigging, happy to be back in the harmony required to sail such a vessel.

Through the scope, Sandoval sees about thirty canoes speeding away from the village heading south. Smoke rises from the land. He is confused. "There seems to be a problem at this village. They are burning something. Perhaps a raid by a neighboring village."

He moves the scope to pick up more area as the ship rounds the point and sees a startling sight. Numerous people on the shore are dead or bloody. Flames rise from huts. Howling from natives now float on the wind, reaching the Lucia and her crew.

Shaken from his task by the sounds, Davis moves to the rail and sees the smoke curling into the sky.

Sandoval makes a decision. "That's it. Some islanders have just laid siege. Too much trouble getting water here." He gives the scope to Fontane.

Kiholo village is clearer from the rail as Davis squints. Under his breath a rasping word forces its way to his lips "Kahekili..." Davis' throat tight with anguish, looks to the Captain.

Sandoval, out of sorts, paces, looking at the map in his mind of the coast. "Fontane, this is very untimely for our progress today. How are we to get all our water? We must move down the coast to the next village."

Davis is astonished at his coldness toward people dying in his view.

Young and Lamakua enter surrounded by chamber guards. Kamehameha leaves the group of chiefs he's conferring with and comes to Lamakua. "Good. Olohana. Where's Akake?"

Having avoided this moment as long as possible, Lamakua can barely get words out, "My king he has gone. Nowhere to be found."

Kamehameha's eyes shift to Young. "What is this?"

Young hands the king Isaac's book of Shakespeare and note. "He told me nothing, sir. It is my prayer you will believe I knew nothing of a plan to escape. He ran away in secret. But, he left this letter for you." Young adds gravely, "He has trained warriors as he promised and you have his word he will not bring your people any harm."

Kamehameha looks at the note as Lamakua translates. He holds the book, remembering times when Davis quoted to him favorite lines from Shakespeare's plays. The king mumbles, "… suffer… slings and arrows…"

Young blinks. "What, sir?"

Kamehameha muses. "… 'take arms against a sea of trou-bells' Akake train me Britannee words… He left these leaves for me." The king glances to guards who have just heard this news. A plan over-takes him – he seems to be in a trance. He mutters, his eyes taking on a mischievous gleam.

The assembled wonder what he's up to. The king opens his arms wide. "Akake good warrior. He work hard for Kamehameha. Akake is wiki-wiki, quick."

Lamakua looks at the king as if he's lost his mind.

Young tries to guess what the king could be referring to.

Giggling, Kamehameha makes a point to speak in enough Hawaiian and English to be clearly understood by the curious guards, "Lamakua, tell Kahuna Lani to not worry. The King has sent Akake on a secret oihana kiu. Oihana kiu for my war plan."

Lamakua is dumbfounded. "You sent Akake on oihana kiu?"

John adds, "Lamakua, what does Oihana mean?"

Lamakua, bows. "Yes, my king, I go." He updates Young. "Olohana, he say he sent Akake on mission of secret for his war. He say, Kamehameha sent Akake away. Not to be worry."

Young is relieved to think the king and Davis could have become friends enough to entice them both to such action. But, this thought is obliterated as Young realizes the benefits to the king to cover for Davis. He will not lose face with Kiana and his powerful, growing faction.

Young gets it. "Yes, sir. I understand."

Kamehameha winks to Young. "I trust Akake to give message Kapene Sandoval. Ask for more powder for musket. Help for big wave in my sea of trou-bells – yes?"

Young sees the irony, "That is very poetic, sir.

The king is curious, "Po-e-tik? "Means – what?

"Sir, not important. How can I serve you in this battle? Where is the attack to be?"

"Olohana, I have new weapons, new ways. But, Kahekili use trick of surprise. Send warriors to attack this island before I am ready to go to Maui."

"Where? Is anyone hurt?"

Kamehameha shrugs. "Do not know where they attack, only know left Maui many hours. Lamakua adds. "Could be anywhere on this island."

Kamehameha suddenly speaks in Hawaiian, "Lamakua, that is right. I see that old octopus wants to trick me, like a fish in a net. Lure me to where he attacks, keep me on this island, running after a few war canoes so he can trap me here. I am not such an easy fish! No, the villages must defend themselves. I will send messengers to warn them and go attack Maui now with my army. I am sure he is there, waiting, thinking I will stay and defend my island. I will kill the octopus at its head and his arms will fall off one by one after that."

Lamakua sees the logic of this. He also thinks it might be the only hope they have.

Young did not understand.

Kamehameha takes Young by the shoulders. "Olohana, I leave warriors to protect you."

"What? You wanted my help, sir. Am I not to fight with you?"

"Olohana teach, not fight. Teach, not die in fight."

A conch is blown, signaling the sun rising. Kamehameha picks up his spears.

Young snaps, "Wait. Kamehameha dishonor Olohana!"

The king spits back, "You not die for my people."

On impulse, Young kneels before the king. "You saved my life, my king. I will fight for you and your people. I owe you my breath. You must not deny me. I trust my life to my God."

Kamehameha is moved by the sincerity. He lays his hand on Young's head. "Olohana. You want? You fight."

Young stays on one knee. "Sir – I ask only one gift. One makana from you, my king."

Kamehameha laughs. "Oh, you trick now! What makana?"

Young stands, even more earnest, "If I prove myself in this battle, may I have Kaoana for my bride, my wahine male? I love Kaoana. Bring her much aloha. Kaoana Olohana wahine?"

The warrior king looks down upon the English sailor and considers his request with a great sense of responsibility. He decides he likes the image of

Olohana and Kaoana together and believes her family would be able to accept him and be served in this union. "If you live, Olohana, Ali'i, Kaoana be Olohana wahine. Come." He leaves.

Young is suddenly struck by the sacred commitment he has just made regarding the native maiden in the heat of the moment to the king of the island of Hawaii, in the middle of the Pacific Ocean, nearly six thousand miles from home. He concludes his allegiance has now truly moved from the king of England to king Kamehameha, but he has not been forced to say such words out loud until now. It sinks in deeper as he rushes after the king and Lamakua into the panicked crowds preparing for eminent battle.

He hurries to get his musket and ammunition.

38

Feet of the Servant

From the deck of the Santa Lucia, Isaac Davis watches in horror as people die onshore, still under attack by remaining warriors in canoes. He is in despair, his mind split – one half turns from the suffering and the other churns with passion to help. He sees an old man in a canoe, hit by an enemy spear close to the ship.

The Santa Lucia's sails catch more wind and begin to take it further out of the bay.

Davis leaves his task and confronts the captain, "Sir, if you would consider offering assistance to these people, I know they would be glad to supply water and much more."

"I'm not risking a boat and men in that turmoil. There's water further south—"

"But, respectfully, sir, you cannot—"

Sandoval warns. "You are my guest, I remind you, Mister Smythe. Do not abuse your welcome on this ship."

Davis sees his mistake. "Sir, forgive me… I have been too long in these islands."

Fontane calls, "Due south, Captain?"

Sandoval moves away from Davis. "Yes, stay the course. Steady on South!"

Isaac moves along the rail watching the old man calling to the vessel, but he falls in the water. It is clear he will drown with the others. Davis, heads below to get away from surging emotions. He turns, suddenly climbs onto the rail and dives off toward the old man.

Two sailors see him. "Man overboard!" Sandoval and other sailors rush to the rail. A sailor reaches to lower a boat, but the captain stops him.

The sailor blinks. "Is he not to be helped, sir?"

Sandoval watches Davis cut through the chop like a dolphin toward the old native, "He is daft, Rudley. I was a fool to take him. He was right, he's been here too long."

Davis drags the bleeding man onshore amid the injured and dying. He hauls him onto the beach and listens for a heartbeat. There is none. He looks up, helplessly. More people swarm the beach, a woman sees him. In Hawaiian she calls, "Who are you?"

Davis, without thinking, shouts, "A'u Akake, I am kanaka hana Kamehameha. *I am a servant of Kamehameha.*"

In the Pu'ukaloa Temple grounds Kamehameha stands before chiefs, chiefesses, and warriors as waves crash to shore behind him. All are in battle dress and loaded with weapons. The king's voice is lower and more impassioned than the warriors can remember. The effect is mesmerizing. Already a head taller than most of his people, he leaps on a nearby rock, looking every inch invincible. He speaks in his native tongue.

"The mountains of Maui are covered with the bones of our dead, killed by Kahekili and his sons in many wars we all remember too well. But, Ku-Kaili-moku, our fierce god has told me their brave souls will rise up to meet us as we push the evil armies up to the highest peaks. There will be no place to hide for them. When we are through, this time it will be Kahekili's dead piled from the canyons to the sea!"

The crowd erupts in cheers, spears raised and shaking in salute.

Kamehameha continues, "When we leave these shores we will not return unless we are victorious. There will be no retreat for such as we. Be ready and wait for my signal."

The crowd roars, "Kamehameha. Kamehameha. Kamehameha."

He jumps off the rock and moves briskly through the assembly. They part for him, prostrating themselves as he passes, no king ever receiving more praise than the ocean of awe washing over him at this moment. He keeps his stature, but in his heart, he embraces his brothers and sisters of the land. His throat is tight with emotion, which he must subdue.

Following him, Kahuna Lani carries the image of the god, Ku-Kaili-moku, his rows of horrible teeth and his large yellow cockade, matching that of Kamehameha's feather headdress. Behind the venerable Kahuna, comes Lamakua, Kiana, Mapala, Young, and the rest of the chiefs, chiefesses and priests. As they pass, regiments of rank and file warriors fall into line.

∂Ю

On the trail North of Kiholo Village, many miles away on the western coast of Hawaii, Davis, in despair, stumbles north, toward Pu'ukaloa. He sees a man running toward him. He begins to hide in the bush, then recognizes Pau Ahi, one of the king's messengers. He steps back onto the trail. The messenger's eyes get bigger as he gets close enough to recognize Davis.

Davis calls out. "Pau Ahi!"

Pau Ahi halts, amazed. "Kahuna Akake. No ke aha? [Why?]"

Davis grabs Pau Ahi by the shoulder. "Kahekili ho'ouka Pu'ukaloa? Kahekili attacked Pu'ukaloa?"

Pau Ahi gasps for breath, "A'ole *No*."

Davis holds him. "Kahekili ho'ouka Kiholo-- Kiholo. *His men attacked Kiholo. I must tell Kamehameha!*"

Pau Ahi sputters, "Au a'o lau kanaka kauhale. E pono 'o 'oe ke hele Kamehameha. Ali'i mo'i send me Kealekakua loa'a koa." *Go! I was sent to warn people in the south.* He gives a gesture of salutation and runs down the trail.

Davis moves north, faster, with renewed determination.

Kamehameha's army marches north on the Road to Mahukona in bright sun, battle gear slowing them down, but deep resolve pressing them forward.

Among the warriors are women – wives who fight alongside their husbands, and other women who carry food and medicines. Slaves carry equipment and supplies.

Young, marches with Lamakua. "I see women wearing battle garments. Are women going to fight? Lamakua looks at him blankly. "White women not fight in Britannee?"

"No. Never. Not in battle. Only at home with husbands. Ha! It is odd to see them. Why did they not train with the other men?"

Lamakua explains. "They train on their own field. We have many who fight. My sister killed thirty warriors with her slingshot."

"Prodigious. When do they have time to train?"

"In idle time with fathers and brothers."

"What of Kaoana? She is a princess. Surely she will not fight? And what of Ka'ahumanu?"

Lamakua comes as close to laughing as he ever does. Only a glint of amusement registers in his face. "No. Ka'ahumanu *not* fight. She is precious treasure to king. Ka'ahumanu go to Mahukona camp to help prepare king, then south to Place of Refuge. Kaoana will come with us to battle. Take care of warriors when hurt."

"She will? That will be dangerous." Young begins to look for Kaoana among the crowd on the road.

Davis, exhausted, enters Pu'Ukaloa village. People rush past, taking no notice of him. He goes to his hut. He enters and sees Opa lying in his hammock, howling, his heart broken.

At the sight of Isaac, he jumps up, his small body still racked with sobs as he grabs Isaac. "Akake. They say you gone." He holds onto Davis, his tears mixing with dirt and sweat on Isaac's chest.

Davis, touched, stands speechless. He seems to see the boy with new eyes, "Opa. Alright lad. I am here. Don't cry, my friend. Where is your family? Olohana? Where is the king?"

Opa blinks. "They go to war, Akake. Gone!"

Davis wipes tears from Opa's face. "Opa, listen to me. I must find Kamehameha. Take me where he is."

Opa grabs his hand. "Mahukona. I show. Come."

The boy nearly drags Isaac Davis down the trail north, creating somewhat of a comic wheel of legs and arms. Opa grabs supplies, handing them to Davis as they rush through the village. Commoners and elderly flee past heading to safer ground in the south.

Davis stops and stares. "They are going south – where to?"

Opa shouts back, "To pu'uhonua. Place of Safety.

Davis realizes for the first time Kahekili is truly on the way. This is the long whispered war feared by Kamehameha's people. As he struggles through the tide of humanity, Davis catches Opa and holds him. "Opa, there will be hard fighting. War. Battle. You go South too, Opa." He points. "Go to place of safety."

Opa shouts above the wind, "No. I take you to king, then I go. Come – wiki-wiki anone."

They nearly fall into Nahena, the sweet-hearted matron who was the sailors' nurse. She embraces Davis, a brief, calm harbor in the midst of a storm. Opa speaks to her asking for food and water. She gives him several calabashes with food.

She stares at Davis for a long moment. He begins to understand that what is coming could change everything Kamehameha's people have ever known.

War for the Kingdom

39

Strategy

O n an eastern mountain road of Hawaii,
Molokoa, a messenger, calls to farmers
in the field, "Prepare for Kahekili attack.
He comes!" They drop their rakes and shout the
warning to others farther down the slope. The
messenger continues, breathlessly running along
the road.

At the village of Puna, on the eastern coast,
several local runners go through pathways calling
war instructions to workers in fields, who drop
tools and run for weapons.

At the same time, on the shoreline of the
east coast of the island, older warriors from the

highlands and Commoners, answering the call, wear the bright red and yellow colors of King Kamehameha, carry spears, cudgels and slingshots or any weapons they can grab. They run onto beaches, haul their canoes into the water, jump in, and begin paddling.

Elder relatives and priests run stumbling after them, yelling good-byes, shoving food wrapped in leaves into the corners of their canoes. Old women and young girls stand at a distance near the shore, weeping, some carve with small stones, bloody marks of sacrifices on their foreheads for their husbands, brothers or fathers, who they fear they may never hold in their arms again. Deep in the pounding chests of these villagers, hope in their beloved king swells like the tide now rising and rolling onto shore.

At dusk, Kamehameha's forces have set up camp near the beach at Mahukona, on the northwest point of Hawaii. They are aware of the rough sea in the channel between them and Maui. Slaves erect temporary quarters, priests chant evening prayers, and new muskets are handed out to warriors trained by the sailors. Some had trained only with a bamboo pole "musket" and are not sure how to hold the weapon. Comrades help them.

On a high slope over the sea, Kamehameha sits with Lamakua and chiefs, calmly discussing plans. At a short distance, Young gathers his men for a drill.

Kiana, watching Young out of the corner of his eye, storms up to Kamehameha and kneels, highly agitated. "My king, I am sorry to disturb you. Rumors are in the air that Akake has escaped to the ship. You see. He has betrayed you as I said he would."

The king gazes at him with disgust. "Is your life governed by rumors? Why do you bother me with this?"

"But you said you would kill them if they tried to leave and now behind your back he has gone?"

Kamehameha springs up. "You will test my patience once too often. Ask me where he is." Everyone within a hundred yards freezes. The king bellows, "Ask me, Kiana!"

Kiana, blinking in shock is finally intimidated. "Where is he? On the ship as they reported to me?"

The huge chest of the king expands as he takes a deep breath, bluffing in a resplendent fashion the likes of which could only be shared with Napoleon, unknown to him and far across the seas. "He is on a secret mission for me. Do you hear? A secret mission. A mighty warrior like you should spend his time drilling men, not listening to gossip like an old woman."

Stung, but not convinced, Kiana backs up, respectfully bowing as he leaves. He turns around to look at the king again and Young, in turn. Young makes every effort to not look concerned.

In the gathering dark, Davis, nearly fainting from exhaustion, staggers forward. Opa, with all his strength tries to hold Isaac up, but feels they may both fall.

Opa whispers, "Rest. You sleep, Akake. Sleep. Mahana."

Davis mumbles, his eyes failing to focus as he loses consciousness. "I must tell the king. How much farther? Mamao aku? Mamao aku?"

Opa looks at the road as tears well in his eyes. "Too far, Akake. Sleep. Sleep." He holds Davis up, moves him to a sandy spot where he falls and passes out, taking the stalwart boy down with him, both landing in the sand. Opa puts a bundle under Isaac's head. His eyes stalk the darkness as he watches his hero sleep, a willing sentry, undaunted and happy to be given this immense task.

The dawn of the second day glimmers on the wake of canoes as the first division of Kamehameha's warriors drive their paddles into the sea heading for Maui. Other waves of warriors waiting to leave, watch them and shout encouragement. These warriors will pretend to be traders and craftsmen when they land on southern shores of the island and kill outpost scouts who will not be able to warn King Kahekili of the advance of Kamehameha. They will arrive at three bays chosen by the king.

On the other side of the camp, Davis and Opa enter, exhausted, their weary eyes searching for Young or Kamehameha's private guards. However, Kiana's men see them first.

A quick exchange ensues as several of Kiana'a men shout to Kiana, "It's Akake and the cripple!" Kiana hurries over in mock friendliness. "Aloha, Akake."

Davis, glad to hear a greeting of warmth takes his hand. "Aloha, Kiana. Where's the king?" Kiana affects a pose of kindness. "Come with me. I show you."

Opa, tries to keep close to Davis, but is swept away by Kiana's men. Kiana sidles close to Davis, walking with him. "Akake, we heard you gone to ship. Good escape you make."

Opa shouts to Davis in the distance but is too far now for him to hear.

Isaac, still dazed and unaware of the trap, tells Kiana the truth. "Yes, I did. I was so desperate to get back to England. But, then... It must have been when I saw the warriors attack at Kiholo..."

Kiana grabs Davis by the arm and begins shouting in Hawaiian toward where the largest group of soldiers stand, "I have captured the traitor. Seize him. Seize him!"

Several of Kiana's men grab Davis, knocking Opa down. Davis resists. "What are you doing? Take me to the king!"

A huge crowd of warriors and commoners join Kiana as he nears the king's temporary hut. Kamehameha emerges. Young runs up from the shore just as Davis is dragged through the crowd, bound and gagged.

Kiana shouts, "We found this traitor spying on the camp for Kahekili. Kill him." The crowd, convinced by Kiana's men join the cry, "Kill him!

Kamehameha and Young are shocked to see Davis.

Young pushes his way through the mob, "Isaac!" Davis, confused, gagged, powerless, stares back.

Kiana continues his rant, "He admitted he escaped to the ship. He betrayed you, my king. Now do you believe me? He told the whites of the massacre. They will send their ships and men to kill us. He must die!" The crowd yells for justice.

Young's voice rises above the melee, "Whatever punishment is his, will be mine!"

Kamehameha moves to Kiana, furious. "Let him go, or I will kill you, you fool."

Kiana, only slightly cowed, motions to his men to let go of Davis. Kamehameha's private guard moves closer to Kiana's men. There is a moment of intense hatred between the two well-trained forces. Finally Kiana's warriors comply.

Young takes the gag off of Davis.

Kamehameha focuses on Isaac in hopes he will understand the plan. He speaks with clear diction to a gathering crowd, "Kiana, I said to you Akake was on a secret mission for me. Whatever he said was to fool you and your men. We are at war and I made him swear before his god to lie to anyone he met."

Davis, expecting eminent death, lifts his head, his eyes reveal panic to understand what the king has just said. He is too exhausted to fathom the king's words, "But, sir, I am… that is to say I was…"

Before Davis can speak further, Kamehameha orders his men to whisk him away.

Kamehameha retorts in Hawaiian, "I have important information to discuss with Akake. Go back to work." The king gives Davis a *hold your tongue and follow me* look as he moves out of the crowd with a hand on Davis.

The retinue moves quickly up the beach under the shade of palms. When safely circled by his men, the king warns, "Wait. No speak."

In the distance, Kiana tries to whip up the crowd, but they begin to disperse. Kiana and his men watch Kamehameha.

In the safety of the inner circle Kamehameha puts his hand on Davis' shoulder and studies him hard. "Akake, I know you go. I know. Tell me true, why you come back? No lie, or I kill you."

Davis, more clear-headed, speaks as Lamakua translates, "My king, I was on the ship with Captain Sandoval heading south when I saw many dying in Kiholo – women, children, old men. I could not see who was doing this, but I knew it was vicious and cowardly. My heart was in despair. I asked the captain to stop to help them, but he would not. So – I jumped off to help as many people as I could. Later, I met Pau Ahi, and he told me it was Kahekili's men. I told him to warn the southern villages before Kahekili's men could attack there. My king, I have come to fight that monster. I have made my choice. I will give my life to fight Kahekili and his armies. This is the truth. You are now my king, not King George of England. I believe my God sent me here for this purpose."

The king's gaze drives into Davis' heart. "You fight for Kamehameha? And next ship come you run?"

Davis hesitates. "All I know is, that day in the mountain pass, you risked your life to save me. Fine men of yours died protecting my life. That is why I will fight this battle for you – *with you.* When I saw people die in Kiholo, I knew I could not leave them. I will fight with all my heart. I only ask for this chance to fight for peace in all the islands."

Lamakua finishes translating.

The king nods. "You see Akake, I bet on you… and I win."

Davis bows low, offering homage, his eyes on the king's feet. "Mahalo, Kamehameha. Mahalo, sir."

Kamehameha looks at Lamakua. "Give Akake his weapons. And I wish for you to return safe from battle with protection from your god."

He leads the mariners back to Kiana and the other warriors. He shouts orders to assemble the other divisions and be ready to launch. He dons his bright yellow feather cloak, the huge headpiece being held by a waiting warrior. He steps up onto a rock and addresses the army, "My brothers, I suspected the enemy would go to Kiholo first, to try to fool us. I sent Akake to warn them and as some have said, he can swim faster than my messengers can run. Ha!"

Brief laughter rises from the army. The king becomes serious. "But, I am sorry to say, he arrived too late. We have a great losses and many deaths in Kiholo, but, he told Pau Ahi in time to warn the southern villages."

A shout goes up in favor of Davis.

"Do not be fooled by gossip, my brothers. Akake is not a traitor. He is a warrior and a brother to Kamehameha. He fights with us." A cheer swells from the warriors.

Young exhales in relief. Davis is dumfounded at the cleverness of Kamehameha.

Kiana crosses to Davis, smiling and taking his hand, lifting his up with Davis' shouting, "I think only of our king and our people. I ask forgiveness of Akake!" Davis is very suspicious, but accepts. The warriors cheer and shout.

Young moves to Kiana and whispers hoarsely in his ear, "I know that you know English better than you let on, so know this – I will kill you if you do not stop this attack on Isaac. Got that mate? I will kill you." Young looks to the crowd with his arm around Kiana's neck. Kiana understands every word as he waves to the crowd.

Kamehameha ushers Davis and Young into a nearby hut, leaving Kiana outside, hiding his frustration.

On the third day the Mahukona shore is in the last, deep darkness before dawn. Faint silhouettes of hundreds of canoes filled with warriors slip in from all sides of the harbor. Hundreds of other men move down the side of the slope to become the next wave to leave.

High above the bay, the king's group, lit by the last firelight of the night, look over a large, rough tapa cloth map of Maui. Kamehameha, Lamakua, Young, Davis, Mapala, Kiana and other chiefs discuss strategy in both tongues. Ka'ahumanu, the only woman ever allowed in the counsel, sits next to the king, looking intently at the map. He explains. "At Hana, they never see red-mouth gun. They will run. This sure. When they run, we get on beach wiki-wiki. On beach, Olohana, you bring Papa kaua with mussket. Mapala come nex. All quick. All one time. Papa kaua shoot mussket.

Boom. More run. We kill who run slow, eh?" He chuckles. "We go to nex valley. Move. Move. All way to Kahului." His finger courses the map up the coast to the north shore at Kahului.

Ka'ahumanu, whispers a suggestion to the king. He thinks, glances to Lamakua who agrees. He continues in broken English, "At my sign, Akake, you take Fair Merikan cannon canoe. Every time see my sign on land, hit with cannon from water. I be bait on hook. They come attack Kamehameha and boom, Akake cannon from sea. Big surprise. Big pu'iwa. Can win many time – every bay – on way North to Kahului. This understand? At Kahului take cannon in canoes, bring on land – boom all way up to Wailuku – up Iao Valley. Not Stop. Kahekili there. He hide. I know. All understand?"

Davis nods, getting the strategy, glancing to Young. "This is a good plan, sir."

Lamakua and the king share a private moment, then Lamakua turns to the sailors.

"The king want you understand only half battle getting to Kahu-lui. We muss be success in break path of his warriors to Iao Valley at Wailuku. Only plan success if Kamehameha army get top of valley. Kahekili high in mountain. Many, many warrior guard Kahekili. He is coward. But, clever rat. He save best warriors to surround him."

Young and Davis understand.

Kamehameha addresses his chiefs in his language, "You each have your plans clear? You understand how there will be musket fire to scare the first waves of warriors in each valley, then our men will kill as many as we can before moving to the next valley – doing this over and over all the way up? Speed is most important. We must catch them unprepared. At Kahu-lui the burning sand log white men call cannon will be brought on land to scatter warriors guarding the opening of the pass and confuse them so we can enter the valley. Gather your courage my friends and speak to your regiments. Then pray to Ku-Ka-ili-moku. Olohana, Akake, we ask you pray to your god of the many leaves."

He lifts Ka'ahumanu to a standing position with him and together they raise their hands. "We sail the dawn to victory."

The assembled leaders cheer. They rise, forming a circle around Kamehameha arm on arm all the way around. There is silence as each man garners courage from the others and makes peace with the possibility of not returning.

The brave princess, Kaoana, dressed in fighting garments, watches from a distance as the leaders break up from their meeting. Young sees his betrothed for the first time since leaving the king's village and runs to her. They catch each other in the tall grass in a wild embrace.

Her soft laughter comforts him, her nose nuzzles his cheek. "I see you Olohana. You look like a chief now." She kisses him on the lips, enjoying the oysterman's custom.

Young looks directly in her eyes. "Lamakua say you come to help wounded men. Why? There is much danger. Please go back to safety and take off these garments."

"Kahekili must die. I fight."

"Fight? If I say not fight, go with Ka'ahumanu? You not go?"

She looks down, disappointed. "My father and brothers be sad if I not go. They teach me warrior, Olohana. I am warrior for my people."

He can see she is crestfallen, as if he has no faith in her ability. "Kaoana, I see many times your skill. You are a great warrior. I only want you to live. My aloha is like the sky for you. I make you my wife, Olohana wahine. I don't want to see you die." She stares at him with a strength he has never seen in a woman. Without words she convinces him not to deny her. "Kaoana, I will pray to my God. His love – and mine – will protect you." She is satisfied. "Mahalo. Yes. John, you fight. Kaoana fight. Is good." He strokes her head, running his hand through her ocean of thick black hair. For a moment, they are both calm.

The golden dawn illuminates the darkness. A conch is blown to announce that the war canoes and the *Fair American* must catch the tide for the attack on Maui.

40

Launch to Death Island

Shortly after, over fifteen hundred warriors sit in canoes silently straining to see the war-god KU, emblem of Kamehameha held high in order to hit the coming sun. The boats are so close they appear to be one endless floating island. Oarsmen hold the side of the vessel next to them waiting to hear the battle cry. Among the fifty men in Kamehameha's outrigger war canoe, are Young, Mana'oi, and several chiefs.

Isaac Davis, with trained gunmen, and warriors-turned-sailors, is in the largest vessel. He has a swivel gun from the *Fair American* mounted on two pontoons constructed on an outrigger balanced on canoes lashed together. Davis leans over to Young. He places his hand on Young's shoulder. "God go with you, John."

Young stares back, knowing it could be the last calm moment he and Davis may have before the battle—a new type of warfare they know little about and never expected to be in. "Also with you, Isaac. It will be good to fight alongside a man for whom I have great respect. You made the right decision."

"Thank you. I am not worthy of your forgiveness, but with all my heart I am grateful for it."

"Where is Opa?"

"Heading to the city of refuge."

"Good. We must train him to fight next time."

Davis laughs. "Yes. He continues to astound me with his spirit. It's enough to make up for five twisted legs, eh?"

They chuckle. Young interrupts, "Look at the queen."

Ka'ahumanu, stands on the highest slope above the beach, draped in lavish ceremonial cloths of Kamehameha's colors, vibrant yellow, red and green, the wind billowing the fabric like flags around her large frame, not a trace of doubt in her deep, dark eyes focused like twin arrows on her king below. Maidens surround her like bright red and yellow tropical flowers, waving palm branches, creating a splendid tableau to inspire the army.

Kamehameha rises up majestically next to Kahuna Lani, who holds the war god up to where sunlight will hit. The king senses the light coming. All hearts and minds are caught in the power surging through them.

On the shore, Ka'ahumanu's huge hand begins slowly to rise as the cue for the armada. All wait for her signal to launch. Her gaze stays on the war god image, as light streams across the water. The fierce face of the god Ku ignites his mother-of-pearl eyes with a fiery glow. All who see it gasp. "*NoKa Lanakila!*" Ka'ahumanu drops her hand, giving the signal. Kamehameha thrusts the standard high in the sun, hurling his deep voice across the harbor like a spear striking into their souls. "Io Wailuku. Io Wailuku. Io Kahekili!" Thousands of paddles slam into the water in unison as warriors shout, "Kamehameha. Kamehameha. Kamehameha!"

The armada is propelled into the dangerous and deadly channel toward Maui, leaving the vessel of Kahuna Lani in their wake as the priests watch, wave, say prayers and hold their robes, whipping in the wild wind.

Moving further on the water, the code of silence begins. They are aware of how fierce the winds and waves can be in the crossing. There will be no shouting, no careless talk as they know sound carries far across water, and as they travel the channel, they must hope for the greatest possible surprise to the enemy outposts at Hamoa Bay, their first point of landing at the tip of Maui. On the shore, tears well in Ka'ahumanu's eyes as she and her servants wave palm branches for as long as backward-glances of the army can see.

In a mountain hut, in Kahelui, in the highlands of Maui, Kahekili enjoys a day of feasting, confident he has surprised Kamehameha. He has no idea his plan has missed its mark.

As land slips further from view, Davis has moments to think before the rough current makes thoughts of anything but safety difficult.

How far to sea would I be now if Kahekili's men had not attacked Kiholo? It matters not. I was meant to be here. It is part of the plan of Providence. What a fool I am. How could I leave John here alone? I must prove myself a good fighter and stay alive. And what's the use? My Lilly has long been happy without me. Time to accept that. I must not get this powder wet or there will be no shooting at all. Davis is distracted by wind blowing too strong on the heavy swivel gun balanced tenuously on the outrigger. He and assistants steady the small cannon as warriors around them dig deep in the water.

John Young paddles his side of the king's canoe lost in thought…

Has Metcalfe gone to all the other islands looking for Thomas? He will never find his son or the Fair American. Isaac is the only one left who knows. Will he return here to make trouble or will his contract with the trading company drive him back to the Northwest for furs? Dear God, please guide me and Kaoana and the army through this fight. Grant us safe passage home. Amen. Home? Ha! It is odd to think of my hut as home, but I must admit I have commenced to do so…

41

Maui Landing

In the channel between the islands, an Alala bird, a large Hawaiian silky black crow, twirls in the sky. It has a view of Kamehameha's armada of hundreds of war canoes silently crossing the deep blue, wild and windswept water, cutting in stealth through the waves.

High on the hillside at the southern tip of Maui a guard sits on a rock at Haou, near the Hana coast. The sleepy messenger hears the shrill cry of a crow and looks up. He searches the horizon carefully and looks back to the wood he is carving. He looks up again and studies the ocean. This time his eyes widen, connecting with an image that seems to be a large number of canoes. He shades his eyes. He leaps up and runs down the slope to another messenger sleeping on watch below, shaking him. "Kamehameha approaches, heading for Hamoa Bay. Hundreds of canoes. Run!"

But, before either of Kahekili's warriors can make any move, four of Kamehameha's men leap out of the brush, strangling them with ropes.

After nearly ten hours of astoundingly difficult paddling, beating against the wind much of the time, and zig-zagging to be able to traverse high swells, they are exhausted. However, surprisingly, they have help from mysterious prevailing winds at times, giving them small breaks to regain strength. The first of Kamehameha's war canoes hit the beach at Hamoa Bay with praise for the gods. Some canoes are missing, a sad casualty of such warfare. The area is deserted except for advance warriors sent earlier to set up camp for Kamehameha.

As canoes come onshore, the warriors don't talk, but drag canoes on the beach, making no more noise than necessary. Kamehameha's war canoe lands, the odd-looking, lashed-together vessel with the swivel gun, which Davis has covered with tapa to look like a load of fish. All are grateful it survived the crossing.

The chief of the advance group bows before Kamehameha. "My king, preparations have been made for resting here tonight." The king squints at the mountains. "Were there many guards on watch?"

"Very few, my king. Most have been called up to join Kahekili's forces in Wailuku and Kahului. Many fisherman have gone into the hills to hide, knowing there will be war."

Kamehameha scans the area, looking for traps. "Good. There can be only a few fires tonight, we don't want anyone passing on the water to know we are here."

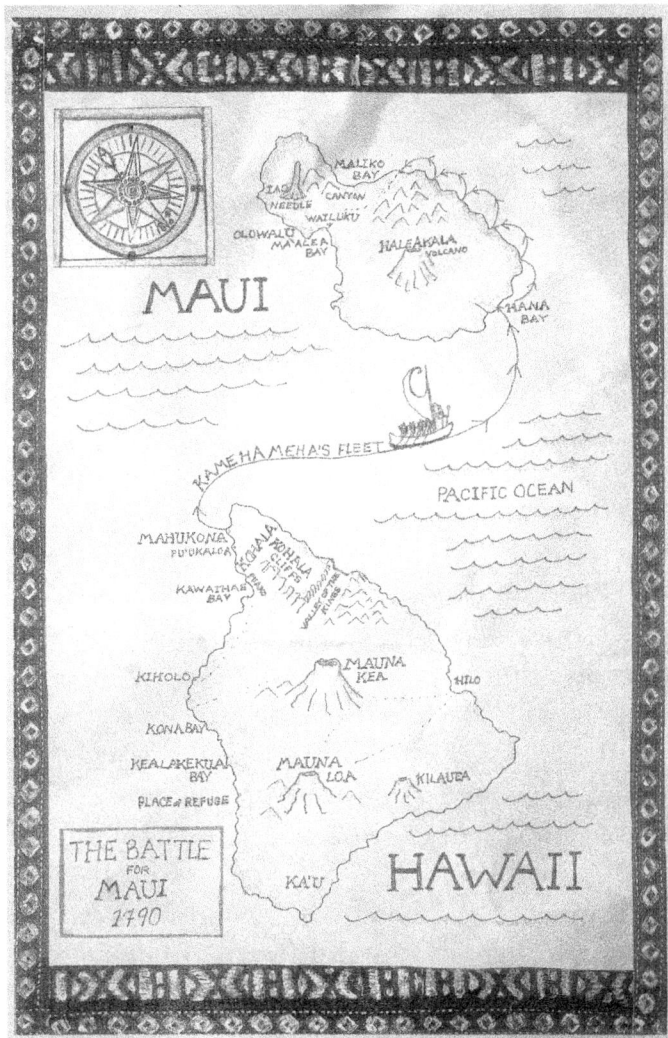

John Young's Battle Map of Hawaii and Maui

42

Chasing Sleep

Young and Davis feel every muscle ache from strain as they toss mats down with hundreds of other warriors near the beach. Servants bring baskets of dried fish, fruit, and water. There is little talk, only what is essential about weapons and strategy. As dark descends on them, everyone keeps an eye out in spite of guards watching all perimeters.

Kamehameha has his personal musket with him, which he has kept near him since the day he got it. He reclines with his head against a palm and positions the musket just under his right hand, with his spears and knives alongside. Two other guards stand near the palm, ready to protect him with their lives.

All night, waves onshore offer soothing music. This brings little comfort and even less sleep for most of the men. In spite of the great exertion of crossing from Hawaii, the warriors chase sleep, their minds twisting on deadly images. Furtive dreams become horrible nightmares, with endless attacks from the enemy.

Kamehameha, awake, alert, searches the night sky for a sign of victory.

43

Pecking Prophet

With first light, Kamehameha opens his eyes, having slept a few hours. He sees a Alae Ula bird staring at him from a bush. He blinks and thinks, remembering asking for a sign. He feels the sign has arrived, knowing the history of this bird and the bright red portion of feathers.

"Ahhh...yes, *bringer of fire.* We will win!"

Young walks up to Kamehameha, with a leaf full of fish and fruit. "Good morning, my king. They told me I could bring this. Did you sleep?"

Kamehameha points to the bird. "Olohana, this my sign! Alae Ula, has mele. When Pele give fire to my people, she send this bird. You see his red there?"

Young studies the bird pecking at the sand. "Yes, I see red on his head and beak."

"Yes. He is my sign burning sand bring peace to us." He nods agreement with himself, jumps up like a contented child, grabs the food from Young and stuffs it in his mouth. "Is good, Olohana. Where Akake and chiefs? We will find them." He hurries off. Young follows, smiling, shaking his head.

Less than an hour later, Kamehameha's huge flotilla moves just off shore, to follow the coast and head to their first target, Hana Bay. Warriors row, jaws set, staring ahead. As long as they can remember, fathers, uncles, brothers and friends have gone to war, many never to return. There is a sense today, deeper than fear, a despondency that the cycle of war will never end. They hope this time might be different.

☙❧

In the bay of Hana, leaders of Kamehameha's floating army see scouts on land shouting alarm. These are not the large regiments of Kahekili's warriors waiting for them up the coast. They are merely groups aware they're under attack. They run in all directions, grabbing spears and cudgels. Kamehameha's canoes come in sight between lava rocks surrounding the shoreline. With his bright yellow feather cape and helmet, the king looks far bigger even than his seven feet, a daunting figure and vision of sure death for whoever crosses his path.

The king's warriors shout epithets to Kahekili's men onshore. A conch heralds in the distance, an alarm being sent up to war camps further north.

Kamehameha's canoe speeds for shore. The double canoes mounted with cannon also move swiftly. The king signals Davis, shouting, "Holoimua!"

Davis gives the command. The cannon blasts onshore. *Boom*! Kahekili's warriors panic. As Kamehameha predicted, the effect is devastating, the new weapons shock the enemy. The king's canoe lands with a heavy thud. John Young and his men jump out and set up battle lines. The first wave of canoes land, warriors leaping out, cheering.

Some of Kahekili's warriors turn back, attempting to counter-attack. Young shouts, "Fire!" The first volley of muskets strikes greater terror in Kahekili's men who race farther up the beach into the hills. The sound of cannon and Young's regiment's musket fire has never been heard or seen in Hawaiian battles. Even villagers seeing from hiding spots in the mountains are astounded.

Kamehameha and several chiefs kill those who cannot escape fast enough. Mana'oi and comrades, feed ammunition to gunners. The king's other regiments move up the slope from the beach in a wild rout. As they get to the hill, dozens of Kahekili warriors rush them from hiding, but are scattered by the musket fire.

However, several spears land in Young's men. Mana'oi picks up a musket from one of the fallen gunners. The unit moves forward, unable to care for the wounded. The artillery having opened the way, Kamehameha's infantry surges up the hill.

Kaoana and several women follow in rear guard canoes. They rush to the wounded, carrying them out of danger. Other regiments waiting as back up in the water, cheer victory, "Lanakila. Eo!"

A flag signal is raised for Davis to order his warriors round the next point of land to attack the next Bay. Opa's head pops up from a nearby canoe. "Akake…"

"Opa!" Davis, amazed and angry at the sight of his young friend diving in the water. "Opa, you lied to me!"

Opa dog-paddles and shouts, "Akake, you fight. I fight. Let me up!"

"Damn." Davis scoops him up, swinging him into the canoe. "Get in." Davis secretly enjoys the shear cleverness required for the child to stowaway for so long. The warriors laugh. "What am I to do with you? You going to be a warrior? Will you follow my orders like these men? Will you – you cheeky runt?"

Opa valiantly salutes. "Yes. I do all you say, Akake."

"Ha! Then it will be the first time – stay down 'til we get round the point."

Kamehameha's troops are on the hillside in hand-to-hand combat above Hana Bay. Warriors in the king's yellow and red colors swarm across the battlefield attacking those wearing Kahekili's green and purple. Kamehameha's women warriors fight bravely and are hard to discern from the men.

Lamakua aims his pololu at the corrupt Ali'i Governor of Hana, a known leader of Kahekili's southern Maui forces. As he hits his mark, the man goes down and a cheer rises from Kamehameha's troops – the king's emblem is stuck into the loose rocks of the nearby temple, a sign of victory. They burn the village huts built for Kahekili, then jump into canoes to speed to the next attack.

At Ka'eleku Bay, Davis, his warriors, and swivel gun have arrived. They look back and see Kamehameha's men on the hill dancing with spears over an easy victory. Dozens of canoes led by Chief Kiana and his men are stationed on the edge of Ka'eleku Bay to go to the next landing, Kalahu Point. A flag from Davis' group signals they have victory there and don't need back up. Kiana's blood-lust is up. He's ready to fight. He's enraged at being left out of the first battles, so he decides not to wait for orders. He heads for the next major target. He turns to his troops and shouts, "Io Kahului!"

All day the fighting continues, as the signal is given. Davis and his cannoneers continue to flush out Kahekili's forces, working up the east coast of Maui pushing ever forward and seizing all villages held by Kahekili – Kalahu, Nihaku, Wailua, Huelo and Honomanu. The siege is so successful they head to Maliko Bay where they gather for the night.

A night of rest is necessary to be able to move all the way to Kahekili's headquarters at the mountaintop. Davis and his men blast the coastline with such force that whole regiments of Kahekili's run off in terror. Not having an effective retreat plan, they scatter up the slopes, becoming targets for the infantry who know well how to use their muskets, spears and cudgels.

Arriving at Maliko Bay, Kamehameha calls together a circle of chiefs as camp is being set up for his bone-tired army. Lamakua, Young, Davis, and Mana'oi meet on the shore. They crouch in a half-circle as the king draws in the sand, speaking in Hawaiian, laying out the strategy for the next day. Lamakua stays near the sailors to translate.

When the king is sure they are all watching, he spreads his arms wide, his eyes sparkling as if he'd just awakened from a full night's sleep though he's hardly slept since they left. His buoyancy outweighs all physical needs. His spirit soars.

"Ah, my brothers. I know many of you bleed and have many pains. You bravely captured many villages today. Ku-ka-ili-moku sang in my heart for each of you as you struck a spear in the core of Kahekili. His hold of Maui has been broken, ripped apart. The beautiful future of our people is within our reach. I will always be proud of you for great courage this day."

He jams the point of his spear in the sand. "But, my friends, hear me. Tomorrow we must do far, far more. We must break the long siege of this fiend at Kahului and move with speed through Wailuku to take the vulture himself in his nest at the top of Io valley. He always saves his best warriors to protect him, so we must be ready to fight days to get up the valley. Eat and sleep, my friends – goodnight and tell your warriors what I have said." He walks briskly away with Lamakua.

Young complains to Davis. "Tomorrow will be 'much worse'? I had hoped they would surrender after so many hundreds of warriors ran from us today."

Davis stares out to sea. "Yes. If my father had any notion what I was up to here, he would have me flogged as a lunatic. We had many dark words over my going to strange lands. Now I begin to understand. What if we lose?"

Young sighs. "Best get some sleep." He turns to Mana-oi. "My friend, join us – get some food and find a patch of sand. Isaac, I expect your ratty little stowaway is hungry as well. Let's go find him before he gets into more trouble."

Davis snorts. "That imp should get a flogging for disobeying me. But, it makes me laugh to think how he popped up like a weasel at just the right moment. He is worth ten of the other young ones back on the island. We must find something he can do to stay out of harm's way."

Young cogitates. "Yes. Have you heard that Kiana's men have been chosen to leave first in the morning? He came back tonight just to get permission. They are to land and draw Kahekili's forces to the north side of the harbor to trick them. The rest of us land on the south and begin to rush them from the other side."

Davis is skeptical. "I heard. I think he's only doing it for show. He is a brave fighter, I'll give him that, but I don't trust him a ha'penny and I'm glad he is not fighting next to me."

As they walk looking for Opa, the boy peeks out from a palm branch and deftly hops after them, bouncing and hiding from tree to tree until they see him and hoot with laughter. He runs to join them. Davis cuffs his head.

It is dusk in "the vulture's nest", a term the king has used to describe Kahekili's hide-outs on the islands he has terrorized. A thick mist surrounds the spiny peak of the Iao Needle near the summit of the Wailuku Valley twenty miles north. King Kahekili, and his sons, Kapa-hili and Kalani sit in a hut with a group of trusted chiefs, illuminated by torches.

They enjoy a hearty laugh with Kahekili. He sneers. "And the real reason Kamehameha cannot beat me is he is so terrified by his gods he hides in his temple and prays constantly. He lives under the skirts of his priests. He has far too many feelings to be a king. He is weak."

Sounds of shouting float up the hill followed by commotion outside. A messenger arrives from Wailuku, prostrating himself before the king. Kahekili turns, vexed at being disturbed.

The messenger gasps, "Kamehameha! In Maliko." A look of surprise and concern morphs quickly into a mask of confidence. "That is not possible." Kahekili, his sons and chiefs fall silent.

44

Wailuku

The army of Kamehameha moves forward in silence. The king signals, "All is ready" with a wave of a small flag to Isaac Davis and his men in the swivel-gun canoe. The pontoon war-vessel glides into place behind the king's, which catches the first ray of sun. Kamehameha grins wide and points to Davis. He pushes Opa out of sight in the hull. "Stay down there all day." Opa, eyes big, ducks down. Davis gestures to his warriors to shove off.

Young is in the flotilla behind Davis. He sits with Mana'oi and three chiefs. They head up the huge body of vessels behind them. Surrounding

Young are his musket brigade, holding their weapons, proudly. He whispers, "Remember, keep the powder dry." His hand goes up and down to signal other leaders in canoes.

The rush of water is massive. In unison, paddles of hundreds of warriors splash in military rhythm as they propel the king's floating island of death into Maliko Bay. They head for Kahului harbor where they expect to meet a large division of Kahekili's army.

Runners have raced far up the Iao Valley. All divisions of Kahekili's on the north coast are manning their posts.

Kiana's men arrive at the north side of the harbor and leap out of canoes. They establish a beachhead at Kahului. Kahekili's warriors arrive at the place and engage Kiana's battalion.

Kamehameha's war canoe and Young's musket regiment arrive at the south bay. Kiana's men are engaging Kahekili's army as Kamehameha's personal guard and Young's gunners move into position. Dozens of Kahekili's men charge them, only to be trapped and killed by muskets, Davis' cannon, and spears from Kamehameha's special guard. However, these are Kahekili's well-trained warriors, and they don't run. They stand and do battle. Kamehameha begins to lose men.

Fighting is hard on the open plains near Kahului Bay. All of Kamehameha's forces have landed and are forging across slopes toward the main valley.

Kamehameha fights with his pololu, twirling and dodging like a dancer, fooling every enemy into being his next victim. He leaps out of the way of attackers. Others around him are getting tired. The king finishes off a man, and fights his way to Lamakua. He shouts, "Tell Akake, bring cannon to land. Push to canyon!"

Lamakua turns and suddenly a spear hits him square in the chest. Shocked, Kamehameha lunges forward, kills the attacker, grabs Lamakua and pulls the spear out of him. He sweeps his dearest friend up with one arm and slashes warriors all the way down the hill.

Young has seen this, but can't help. He shoots his musket, it misfires – he has to grab his short spear and fight off several warriors. Mana'oi covers him bravely with his musket. Young struggles his way to Mana'oi and shouts, "Pass it along—*Ka-hawai. 'onou po'o kahawai.* Meet at canyon!"

On the slope of Kahului Bay, Isaac Davis and his regiments have the high tide on their side, so landing the swivel gun has been easy. They move it onto a tapa sled carried by slaves.

The soldiers load and re-load, blasting cannon balls into Kahekili's forces, opening the main path to the Iao Valley. Many more divisions of Kahekili's warriors are in hiding. The first and second lines have run away but divisions behind them are out of reach of cannonfire – waiting in the valley.

Kamehameha's army must move in great haste or lose momentum. A messenger shouts to Kiana and Davis, "Push to canyon!" Kamehameha, carries Lamakua, bleeding heavily, to a ravine, where women and older men care for the wounded. Kaoana runs to him. "Cousin!"

"Save him. Do what you can, his heart is strong." Kamehameha looks deep into Lamakua's eyes. Lamakua grabs his arm. "Go, my king. Claim your victory…"

"Do not die. You will see it with me."

Kaoana, in tears, motions the king to go.

Kamehameha hurries up the hill. Lamakua watches him go, praying for the man he has served for twenty years. The king disappears in a sea of spears and colors. Kaoana sees the light leave his eyes. She screams but no one hears her in the midst of the howls of battle.

Near the top of the hill, John Young looks around for Kaoana as he fights alongside his men. He is nearly gored by a spear but regains his focus.

At the bottom of the hill, Kaoana takes Lamakua's dagger from his belt and runs into the fight.

Princess Kaoana as warrior

45

Trick

The afternoon sun protects Kahekili. It shines in the eyes of Kamehameha's army as they rush into the entrance of the valley. There is only one way in, and they must push that line to break through to Kahekili's headquarters in the mountain compound.

Kamehameha and Davis meet in a glen near the fighting. The king grabs Davis' shoulders. "I will go mock them from rocks. They throw spears. Ask your god of leaves move sun down! Move down!" His hands describe his strategy, adding to his rough English. "Akake, take cannon up hill. Olohana and Kiana army go. We follow. Yes?"

Davis is unsure. "Olohana's troops have enough burning sand?"

"All musket sand with Olohana. Yes, bring cannon!"

Behind them rises a high and ominous tower rock, like a sentinel, near the summit. Kamehameha glances at the gigantic spire, knowing it is near the last place where Kahekili will stand his ground. The Hawaiian king climbs on nearby rocks. He can see Kahekili's armies waiting in the upper valley beyond. He sees Davis, Young, Kiana, and the cannoneers getting into position near the path of the steep trail. He shouts and jeers at the warriors below, taunting them, offering himself as a target. They take the bait. Regiments move in. He dodges dozens of long spears, hooting as they hurtle by him. Some he catches, throwing them back with deadly accuracy.

In the chaos, his army finally breaks through enemy lines. The decoy trick has worked.

🙶🙷

In the steep mountain there is a plateau where Kahekili and his sons hide in a well-supplied hut filled with warriors. Kahekili speaks in icy outrage. "Kalani, you fool. How could they have surprised you? Didn't you have loyal runners on Hawaii? How close are they? Is there anyone here I can trust?"

"Father, please. No one has ever been able to get up here. We have five layers of men in the entrance to the valley. No one has ever broken through that pass."

The sound of distant thunder comes to their ears.

Kahekili's eyes widen. "What is that?"

All turn to the sound. It is a sound they have never heard – Davis' cannoneers.

Down the mountain, on the other side of the rocks, hundreds of Kahekili's men hold the last portion of the pass against Kamehameha's army. At that moment, the sun moves enough to give Kamehameha's warriors a clear view. They surge forward.

For many minutes, the forces of Kamehameha gain essential ground in the canyon. But, Young and other chiefs with their units are in danger of getting cut off. A vanguard of Kahekili's army has burst through and fights with new courage.

John Young sees Mana'oi near a pocket of warriors with no back up. He shouts, "Mana'oi get behind cannon. Now!" Mana'oi grabs a spear from a dead man and fights harder, moving close to the cannon. Young and Mana'oi join a group of other warriors against the onslaught.

Kamehameha continues as decoy. He jeers and blocks each attack as he waits for all his troops to get through the pass into the canyon, where he can join them.

Davis and the cannoneers have moved forward. From a ledge above the main path, they prime their cannon. They shoot straight into the widest part of the gorge. *Boom*! Hundreds of retreating enemy run faster to get away from the blast, but many are hit. Kamehameha's army is like a tidal wave washing up many Iao valley trails slamming toward the top of the mountain.

Seeing his men have broken through, Kamehameha raises his hand and shouts over and over in Hawaiian, "To Wailuku!" The cannoneers continue. *Boom*! Enemy lines are blasted, splintering divisions.

A conch is heard, blown by messengers, sounding a retreat, echoing to the nether reaches of the summit. The second wave of Kiana's men and other Chiefs move in. Kiana shouts, "Kamehameha. Kamehameha! A Wailuku!" An enemy warrior singles him out.

"Behind you!" yells Davis, but Kiana can't hear. Davis throws his dagger at the warrior, who goes down. Kiana turns in time to see Isaac Davis has saved him. A look of shock crosses his face. He turns back to fight.

Wailuku Valley is now a sea of Kamehameha's colors, yellow and red streaming in from the entrance to the canyon and wending its way toward the highest mountain where Kahekili's compound is hidden. But, there remaina a hundred-man strong contingent of Kahekili's men fortified in this top part of the gorge.

Davis' and his cannoneers drag the swivel gun to a higher ledge, sweating and groaning as they go to be able to pound a bigger hole in enemy lines.

The armies collide as if in a huge green bowl, thick with vegetation, streams, and gullies. Kahekili's men are pushed deeper into the valley, with no way out.

The sun is setting on the Iao Needle. The mountain streams are a mix of glittering gold and fresh blood from corpses damming them up. The armies fight in close combat.

Young fends off two warriors at once. He is helped by a clever warrior with a short spear, which lands in the chest of his opponent. He is jolted to see Kaoana by his side. She yanks the spear out of the warrior, brandishing her ever-present knife to protect Young while he re-loads and grabs a spear from a dead enemy. They make a magnificent couple, as they push on, protecting each other from attackers.

Mana'oi is sparring well when he is hit by a rock from a slingshot. Blood spews from his temple. He calls to Young who attacks the warrior before he can do any more harm. Young drags his friend to safety. Mana'oi looks up. "Leave me! Help Kaoana, Olohana!"

Young's face is riddled with hesitation. "I will return." He joins Kaoana who is fighting several of the enemy. Mana'oi hears others approach. He tries to crawl into the underbrush. As he rises, a warrior stabs him from behind. His eyes lock on John Young and Kaoana fighting in the distance. His spirit is lifted, knowing he helped them find each other. It is his last thought.

46

Man to Man

Davis has run out of ammunition. He drops his musket and fights with spear and dagger. Kiana sees him in danger. In a rare moment of gratitude, he surprises Isaac, killing his attacker with a slingshot. He nods to Kiana.

Kamehameha fights alongside his men as they struggle up a rocky trail. Across the canyon he sees Kapa-hili, Ka-hekili's oldest son, taunting him – their eyes lock while he stabs Kamehameha's messenger, Wakana, who falls from the ledge to fifty feet below.

Kamehameha grits his teeth and shouts to Mapala. "Did you find out?" Mapala points to the upper trail. "Kahekili is not to be found. Only Kapa-hili and Kalani-Kupule. Kamehameha shouts back, "Send the challenge before they run, too!"

On the other side of the canyon, Kapa-hili fights off several of Kamehameha's special guard savagely. A messenger waves a tapacloth on a long stick as he runs toward him. Kapa-hili knows what it means. He raises his hand. Kalani, his brother, holds up his hand, shouting for his men to halt. The call spreads quickly across the armies that the battle for the island of Maui will be decided by hand-to-hand combat. Messengers scream, "The kings will fight. The kings will fight!"

Young and Davis are startled. They were not warned of this stratagem. Nor are they sure they understand why it is happening. They stop fighting as warriors on both sides pull back and watch Kamehameha head toward the other side of the canyon, followed by several bodyguards.

∋⊂

A fight area is staked out near a precipice. All warriors stand breathing hard in silence, relieved to rest while the two kings fight. However, each side knows if their man goes down, they must be ready to run or to massacre the losing side. Kapa-hili prepares. Kalani watches from a safe distance.

Young and Kaoana stand with Davis. Isaac whispers to Young. "If Kamehameha loses?"

"Then we are dead."

In the bay below the Iao Needle, King Kahekili, looks back as he escapes in his war canoe. He winces in pain. A servant nurses a wound in his shoulder from one of Kamehameha's warriors. He hears shouts from the mountains above. He looks back to the bay ahead, disgusted with himself for running away. He scowls at his slaves, attacking the waves with their paddles. "Can't you move faster? I must get to Oahu."

On the mountain ledge, Kahekili's beloved son, Kapa-hili, and King Kamehameha square off with short spears. They are physically quite equal. They circle. Kapa-hili snarls as he fends off several lunges by Kamehameha. Their spears crash in volleys, which echo down the gorge.

Both armies cheer their side with every hope of winning.

Kamehameha, caught off balance, loses his spear. The crowd gasps. The weapon clatters out of reach. Kahekili's warriors cheer. Kapa-hili seizes the moment to throw Kamehameha to the ground, but the fearless king catches the top of Kapa-hili's spear with his bare hand. Kamehameha barely keeps the spear's sharp point away from his throat, blood spurting from his hand.

Kahekili's forces howl with joy raising their fists. Young instinctively moves to help. Davis grabs him. "Stop." In one movement, to everyone's amazement, Kamehameha pushes Kapa-hili off of him. Kamehameha's forces whoop in support. Kapa-hili loses his spear as Kamehameha clamors to his feet. Weapons gone, they circle again, meet hand-to-hand, struggle back and forth, moving closer to the edge.

Legions of warriors sway as one leader gets the upper hand, loses ground, then regains control again. They break up briefly, circling, and back into a locked embrace. Kamehameha gets an arm free, wraps it around Kapa-hili, places his foot at just the correct angle, and stares into Kapa-hili's eyes. Another deadlock. A guttural sound comes from deep in Kamehameha as he takes Kapa-hili in one swift motion, flinging him off the precipice. "Eeeeyyyaaa," echoes down the cliff. Every heart is taken by surprise. A mysterious silence fills the gorge.

Kahekili, in his war canoe, hears the eerie scream float on the wind. He looks back and listens. His eyes close briefly. He faces forward again, toward Oahu, the last major island he must hold in his power. His expression turns to stone. His attendants claw the water with their paddles.

Up on the mountain, warriors from both sides watch as the body of Kapa-hili bounces off two ledges and lands far below in a streambed. All eyes turn to Kamehameha. He raises his hands slowly in victory. Men in both armies realize what has happened. Kamehameha's army cheers. The king gestures a challenge to the remaining prince. Everyone turns to see his reaction.

Kalani, hides in the crowd, shakes in terror and disappears behind his brigade. Kahekili's forces turn to run, but Kamehameha's warriors charge with new fury. The slaughter begins.

∞

The wind blows white caps over a dusky sea. Death has silenced the shouts of battle. Fallen warriors blanket the landscape from the Iao Needle to the shore. The only sound above the whine of strong wind is the constant moan of the wounded and dying. A trail of dead warriors, largely those in Kahekili's colors, begins at the summit of the canyon and continues down the valley to the bay. Dark, blood-filled water courses over bodies in streams, gaining speed, crashing over ledges, becoming red waterfalls chiseled across the cliffs pouring into the bay. Waves roll on the beach where more bodies are strewn along the shore like so many dead fish. Kamehameha's prophecy has come true – the blood of Kahekili's men "will run from the mountain to the sea."

Young and Kaoana, both wounded, search for Davis and the king. Others call out for their companions as they wander through layers of bodies. Young calls as he walks across a small lagoon, "Isaac? Kamehameha?"

Kaoana searches near him, shouting, "Akake?"

Davis and Opa appear on a ridge above them. They carry a wounded man. Davis's arm is heavily bandaged. "John. Kaoana. Up here!"

Opa shouts with relief, "Aloha, Olohana. Kaoana!"

Davis struggles to help the wounded warrior. "Must stop the bleeding." John and Kaoana hurry to help, stepping over bodies and rocks. John is the first to reach Davis. He calls to other warriors, "Help. Kokua. Eia!" "Are you hurt badly, Isaac?"

"No. I am fine." Warriors take the wounded

man from Davis. "It's not bad. But, Lamakua - is he…?"

"Sit on this rock. Yes. A good man. A fine man. He's gone. How quickly it can be over." Kaoana wipes blood off of Davis' wounds. Isaac looks at Young, "And Mana'oi…?" At the sound of Mana'oi's name, John cannot speak. He shakes his head and sits next to Davis.

Davis avoids his eyes. "I am so sorry. So many… many."

Young wipes tears from his eyes and gets control. "We must take care of his widow. Nakui will need friends. I will make sure the king knows how bravely he fought."

"Yes. We will help her all we can."

John spots Opa sitting near Davis on a rock. "Opa? I was told you were sent to the city of refuge."

Opa lifts his short spear. "You fight. I fight."

Davis looks stern, but eyes Opa with love. "He was a ratty numbskull not to listen to me. But, now he's taking orders very well." Opa beams.

Young gives the boy a warm English handshake then takes him by the shoulders. "You are a good man. But, you must stay back on the next one. Promise?" Opa smiles.

Davis looks around. "Where is the king?"

"No one knows. They can't find him."

"The king is *missing*? Preposterous. Is it possible we have misplaced our king?"

Young shakes his head. "We have looked everywhere and even the highest command cannot find him. They say there are times when he disappears and cannot be found for many hours. They want to wait at the canoes for him to return to the shore, but we have decided to keep looking. They will blow the conch if they see him."

Davis looks toward the mouth of the valley. "Let me help you search. It is better than sitting here in pain."

Much later, several hunting parties search near the bay in Kahului. Hundreds of warriors sit on slopes near the mountains, resting, eating, laughing and talking.

Young, Kaoana, Davis, and Opa search with a group of warriors combing the Iao Valley. Shouts of "Kamehameha. Kamehameha" echo up and down the gorge, but to no avail.

Young squints at a crowd of men down on the beach. "It looks like Kiana is giving up the search, gathering his men in canoes. Doesn't he care where Kamehameha is? Let's try that trail."

Kaoana speaks up. "What about that ridge? He is not down here, so perhaps he went up the gorge."

John agrees. "Akake and I will go to the top and work our way back down if he is not there. Stay with Opa here."

John and Isaac move up the slope of jagged, lava rocks. The setting sun throws a cape of crimson over them as they climb.

47

Ocean of Blood

An hour later the mariners move around the far side of the canyon, stepping over more dead warriors as they ascend higher.

The wind is fierce closer to the summit. Young and Davis find it difficult not to search for Kamehameha's warriors who may still be alive, but decide to focus on finding the king first.

As they reach the top plateau, Young sees a figure in the distance and points. It is a person sitting, holding a dead warrior. From the size of the man, even in silhouette, they know it is Kamehameha. He looks up and sees them approach. He does not move.

When Davis, who carries the conch, is sure it is the king, he raises it to his lips, but Young stops him, "Wait." They stay where they are and watch from a respectful distance.

Kamehameha looks to heaven. Tears pour from his eyes. *"Ku-Kaili-Moku. Today you honor me. But, you have not made me king of Maui. I am king of the dead! When will you be satisfied? Must I swim in blood forever? Kahekili escapes again and more will die. Always more and more."*

The wind howls around the sailors. They stand in silence.

The king looks up again, nearly mad with grief. The sailors move to him with caution. He becomes aware of them and looks down at the corpse he holds. "This warrior, Kahawai, was a friend of my mother's from my childhood... we played in the sea." He points to another part of the plateau. "See... a cousin, and see in the tree... a man who I fished with. We talked of women..." He cannot finish his thought. He takes the man in his arms, lays him on a bed of leaves, takes the warrior's cape and covers him.

At that moment Young and Davis notice the color of the cape of the dead man.

Young gingerly approaches. "Sir, these warriors are all the enemy, are they not?"

Kamehameha lifts the cloak and rubs his hand in the blood of the dead man. He mixes it in his hands in the blood from his own wounds, and gestures. "Blood is same... no? These all my people. Many more will die. Many, many before peace."

Davis moves to him. "But, now certainly they will ask you for peace. Will they not?"

The king grabs a rock near him and shatters it on a boulder. "There will be no peace before Kahekili is dead. As I speak, he plans the next attack. I am a fool. I let him escape. I was sure I had good trap. The mountain would be my friend. But, he is gone." His hands fly up. "Olohana. Akake. Friends! I forget joy. Happy you fight well, my brothers. So Brave. Gods keep you." He touches bandages on Davis' wounds. "Ahhh, how is Akake? You pain?"

Davis is ambushed by feelings for the king, shakes his head. "No. No."

"And you, Olohana?"

Young flexes his wounded arm. "Not bad, sir. See, still works. We shall both live to fight Kahekili again."

Kamehameha's tortured spirit is elated to see them alive. He pounds his chest. "Now I know you not hurt my people. I win bet on you. Yes! Many chiefs owe me now. They lose bet you betray me."

Isaac and John glance at each other, surprised. The king puts a hand on the shoulder of each of them. "My friends. Brave friends. Now I give you freedom. You free to sail Britannee. You go."

Young gulps, "What? Sir. That is very generous, but you do not mean to go... home?"

Having so recently embraced the notion of staying in Hawaii for the rest of his life, Young trails off at this bizarre turn.

"You mean..." Davis fumbles words, "You would – my king – let us go back to England?"

Contented, the king gestures with open arms. "Yes. Go home friends to Britannee king. Kamehameha trust you now to say good report to King George."

The sailors stand mute. Having expected his prisoners to be exuberant the king is stunned "This not make good feelings for you? I think you jump into joy."

Davis tries to respond, "Of course, sir, I am grateful. Very grateful. I am sure we both are, but it is only that..."

Kamehameha's studies them. "No? This strange. I want you stay, my brothers. Fight with me. I give you lands. Make you chiefs. You have many wives and days aloha with Kamehameha. What you want for happy? I have no ships. I can give land – I can give women – many women – huts – food -"

The Englishmen are astounded. Young grabs this moment to plant his flag. "Sir, I want only one wife. If you will grant me that. I fought and I lived today. All I want is Kaoana. To marry her would bring me great happiness."

Kamehameha, satisfied, unleashes his powerful rolling laugh, coming from somewhere in his core. "As you wish, Olohana. Kaoana wahine have only Olohana. One man. It be you."

John, amazed, overcome with gratitude, bends his knee to the native king. He places his hand over his heart and bows his head. "Agreed, my king. I am most grateful." Kamehameha lifts up Young and stares directly into his eyes. Young can only blink back. The king, understands, lets him go and turns to Davis.

"Ahhh, Akake. You stay? You fight with Olohana and Kamehameha more?"

Davis is in a muddle. "Sir, you said you would give us land? How do you mean 'land'? Land to own? Make farm? To build a house? On my own land?"

Kamehameha laughs. "I give! You stay, not run to ship. Or swim away like fish. I give land if you serve me. You stay. You have."

The moment is broken by someone on the precipice. Opa pops over the top of the ridge. "The king. The king is here!" he shouts down to others as he prostrates himself.

Kaoana follows over the ridge, huffing and puffing, but happy to find the monarch alive. John goes to her side. Kaoana calls to Kamehameha excitedly, "Uncle, my king. Chief Lunakia will present the wreath of surrender to you at dawn."

Behind her, out of breath, is a young priest, Kokua, sent from Kahuna Lani to watch over the king. He begins fussing at him in Hawaiian, "My king, we have looked everywhere. We must wash your wounds. Night comes, sir, and you must sleep. You must eat. Please come. And in the morning your army is ready to return. The tide comes early." Impatient, he stares at the king's silence.

The king holds up his hand. He looks to the sky and back to Young, Davis, and Kaoana with a look no one can describe. They are not sure what to do. The wind howls. He takes a deep breath, his mind still contemplating the unexplainable and begins the long walk down. He picks up the cape of his enemy.

The others follow in silence, knowing their destiny in this world is tied to this man, for good or ill, forever.

48

Sweetest Wind

The morning of the next day is deceptively beautiful, hiding activity in the deep carpet of rich green slopes. Under the protection of vines and bushes, the Maui people watch, unsure of their fate until the surrender is real and the ruthless adjutant of Kahekili is gone. The mountains rise and meet the piercing blue sky, but a mysterious morning haze of death hangs in the air.

One old Maui man whispers to his grandson, "You can see there, the mist filled with many souls, hovering – waiting to depart to the next world."

Natives from villages come to carry off the wounded. Many more wait in the undergrowth to seek for and wash dead bodies of relatives in salt water to purify them, the beginning of the burial ritual. First, they must be sure the old leaders' canoes have sailed off.

Opa sits on a rock remembering the horror of battle. He hears a conch blow and rises to watch the surrender ceremony.

Kamehameha, in his feather cape, followed by Kahuna-Kokua his personal guard, many chiefs, Kiana, Young and Davis, in a procession, move to the place where Lunakia, the representative of Kahekili waits to present the wreath of surrender near the shore. Hundreds of Kamehameha's canoes are loaded and wait in the water. The warrior army, their bodies riddled with wounds, cheer in tired, but exuberant love. The sound of their praises and beating of drums sweep across the water, rising across the land, up the valley, echoing in sweet victory, "Kamehameha. Kamehameha. Kamehameha poʻokela *Kamehameha the great*."

General Kiana leads a shout from his warriors, "Kamehameha poʻokela." making sure all see how loyal he is to the king. It is a very convincing show.

The surrendering general, Lunakia, steps up and places the wreath in the king's hands, stepping back and kneeling in a gesture of submission. Two other chiefs with him lay trays of shining treasures and food across the rocks near him.

Kamehameha holds the wreath high. From the verdant mountains, hundreds of Maui villagers rush out from hiding, the terror of the brutal King Kahekili finally lifting off of them. Streaming in from everywhere they shout passionate allegiance to their new king. Many more trays of food wrapped in tapa leaves and flowers are brought and loaded onto war canoes by singing villagers for the trip back to Hawaii.

The king feels great love for them as the fleet pushes off.

The crowd roars again, "Kamehameha po'okela. *Our hero king*!"

The villagers run along the shore as the flotilla of canoes move into the bay. The joyful salutations and singing continue. The wind ruffles the vibrant yellow feathers covering the king's royal cape. He stands in the prow. Drummers beat a victorious cadence. He relives the achievements of his battles, mourns the loss of Lamakua and valuable warriors. The salt spray kisses his face as he conjures up visions of his adoring queen waiting at landfall.

The warriors sing, as their canoes sweep through the brine, grateful they lived through the fight. …

E Kuamu e Kuamu, Mu.
O silent ones, hold your silence.
E Kuawa e Kuawa, Wa.
O loud voiced ones, shout loud!
Wa i ka ua lanakila uwa. Uwa.
Shout aloud of victory. Shout!

The trip back down the coast is pleasant and the wind is with them. After a peaceful night at Homea Bay, where sleep was deep, they set out for their home island. The many hours fighting the channel again, seem not so bad to the returning victorious army. Each man squints to see beyond the water ahead for the first sight of Mahukona, the shore at the tip of their beloved Hawaii.

Isaac Davis, in Kamehameha's canoe, sits near Young, relieved to be alive, but sad to have lost friends. He tries to navigate his ocean of emotions as they move into the calmer sea, dolphins leaping in their wake.

Opa paddles and sings with the rest. Davis looks over to Young and Kaoana in an embrace. They return his warm look as the wind luffs Kaoana's dark, shiny hair. Isaac muses.

*Her beauty is so vibrant and calm, it is hard
to accept her fighting so aggressively with spear
and knife in battle. I must find a way to think
of women differently.*

His eyes drift up to the sky and towers of billowing pink clouds.

John studies Isaac. He tries to draw him out, "Why so thoughtful, mate?"

Davis raises his eyebrows. "I am observing the beauty of these islands. It is as close to the Almighty's Garden of Eden as I could describe. And there are people here who are... different. I know there is barbarism. And we must not ever give up trying to change it, John. But, I see my mission is somehow with them. I do not know why I never saw it before."

"Aye. A mystery. And of course, there is also the grand beauty of Miss Paloa."

Davis is embarrassed at the sound of her name. "Yes. She will make someone a good wife. She is extraordinary."

"Perhaps it is time to ask? What about your wife back in England?"

Davis watches the spindrift. "I don't think she will miss me. She never has before."

Silence. The hull slaps and thuds on bigger waves in the channel.

Davis continues, "What about you? Won't you be missed in England?"

Young stares at the towers of golden clouds. "Perhaps. At times. But, not enough to return. Besides, I have come to realize I am only a man. The wind has blown me here in spite of all my well-woven plans. Best not to go against it, *kumakani*. That's the Hawaiian word for it."

"What?"

"*Kumakani* means *against the wind*. I will fight my fate no more."

Kamehameha gazes from his perch in the prow at his English warriors. They decide to salute him. He chuckles. They chuckle. He continues to sing with his men.

Wa i ka ua lanakila uwa. Uwa.
Shout aloud of victory. Shout!

The wind blows stronger, filling the sails of the king's canoe, sending the craft careening over a large swell, seeming to surge with the hearts of the army. The water itself is so sparkling and mysteriously joyful to the eye of the king, he imagines it to be a buoyant old friend, embracing the hull and singing along with the warriors as only the sea can, when, and for whom, it wishes.

49

Victorious

Ka'ahumanu, Paloa, and many royal Ali'i women, priests, and villagers laden with flowers, wait for the returning army. They cover the slopes and hillsides of Mahukona, playing games with strings, marbles, and rocks or make leis to give the warriors whether in victory or defeat.

The queen's head rests on a pillow as slaves wave fans to cool her. Her dark brown eyes flutter slightly in the end of a pleasant dream and she wakes, rising on one elbow, shading her eyes to see as far as possible. Out on the ocean, warriors are able to discern the coast and a hurrah explodes. Back on the hillside, a scout observes canoes on the horizon. He hollers down, "They come!" Ka'ahumanu pins her gaze on the channel and begins to sing. Others stop their tasks and jump up to catch a glimpse. Scores of women, elderly and young children run toward the shore, as if the sound of their voices alone could bring the army faster.

As soon as he feels he can be seen, Kamehameha raises his hand in his deliberate fashion, high in the air, indicating they have been victorious. This ignites wild acclaim and dancing from the people on shore.

As the canoes begin to land, hundreds of men, ecstatic to be on home shores again, are received by the adoring crowds. Some of the men are badly wounded, some bleeding, others leap out and swim ashore amid songs of victory. Flower leis abound, being thrown over heads as warriors fall into embraces of loved ones.

Ka'ahumanu resists with dignity until the king has come onshore. She then spreads her arms and welcomes him, laden with the longest, most magnificent leis, made out of the finest fragrant ginger and pikake flowers that could be found. She drapes them over him and gently touches her nose to his, in a passionate Hawaiian kiss. Tears run freely down her cheeks, "My prayers have been answered. You are walking, smiling, and alive my king. You are victorious and I love you like the sky loves the earth. You must feel this love flowing from each one of us. Do you feel it?"

The king holds her. "Ka'hu, Ku-Ka-ili-moku was ever before us, and your great strength in my heart filled every moment with power. I needed nothing else."

She looks in his eyes. "Is he dead? Did you kill him?"

Kamehameha winces at the memory of his failure. "Kahekili tricked us. I killed Kapa-hili. Kalankupule scampered away like a child and the father escaped me, crawling back to Oahu. However, Kahekili's army is completely destroyed on Maui. It will take many years to gather a new one and train them."

Ka'ahumanu pours as much comfort into his heart as he will allow, "My king, I am sorry he is not dead. But, you have this victory. You have won Maui. You killed his favorite son. We must all celebrate. The people are hungry for it."

Isaac Davis, still in the canoe sees Princess Paloa on the shore with hundreds of others. He throws his musket to Young and leaps in the water. To the amazement of the people in view of him, he swims like a fish to Paloa and pops up out of the water near her. She screams with surprise and opens her arms. He sweeps her in an embrace, kissing her on the mouth passionately, shocking her as well as himself and the crowd. Though she finds touching of mouths very strange, she is so much in love with him even his slightest touch sends an ecstatic pulse through her so powerfully pleasant she decides he can do anything he wants with her.

Davis reads this countenance of complete acceptance on her pristine face and takes courage. "Paloa Kamaulii, will you be my...Christian wife?" He gets down on one knee on the beach, further confusing Paloa, who thinks he has been injured. "Paloa, this is English way of Aloha. Will you marry me, ho'ao, and not go with any others, Mau loa ... forever Isaac for you?"

She is still distracted from the pressure of his lips. She grabs his arms and manages to stammer, "Husssband?"

Davis repeats, "Yes, husssband."

The people around her crowd in. Davis, victorious, rises, picks her up, and hurries to Kamehameha. The sea of villagers parts for them with cheers, aware of their passion.

John Young steps forward from the crowd beaming, eyebrows raised. "Isaac, you have won a different battle I see."

Kamehameha pats them both on the head with his approval. "Akake. You are capture Paloa."

Davis puts her down, kneeling to him. "Most Great Kamehameha, I have a fervent wish to take this woman, Paloa to be mine forever, as my wife. May I have your blessing – I mean your permission – to marry her?"

"Akake, what is this *per-miss-son?*"

Davis loses patience. "It means, you, as king, give me, a poor subject, the right to be her husband forever – to live with her, only her, Paola, the rest of my life. Me only! No others! Do you understand? Do I need the permission of her father, too? Or anyone else?"

The king considers fitting this match into his vision of the future. He studies Paloa's eyes to feel sure he can count on her to be a good wife, since keeping Davis happy in his service is now essential to him. Paloa gives him her rapt attention. He speaks, "'A'ole kekahi Paloa. Mau loa." She nods in all sincerity. He takes Paloa's hand, placing it in Davis'. He puts them on top of each other and turns them back and forth several times. "Akake, is done, *Permission*, yes?"

"What?" Davis bridles. "No, my king, we want – I mean, I must have a ceremony, a Welsh Christian ceremony to make the marriage complete."

He points to John. "I believe Mr. Young can do the honors."

The king knows he will never understand these *haoles,* so gives up. "Akake, you and Olohana have English ways – do what you wish."

Davis sighs in relief. "We will plan and visit you with details."

Kamehameha claps. "Details? I know this word *details.* Yes. Now, time we make my warriors much Hawaiian aloha." He embraces Ka'ahumanu. They begin the triumphal walk as hundreds of commoners prostrate themselves as they pass.

Behind the king and Ka'ahumanu are many priests, kahunas, chiefs, Young and Kaoana, Davis and Paloa, Kiana, Mapala followed by generals and officers in the army.

As the two mariners-turned-Hawaiians walk through the crowds of revelers, they feel the perfume of love from people they now think of as family. The eyes, hands, flowers, winsome smiles and many words they have come to know the meanings of, resonate into ribbons of affection previously unfelt and nearly indescribable to two English hearts. After risking all in battle they have come home to an island of welcome and acceptance in ways their native English countrymen had never given them, nor likely ever would.

50

Icy Channel

On Maui, the sun sets on the third day following the battle being called by locals, *The Damming of the River.* So many hundreds of dead bodies clogged the streambeds that only a red bloody brook was left of what had been rushing creek previously pouring into the sea.

Nothing will ever be the same for the Ali'i or Commoners in all the islands. The word has gone out, runners and fishermen spread the news, "Kamehameha rises." It sweeps across the sea and up green valleys and tumbling falls, even into hideouts of hermits in the mountain peaks.

The headstrong king of Hawaii has turned the tide of his fortune. But, the haunting image of the house of bones on Waikiki, and the stench of death flowing from the most powerful reigning monarch is still on the wind. Everyone knows that. He has won Hawaii and Maui. But can Kamehameha win all the islands?

On Hawaii, Kamehameha knows he will have to kill that one man. In every waking hour, he plans his attack on Oahu. He cannot rest.

On Oahu, Prince Kalani-Kupule and the remaining divisions of warriors arrive exhausted into Honolulu Bay to the reception of quiet crowds under the rule of King Kahekili. Villagers there, in fear of Kahekili, give the warriors a semblance of support, but it is a paltry performance. Warriors, many wounded and bleeding, disembark from canoes and embrace loved ones on Waikiki beach in pain and sadness.

The trip has been delayed by Kamehameha's forces who burned many of Kahekili's canoes and took the rest in the victorious sweep. Kalani-Kupule's men had to steal villager's canoes to bring the army home. Many Maui men, in the heat of their newfound freedom, fought Kalani-Kupule's men for the canoes.

Kahekili's notorious house of bones looms

ominously near the shore and is more heavily guarded than before. Kahekili, in pain due to his wound, sits in front of his hut nearby. He turns away when he sees his son coming up the path. Kahekili is suspicious of everyone. Anything he uses is burned afterwards, because he is so fearful someone will perform sorcery or send a curse to him. The wind whips the king's banners as Kalani-Kupule stoically enters the compound. "My father, I have returned with as many fit men as I could find. You received my messenger?"

A tense moment passes. Kalani waits, aware of the coldness coming from his father.

Kahekili sits like a statue. Finally, he speaks, "My son is dead. I have no need of messengers." Still not looking at Kalani-Kupule, Kahekili continues, "What did you do after your brother was thrown off the cliff? Did you run away and hide? Run from Kamehameha and his minions? With the speed of your arrival here you must have run, you coward. You let your brother take the fight and you ran. I killed your messenger, but I should kill you."

In a startling move, Kahekili rises up, throws his arms around his remaining son. "You must kill him, Kalani. You will never reign until you kill him. I cannot do it for you when I am gone." Kalani-Kupule weeps. "Father I will. I will do as you say. Give me time to rebuild my army and you will see his skull and bones decorating your house before you die." He embraces his father. "You will see that day. I promise you. Now let me have your love and trust, my father."

Kahekili holds him, trying to believe.

51

Ripe Fruits

For six days, the entire court of Kamehameha, including priests, Ali'i royalty, Commoners and country people celebrate and praise the feats of their king and his warriors in dances, songs and games in one long festival, *aha'aina laulima.* Even the lowest outcast kauva slaves have not been forgotten during the festivities, being surprised and grateful for tapa leaves filled with breads or poi left for them on outlying rocks. After so many months of constant fear, war preparations and training, a spirit of great fulfillment has over-taken the hearts and minds of Hawaiians. From Kau to Kealakekua Bay, people are celebrating victory with poetic meles and boxing matches. Some Maui people have come from their liberated island to join the celebrations, happy to be out from under the reign of death wrought by Kahekili.

The seventh day finds Isaac Davis in his hut preparing for his wedding to Paloa. He reaches for his Bible and reads.

Young comes to the entrance of his hut. "Have you chosen the scripture yet?"

"Not yet. I have gone over so many of these, and not finding the correct passage is making me even more muddled." He hands him the Bible. "Here, you are going to be the Holy Father, please pick what you will say."

"I will try my best, Isaac. But, tell me, where is the union to be consecrated? Have you decided?"

"I refuse to marry her at that blasted pagan temple. I have prepared a bit of an arbor for us up on the slope. Once we've done a ceremony there, they can dance and do whatever rituals they wish. I will go with Paloa and her father to the rites, but I will ignore them in my heart."

The next day, the entire village has turned out to see the burly mariner, Akake Davis, and their beloved and sacred Ali'i maiden, Paloa, enter into a public ceremony to unite them in an

"oysterman way" of marriage. The sailors themselves not being versed in the customs of English
weddings in general, are only too happy to keep
it brief. Nevertheless, they see a gentle opportunity to weave some English Christian culture into
the hearts and minds of their new countrymen,
with the hope of bringing peace eventually and
ending human sacrifice and slavery of all the
Kauva people in the islands.

For today, Young has abandoned the more
difficult goal for simply a reachable one – a short
Christian marriage ceremony for his comrade.

Having suppressed all passion under the kapu
and under his own discipline, Isaac Davis is now a
man with a purpose – to make great love to Paloa
as soon as circumstances will allow and to make
it for them both like a magnificent, rolling wave
crashing on the shore.

However, unbeknownst to Davis, the preparations of a Hawaiian maiden given to a young man
are all too similar to the average English maiden
in pursuit of the perfect ceremony to consecrate
their love. Davis enters the arbor area and stands,
waiting. And waiting. And wondering. And fuming.
Finally, two small, enchanting children enter and
lead the procession of Paloa's entire family – a long
and tedious entrance into the wedding arbor of

aunts, uncles and cousins as far away as Hilo. Davis is completely unaware of the many tendrils and extensions of Paloa's relatives and the minutia of respectful smiles he must apply to the hierarchy and position of each personage.

Young, as the clergyman officiating, sees the adverse effects on his groom. He smiles and passes Davis a small calabash of *refreshment* to calm his nerves. However, the need for clear speech and thought and his reverence for the event, keeps Davis from drinking any more than needed to quell his anxiety.

At last, everyone is accounted for and seated in some fashion. Now, all kneel or prostrate themselves as Kamehameha, Kahuna Lani, and the chiefs enter and stand in a semi-circle in the arbor. The king stands next to John Young, creating a tall and beaming centerpiece to the picture.

From nearby, pipes play a melody, and Paloa emerges, walking with her mother on her right and her father on her left. More little children lead her in, giggling and throwing flowers in her path. Her appearance is one of quiet joy and humility. Her head is adorned with a halo of tiny pikake flowers. Her long hair, cascades around her shoulders like a garment.

Davis sucks in a breath, awed by her beauty. A

few yards of thin, creamy silk cloth recovered from the *Fair American* are wrapped gracefully about her body, including her breasts, a request by Davis for this ceremony. From the skirt, hang rows of tiny dogs' teeth, which make a lovely sound as she walks. Her wrists are festooned with feather bracelets and the largest hog tusks that could be found. Black, red, and yellow feathers caress her neck and ankles.

The assembled crowd stares in wonder at her eyes, fountains of love focused only on Davis. The assembly rustles with anticipation as she arrives next to him.

Paloa is aware of the unique adventure she is about to embark upon and trembles with fright. Sensing this, Isaac takes her hand, and they turn to face Young, who stands in front of the congregation. Knowing full well only a modicum of what he will say will be understood, John nevertheless wants to keep the greatest possible propriety for posterity, also knowing he is officiating at likely the first marriage of its kind within thousands of miles.

"Dearly beloved, we come here with God and these witnesses, to bring this man and this woman in holy matrimony." He opens Davis' well-worn Bible and lifts it for all to see.

"These leaves I hold, contain the words of the great God of Akake and Olohana, who, in His infinite knowledge and mercy, guides all creatures through the many perils of life in this, His earth."

He locks eyes with Davis for a moment in a flash of memories over the past year and then reads:

Who can find a virtuous woman? For her price is far above rubies. The heart of her husband doth safely trust in her. She will do him good all the days of her life. Give her the fruit of her hands and let her own works praise her in the gates.

Turning to another page, Young continues, sweat dropping from his forehead in concentration of his effort to control his emotions, which have ambushed him. As he tries to speak, more memories flood his mind of himself and Davis, kidnapped and destitute for months, and so recently in war, having made their way still alive in such dire circumstances to arrive at this, a happy wedding day.

He stumbles over the words.

Husbands, love your wives, even as Christ also loved the church and sacrificed himself for her... He that loveth his wife, loveth himself. For this cause shall a man leave his father and mother and cleave unto his wife, and they two shall be one flesh. This is a great mystery.

He closes the book and looks at faces before him. "Isaac Davis, do you wish to take this woman, Paloa, to be your lawful wife?"

"Yes, I take Paloa for my wife." He takes several thick flower leis from her handmaiden and places them upon her neck, touching his nose to hers. The crowd explodes in wild cheers.

Kamehameha holds up his hands and silence is restored.

Young continues, "Paloa, do you take Isaac – Akake – Davis to be your husband?"

"Yes. Paloa take Akake Da-vis to… hussband – mine." She takes leis from her handmaid laying them over his neck and touches her nose to his cheek.

Young holds both of their hands. "May God bless you both eternally, in the name of Jesus Christ, our Savior. My king, this ceremony is complete."

Kamehameha, is cautious. "You say this like true Britannee marriage wedding? Yes?"

Young clears his throat. "Yes, sir, it is as best as we can recall, sir."

"Ah -Aloha!" The king raises his hands. The assembly erupts again in hoots of glee.

Davis embraces Paloa for the first time as her lawful husband and kisses her on the mouth. The crowd is confused but decides this is just a part of the great challenge for Paloa as the wife of a foreigner.

Kamehameha silences the crowd as Kaoana enters from the other side of the glen, looking as beautiful a bride as Paloa. Opa and others play their pipes again.

Young and Davis exchange places. Young hands the Bible to Davis, who becomes clergyman for Young and Kaoana.

Young grins. "Hey mate, grateful you are going to get me through this."

"John, I would not wish to be stranded on an island without you. You are a fine man. A very fine man, indeed." He becomes aware of the eyes of the assembled and begins the ceremony.

It is a day of celebration and joy, and one of deep and holy promises. It is one of the happiest of all their days on the earth.

52

Foulest Thunder

O n the ninth night since his return from the battles, Kamehameha and Ka'ahumanu sit alone on a high cliff in Kohala and talk quietly. They drink pleasant Hawaiian rum out of a calabash, *awa*, and watch *aka'ula*, which is the reddest kind of sunset. A night heron flies silently by. The sound of their laughter rings along the rocks bouncing down hundreds of feet to the surf.

Kamehameha focuses on something beyond the gentle waves rolling below. Ka'ahumanu has seen this look before, when her hero and lover seems to be somewhere else. She knows better than to try to get him out of a dark place too soon.

Finally with bitterness, he speaks. "Ka'hu, I let him get away, right through my fingers he floated away. I should have posted a guard on that side of the island. I am a fool. I took the bait to fight Kapa-hili and thought for sure I saw Kahekili watching us. I wanted him to see me win, and to see his son die before his eyes. After I threw Kapa-hili over, I looked back where he had been and he was gone." He stops.

The queen moves closer to massage his temples as she wonders how to comfort him. "My king, I believe you did something better. Here it is. My sweet, you killed his favorite son. You threw a spear right into his evil heart. And rumors I hear are Kahekili was badly wounded as he escaped. They may be true. Perhaps he is dying even now of his wounds."

Kamehameha, refuses to be comforted. He drinks long from the calabash. "He should be dead, Ka'hu. I went to kill him, him and both his sons, and all I did was kill Kapa-hili. He tricked me. He tricked me again. I am not a 'man of word.'"

"What is 'man of word'?"

"What Olohana and Akake say. It means a man must do what he says or he is not a man. I promised my warriors we would kill that spider and I did not. I must gain a better hold on Maui. I must let one harvest season pass. Then, I must go and kill him, right there in his house of bones on the beach, right in front of his last loyal guard, only then can we hope for true peace."

Ka'ahumanu studies her powerful lover. He appears to be drunk, something he never does or very rarely does. He drinks, but he never gets confused or maudlin. However, tonight, his eyelids look heavy and his demeanor odd. Ka'ahumanu has been drinking with him and now is feeling her body humming with drink more than usual. While she thinks about this and watches him, he continues sullen, rolling back on his arms, giving in to sleep. She moves closer and realizes to her amazement, he is unconscious. She cradles his head in her arms as she positions herself under him. He ends up with his head in her lap, sleeping contentedly. She feels comfortable, cradling the king, the man who could order her death, who lays vulnerable and trusting in her care. She breathes deep, enjoying the moment of bliss. The crimson sunset wanes and she lifts her hand, gesturing to servants nearby.

Two strong guards appear in the dusk. "Your wish Ali'i Ka'ahumanu?"

"He needs help getting back to his huts. Go in the back way to avoid him being seen. Let him sleep until dawn."

They gesture to others in the king's guard. They help the muttering monarch to his feet. Ka'ahumanu gently places his cloak around him. He mumbles orders and seems to be on a battlefield. They walk him back towards the compound, moving in a phalanx.

Ka'ahumanu is drawn to the last moments of magnificent magenta sky. She gestures to her servants to go as well. When she feels she is alone, she begins to whisper a song,

> *... from the rising reddish mist of Kane,*
> *From clouds blazing in the sky, lovely horizon*
> *clouds*
> *Restless desire for Hawaii, seized Pele...*

Feeling she is no longer alone, she squints into the evening mist and blinks. She sees Kiana staring at her from behind a rock. "You frightened me. I didn't see you. What are you doing here? Are you looking for the king?"

Kiana doesn't move. His voice rolls across to her. "No." He is relaxed and calm. He is also looking extremely handsome, as always, but in the haze of her drunkenness he looks even better. She has always been attracted to his body, but his spirit and mind were clearly deceiving and consumed with power, so she kept her distance.

She repeats, "Who are you looking for?"

Kiana speaks with confidence. "You."

Ka'ahumanu shakes her head. "No. You are not looking for me."

"I am not?" Kiana blinks.

"No. Because…if you were looking for me, you would have found me. I am not here." She giggles at her silliness. Her words did not come out the way she had hoped. Her senses are more confused than she thought. "I am going now." However, as she tries to rise, she finds her body doesn't have the same idea. She supports herself on her elbows and decides not to get up until she feels steadier. *Why did I send my attendants away?* "Holloa!"

"Too late. They are gone." Kiana moves forward.

Ka'ahumanu fights her mind. She is drunk and in a trance of desire mingled with revulsion.

"Ka'a, you know the fire I have for you. Brighter than that sky. Brighter than Pele's fire below." He comes near and sits next to her. "You have seen it in me and I know, and you also know, all the times he has taken you together cannot please you as much as I can. If you will only let me show you. Just once."

The effects of the awa have attained their full power. Kiana, sensing the most opportune moment and Ka'ahumanu's weakness, leans over to her. He gently strokes and kisses her hair and massages her temple.

"Close your eyes Ka'hu, just feel my love pouring into you. Only this once."

He moves down to her breasts, making her forget every other thought but how delicious it feels. He works his way downward, at a leisurely pace, aware of his gifts of enticement. The desire to stop him becomes ever weaker in her. She yields herself and lapses into him, moaning with pleasure against her better judgment and any ability left to refuse. Images of Kamehameha and Kiana begin to swirl together in her mind.

The last blaze of sun fades as Ka'ahumanu slips ever more deeply into Kiana's spell. The sun sinks, relinquishing the last of its pristine hues into the darkness.

On the other side of the village, John Young and Kaoana find peace in each other's arms. They talk softly, their dreams and plans float up from them like seeds being blown in a fertile wind. Young stares out at the blanket of stars through their hut window, continues an astronomy lesson, "… and that one we call The Dog Star."

Kaoana laughs. "Ilio?"

"Yes. Ilio Hoku. Dog." They get more comfortable in their new straw bed, festooned with decorative flowers and leis. "Kaoana, do you wish for me to speak in your language or mine?"

"I want Britannee speak. I want speak love to you in Britannee, bigger than Britannee lady tell you love."

"You do not need their dry, empty words, Kaoana. What you do and who you are is love itself. You are aloha. Please, believe me, no Britannee woman I have ever known or even heard of can throw a spear and stand in battle much less be a soft sweet woman who can kiss like... like an endless wave. I am very happy, Ana. And I am so grateful you were not hurt in the battles. I thank my God for your safety."

"He is great god if he made you." She runs a hand through his blond locks and joins him in a passionate kiss. The wind whips up and rustles palms outside.

In a nearby hut, Paloa and Davis are making love, their bodies undulating in a shaft of moonlight coming through the window. They move easily from one exquisite moment to the next as if they had given each other pleasure for years. Months of daydreams they each had imagined have now come true. They each are surprised to find their fantasies were amazingly accurate, but with added, pleasurable, nuances.

For Davis, a thousand bitter lonely nights at sea have melted away.

For Paloa, all visions of how life as an Ali'i Hawaiian woman would be like have been replaced by new dreams of the many ways she can love the heroic man who floated in from the sea one day. She also longs to learn more about the one he loves called *Khake-speare.*

At a far corner of the hut, unknown to them, Opa watches through a slat near the bottom of the wall. His eye grows big and he pulls away, but he stays sitting, wide-eyed in wonder. Life has become too complicated for the moment, and the boy wanders down the lane between the rows of huts.

Inside the monarch's sleeping hut, Kamehameha jumps awake and calls out, "Ka'a."

Opa hears the sound and is afraid to be caught roaming the village at such an hour. He darts into the darkness.

Kamehameha, sees the empty space next to him. Thunder rolls in the distance. He is worried where she might be. He tries to clear murky thoughts. He gets up and moves through the hut solely on instinct. He mumbles to one of his personal guards, "Where is Ka'ahumanu?"

He sees the guard blinking. He grabs him. "Where is Ka'ahumanu, do you hear me?"

The guard stammers in panic. "My king, she was – she was on the cliff when we brought you back here to sleep. She said let you sleep undisturbed."

Kamehameha lays a strong hand on the guard's chest. "Do not follow me. Wait here. Tell the others I have gone to the hills to pray." He leaves the hut, following a nightmare image in his mind, goes up the slope, gaining speed as he leaps up the side of the mountain.

The guard watches confused. Others join him, curious.

In the darkness on the deserted cliff, the wind rises and whips the fronds of the palms. Lightning flashes. A storm has swept in. Pelting rain hits the rocks. Thunder rolls.

Ka'ahumanu and Kiana's naked bodies move in the spot where she had been with Kamehameha hours before. They do not hear Kamehameha approach. Their passion is so focused on each other they cannot tell where they begin or end. They have no time to part. The king grabs Kiana and unleashes his rage with such power the Kauai prince is literally thrown many feet from

Ka'ahumanu, who screams and crawls away in horror. She grabs cloth that had been around her and stumbles to her feet.

"All along. You have betrayed me – all along, and I believed you." Kamehameha, blinded by fury, catches her and throws her to the ground.

She screams, "No! No!"

He jumps on her, his hands tighten around her throat. It is only by sheer chance Ka'ahumanu is able to twist from his grasp. She howls, startling the king so much he realizes he will kill her. She scrambles into the darkness, weeping and running.

Kiana has recovered enough to sprint away as well, fearing death.

Kamehameha pounds the dirt. Tears flow. He doesn't move when a squall of rain lashes him, ribbons of lightening move in closer. He wails, his guttural moans turn to howls, like a huge, wounded wolf, he challenges his gods in the tempest, his eyes flash with rage in the lightning.

53

The Search

Ka'ahumanu darts through the downpour and rushes into her hut on another side of the village where women's huts are clustered. She knows if she can get to the City of Refuge many miles south in Kealakekua, even the king will not be able to hurt her. She will be safe with priests and the kahunas who will protect anyone who comes under their authority. She disappears into a hut and, moments later, emerges carrying a small dog, and a ragged bundle. She looks about furtively, covering her pet from the rain. She runs into the brush. Two female servants appear after she is gone, shaking off sleep.

At dawn, Kaoana and John Young are awakened by loud voices.

"Get up! She has disappeared. We must go. Hurry," is all Young can make out as he rubs his face. He gestures to Kaoana to stay where she is and leaves the hut. Four of the king's guard stand in front of Young's hut, some of the most fearsome warriors in the whole of Hawaii and beyond. Young queries, "What is wrong? Is the king safe?"

The one with the most command of English responds, "Olohana, the king is send to hunt Ka'ahumanu."

"What happened to her?"

The warrior bows his head slightly. "We bring to Kamehameha."

"Why?"

Before the guard can answer, Kaoana comes out of the hut and talks with the guard in hushed tones. Young hears the word *Kiana* in their chat followed by a gasp from Kaoana.

Kaoana reaches out to Young. "Olohana, Ka'ahumanu has betrayed the king. Please hurry to him. Beg for her life. Hurry."

"Ask for her life? Why? Is the punishment death?"

Kaoana nods.

He takes her hand. "We must go together to the king. Come."

"No, Olohana, John, you go. Woman no ask. He listen to you. Go." She grabs his shirt and helps him on with it. He hurries to rouse Davis.

At Isaac's hut, he knocks on a pole. "Isaac?"

"Can't a man have a good night of rest with his wife on this island? What is it, John?" Davis is inside, pulling on his trousers.

Young would like to keep this quiet, but the conch is blown from the king's compound.

Davis emerges. "Has Kahekili returned?"

"Ka'ahumanu has betrayed the King. I heard the name *Kiana*."

"*Kiana?*"

"Yes. That fiend. He never stops. Come. Apparently, to save her life, we must plead for mercy."

A general chaos has ensued as the whole village is awakened to the dreaded news of Ka'ahumanu's betrayal. The king has indeed ordered her death, and anyone seeing her must kill her on sight or suffer consequences.

As Young and Davis trot through rows of huts, Davis speculates, "I wonder sometimes if it was a bad thing for Kiana to sail with Captain Meares in '87. What he learned by going to China and the

American coast likely only made him more of a deceiver than before. Our ways are bad weapons in the wrong hands."

"No, Isaac, I disagree. Kiana would be a bad sort no matter what journeys he went on or what company he kept. But, I believe Kamehameha has been far too impressed with Kiana's travels and his study of English. The king is too impressed with him and gives him too much latitude. So, Kiana thanks him by duping him and taking what the king loves most. He is a shameless weasel. I never trusted him."

"This edict makes no sense, John. The king can have any woman he wants. You have seen others have many liaisons. Why must she be faithful if he is not?"

"Jealousy is a vicious demon. And he is king. If he wanted her to be faithful, she must have known what could happen if she was not."

They come upon a group of bewildered Commoners, including the queen's family. They have great love for Ka'ahumanu and cannot believe the king has ordered her death. Her parents openly weep and hold each other in despair. Some women around them press rocks into their foreheads. John and Isaac have never understood this custom and look away in sadness.

Ka'ahumanu's father catches Young's arm begging for help. "Olohana! Kamehameha huikala. Akake. Olohana Kamehameha Huikala Ka'ahumanu!"

Young encourages the father. "Come with us, Ke-e-au-moku. We will talk to the king." The men hurry down the path to the king's compound. Guards prevent anyone passing except Young, Davis, and Ke-e-au-moku.

In the hut, Kamehameha sits on his throne, a simple but beautifully carved wooden chair in the middle of the dirt floor covered with mats. He stares off when they come in, now in a state of resolve so complete he can see the whole execution in his mind. He does not acknowledge them, but his voice rolls in their direction with icy authority, "She will die. You cannot save her. She is dead in my heart already."

Ke-e-au-moku throws himself at the feet of Kamehameha. "Most forgiving king, I beg you to spare my daughter's life. I beg you to show her mercy, my king, mercy, like English speak – like these Christians. Please, please consider the many years she has loved you with all her heart."

Kamehameha leaps from his chair and descends upon the prostrate chief. "You do not know. They have been behind my back all along. There is nothing for it. Do not press me, Ke-e-au-moku."

Young kneels before the king. "Kamehameha, we clearly understand your anger. We know how you feel, but please hear me speak before you take this terrible action."

"You shall hear for yourself." He shouts to the guards to bring in Kiana. From the other side of the yard, several guards bring him into the room. As he sees the sailors and Ka'ahumanu's father, he stiffens.

"Now hear, my brothers and see if you would not do the same if it was your wife. The woman you gave your heart to." He turns to Kiana. "Tell Olohana and Akake."

Kiana straightens up and looks fearlessly in their eyes. "Kiana hala 'ole. Ka'ahumanu say many times she want Kiana for her bed and I say, 'No, Ka'ahumanu. Kamehameha my king. I wish not to betray him.'" He looks appropriately embarrassed to reveal Ka'ahumanu's lust for him as he glances to see the king's rage further enflamed against her.

Young, outraged beyond control, steps forward. "My king, I believe these to be bold and callous lies. He lies! Why can't you see it?"

Kamehameha springs up. "Olohana, remember I am king. If I say 'die', the bones are washing in the sea by the next moon. Speak careful to me."

"I only ask you to please hear my words about this man. I know your love for truth and I have truth to tell you about Kiana."

The king thinks. "Olohana, speak."

Kiana considers interrupting but, decides to see where this is going.

Young launches in. "One day, last Maka-hiki season, Lamakua and I were in the munitions hut. Kaoana was coming to find me to talk to me about my watch, but, she told me later, she had seen Kiana waiting for Ka'ahumanu near the path. Kiana stopped Ka'ahumanu. He thought no one saw him, but Kaoana watched him try to hold Ka'ahumanu strongly and she shoved him hard away and left him on the path. My king, this is proof she did not, at least then, have any interest in this man. She was alone with him and was free to behave as she wished. She pushed him away. This is the truth."

The king considers this. Kiana squirms under his gaze. "Kiana, speak."

Kiana defiantly tosses his head, speaking quickly in Hawaiian, "My king I do not expect you to believe me. Ka'ahumanu, as you know, is a very persuasive woman, and I must admit that day on the path I remember well. She was angry with me because I was loving another woman the night before. She pushed me away because I did not meet her when and where she asked me to. I know, my king, I was wrong to get involved with her, but her charms are many and she is hard to refuse." Kiana sees his arrows are hitting their mark. Now he takes the ultimate leap. He throws himself on the ground at the feet of the king. "If I must die for this offense it is because she is able to put a spell on a man. I fell under her magic." He weeps. "My king, most great king, I have served you in battle with all my heart. But, I have failed miserably to keep from falling in love with her. I am guilty."

Young and Davis are confused. Kiana was speaking Hawaiian too quickly for them to know his deception. Kamehameha sits like a stone. No one speaks. The king considers what Young has said, then reminds himself, *I believe Kiana is hiding something, but to win the war against Kahekili, I would do well to have Kiana and all his men on my side, and with Kiana dead, Kiana's men could become a rogue battalion against me. Kiana has been brave and successful in the field... killing Kiana could have serious repercussions. Killing Ka'ahumanu is justified. She betrayed my sacred trust. I saw it. I caught her. I have given the order.*

The king straightens up. "Kiana, you will live." Kiana collapses in a frenzy of tears and gratitude.

He grabs the bottom of the king's garment. "I will serve Kamehameha forever. Your mercy is as vast as your strength, O mighty one…"

Davis and Young and Ka'ahumanu's father are astonished at the king's ability to believe this cunning liar. Kamehameha gestures to the guard. "Take him out." Kiana moves to leave. The king catches hold of him. "Watch your evil ways. This mercy I show only once." Kiana hurries out. The king looks back at Young and speaks in English, "Do not be anger to me, Olohana. I need Kiana and his men in my wars. Kiana good general and brave warrior. Long time. Long time."

Another silence fills the hut as the defenders of Ka'ahumanu try to come up with any kind of statement that will prolong her life. Young tries a new tack. "My king, I sincerely hope you will not live to regret this action against your queen."

"What if that man is lying to you?" Davis pleads. "What if he is a liar? Will you not even listen to her side of this story? Please understand, our King George would always hear the side of the accused. Always. It is only fair. In Britannee, the one accused always is given a chance to speak before any judgement."

"Yes. Isaac is correct," Young jumps in. "I am sure Kamehameha does not wish to be known as a bad king, an unjust king. We only beg you to hear her side before you sacrifice her. You listened to Kiana. Let us bring her here to you to tell you what happened. This is all we ask of you."

A barely perceptible growl wells up in the king, who feels his leadership is in question. Davis senses it and empathizes. "My king, you will lose no respect from your people to give her one chance to speak. Your people are out there right now, hundreds of them, along with Paloa and Kaoana, all praying to your gods for her life to be spared. You would show great wisdom to your people to hear her before taking an action. A great leader would do this, sir."

The three advocates patiently wait for the king's answer. Beads of sweat stand on Kamehameha's forehead. He rubs his mouth. "Go. Find her. Bring her here to me." Ke'e au-moku sinks to the floor weeping openly in relief. Kamehameha stands and orders his guards. "Find Mapala. Tell him to not kill her if he finds her. Tell him to bring her to me. Inform the assembly the order has been changed. Go."

54

Judgement

In a deep thicket of undergrowth, Ka'ahumanu crouches, hiding near a hut. Dawn inches its way up the horizon. She knows she must get to safety before the sun rises. She hurries to the side of the hut and whispers, "Kaloli. Kaloli. It is Ka'a." A moment later, after rustling in the hut, an old man emerges. Surprised to see her, he drops to his knees and prostrates himself, but she pulls him up. "Help me, Kaloli, the dawn is coming, I must get to the city of refuge."

"Ka'ahumanu, most royal queen, why are you alone and so fearful, my child?"

"I have betrayed Kamehameha, my king, the only man who has ever had my heart. Kaloli, I deserve to die. My only hope is to get to the kahunas in the City of Refuge. Maybe the priests will help me."

With years of habit as a healer, the wizened kahuna grabs a paddle from the side of the hut and takes her by the hand. Silhouetted against the grey light, they run together to the beach, Ka'ahumanu sweating profusely from her ordeal, her long, thick black hair flying in the wind. Her bundle has a small furry head protruding from it, his eyes bulging in wonder.

"Careful, my Queen," Kaloli whispers as he helps her scramble into the canoe, her huge frame settles into the hull. The kahuna leaps in and paddles as though it were the greatest event of his life. Epo, the dog, not recognizing the kahuna, begins a low growl.

"Epo, no," Ka'ahumanu admonishes, pushing his head back into the bundle. She scans the shore behind them for signs of the king's men.

Kaloli propels the canoe furiously across the bay. The statues of gods of the Pu'u'a-nua Ho-nnou-nou, the City of Refuge, are in view as the prow cuts through the glassy pre-dawn water. Torches from the night guarding still burn, reflecting on the water, warding off evil spirits and creating a fiery carpet for the canoe sliding to shore.

Ka'ahumanu disembarks and hurries up the sandy slope. The old kahuna knows his beloved queen must travel the rest of the way alone. Starting up the beach, she turns with great haste, runs back to Kaloli, catching him in her arms. "I will never forget." He drops to the ground. "My queen, my queen. I will pray. May the gods keep you." She makes a sound so pitiful he must ignore it. He remains prostrate on the beach until she is out of sight.

Once safe on the sanctified ground of the highest priests of the island, Ka'ahumanu slumps, gasping. She approaches the guard hut and calls out, her voice breaks the holy silence. "It is I, Ka'ahumanu, begging sacred refuge from Kapou-haki, your priest."

From inside, are sounds of guards leaping up from sound sleep. As soon as they realize they are face-to-face with their queen, they prostrate themselves, after which the head guard runs to the high priest's hut next to the temple.

Kapou-haki, having heard the disturbance, lumbers from his cot to the door. Several other guards have arrived and await instructions. They see the queen and prostrate themselves.

The high priest peers at her curiously. "Ka'ahumanu, why have you come, my child? For whom do you seek refuge?"

Ka'ahumanu tries to speak. The lump in her throat makes it almost impossible. "Holy One, I am a wicked woman who has betrayed her beloved king and shamed her father and family. I seek safety in hopes of forgiveness."

The wise kahuna reveals no sign of concern, but offers a gentle hand to the dishonored woman. He asks no further questions, but turns to one of his guards and whispers a location where the queen may hide. "My Queen, go with Maloi to a secret place and wait until I send for you. Do not move from there. We will bring you food and tend to your needs."

"You are kind. So kind." Ka'ahumanu, broken, follows the servant priest down the lane. They hurry over lava rocks, the queen stumbling here and there, being helped by Maloi. She comforts Epo and glances back from time to time.

❧

On the far shore, a search party of men comes through the underbrush. Four warrior guards, Mapala, Young, Davis, and Ke'e-au-moku appear on the trail. They step into canoes not belonging to them, but always available for purposes of the king. Kaloli hides in the thick bushes, watching them shove off in the bay, just as the sun shoots first light across the bay.

Upon a slope, Ka'ahumanu looks back across the bay and sees the group coming across. She grabs Maloi and they disappear into a cave.

Once inside, Ka'ahumanu says a prayer under her breath.

Oh, gods, you know all things. If there is a chance to live, let me find it.

Epo moves about in the satchel as she shoves a piece of breadfruit into his mouth. They are silent for a moment and then hear voices on the wind.

She goes to the opening of the cave and in the distance she sees John Young and Isaac Davis talking to the high priest. Behind them she sees Ke'e au-moku. "Oh, my father. My dear father."

"Maloi, they have come for me. I am dead now. The king will use his powers with the priests. They will give me up to him."

Maloi studies the movement of the High Priest as well as he can. The priest's face is unflinching as he seems to not know where the queen is. A small rodent skitters across rocks in the cave. Epo catches sight of it and barks, trying to leap out of his mistress's arms. The queen and Maloi duck deeper into the cave, but it is too late, their position has been discovered.

Quickly, John, Isaac and their party move up and across the rocks with warriors following close. When they have come near enough to be heard, Young calls out to Ka'ahumanu, "Do not be afraid, Queen Ka'ahumanu, we will not hurt you. We did not come to bring you harm."

Ke'e-au-moku shouts, "Ka'a. Ka'a. Come, my daughter, to plead your case. I know your heart is pure. There is a misunderstanding. We will cry mercy. Come with us."

In the shallow cave, there is no further place to hide. The queen feels life ebbing away, convinced of her fate. She gathers herself and decides it is time to face the king with as much courage as possible for the sake of her father and family. She reaches into her bag and takes out an amulet she grabbed when she rushed into her hut. It is a carved wild boar tusk in the shape of a goddess tied to a piece of long grass into a necklace. She puts it around her neck and moves to the opening of the cave.

Maloi jumps in front to shield her. "My Queen, we will protect you here. Make your appeal to the High Priest. You are safe."

Ka'ahumanu lovingly pushes him aside. "I am here," she calls to John Young and her father. She stands up to her full height outside the cave and watches John approach, breathless in his journey up the hill.

Davis and the others take in her tear-stained face, the dirt on her clothes, and the red eyes. But, there is something especially poignant about her mouth, the way it is set in humility, no fight left.

"Most gracious Queen, we have come from the king where we have reasoned with him with all our hearts," Young stammers.

Ke'e au-moku holds out his hands and opens his arms. His daughter comes into his embrace, weeping. "My sweet child, the king is very angry, yes, it is a great danger for you. But if you come and tell your side of this, I know you will turn his heart. It is the only way."

Ka'ahumanu looks at her father, then to Young and Davis and back to her father. "My father, if I stay with the priests I will be safe. Why must I leave? What did the king say? He tried to kill me."

Ke'e au-moku wipes sweat from his brow. "He had ordered you to be killed. We have spoken to him, and he sees he must listen to your story before he does such a thing. Kiana said you had seduced him for a long time and he is innocent."

Ka'ahumanu stiffens. "He is a most vicious and devious man. It is he who has tried for many seasons to lure me into his arms and only last night, only one night, my father, when I was drunk with awa, did he wait for me to be alone and sprang upon me. I am the one who is innocent of the charge of seduction. But, I am guilty of not fighting him hard enough. Everytime before I did fight him. I pushed him away. But, this time I was too drunk and foolish and could not even get up to run away. And now I have lost the only man I could ever love."

Her father opens his hands. "Will you come with us to explain?" The sound of waves crashing on the shore of the temple fills a long silence. Ka'ahumanu holds up her hand. "My father, I will not go there. It is too soon."

Her father hangs his head. Young and Davis look away, hopeless.

"But, you could tell my story to the king. And you could beg for me to be allowed to stay here, with the priests, in exile. Perhaps after some time, he will remember the power of my love for him, and if it pleases the gods, he will miss me and come to visit me here. But, I will not go when he is in his rage. It is not wise for me. Kiana is very clever, but I believe my love will speak louder to the king as days go by. My love is true, and it will speak to him. Whether he will listen or not, that is out of my power. Will you tell him my story? Just as I have told you?"

Ke'e au-moku is astonished by her ability to strategize while in such a crisis. "Yes. I will explain to Olohana and Akake as we travel back. I know they will help me plead your side. Oh, the people, my daughter – it would make your heart swell. They weep for you. They believe your love for the king and they love you, Ka'a. You must know you have many friends who cry for mercy. I know the gods will hear them too, you can be sure."

She holds him. "You take my heart with you, my dear father."

55

Appeal

The face of the huge man called "great" by his people, seems very tense as he sits in his throne, morose, miserable, ruminating. Ke'e au-moku has finished his tearful story, and Davis and Young have both offered their advice. They all watch the king for his response. The silence is broken only as rain pelts on the king's hut in torrents.

Davis cannot keep quiet any longer. "My king, please explain to me. Ka'ahumanu's offense does not seem to deserve death. You are angry, we understand, but you have many wives, why should she not have more than one husband?"

Ke'e au-moku winces when he catches the meaning of Davis' question. He shakes his head. *This is not doing my daughter any good!*

Kamehameha's eyes turn full onto Davis as he rises. "Akake, Ka'ahumanu be above all others. She must only have love for Kamehameha."

Young jumps in, "Sir, Isaac is only trying to find a way to make you happy again. He believes you will be a truly great king, indeed, if you show mercy to Ka'ahumanu. We have seen her face and we believe her story. The people will see your heart is a king's heart and bigger than that of all other men in your land." He gestures with hands wide as he takes the chess piece king from the nearby board and raises it up, as if rising above the people to some exalted state.

Sounds of wailing outside can be heard in spite of the deluge.

"Have mercy on her!"

Kamehameha goes to the hut window, letting rain pour onto his hand. He hears some of the women weeping, their foreheads bloody from rubbing rocks across them. He studies the faces and outstretched hands of many of his warriors who have come to plead mercy for Ka'ahumanu. His eyes glaze over. He turns back to the waiting group and makes his edict, without raising his voice, "I not kill her. I send her to live in Kau forever. Olohana, do this. Tell my people. Ke'e au-moku will send canoes to take her there."

Ke'e au-moku collapses in gratitude. Young is confused. "What is Kau?"

Kamehameha stares out the window. "It is lua Pele – a place where few live.

Within three days of the visit from her father and the king's men, Ka'ahumanu embraces the high priest and prepares to leave the sacred temple on the west side of the island of Hawaii to travel to Kau, the southernmost district on the island, a sparsely inhabited place near two volcanos.

The priest weeps. "My Queen, your mother gave me many soothings as a child. Many times if I fell on the rocks or fought with my brothers she was always there with her eyes of healing. I prayed last night the gods would give me her eyes to look upon you today as we part."

Ka'ahumanu embraces him. "I am so grateful to you. I have always seen the care you have for our people. You are kind to each one who needs you, and have been most kind to me. Be at peace, my kahuna."

She takes Epo from the arms of an attendant and walks to the waiting vessel.

The high priest waves to her. "We will continue our vigil for the king's forgiveness."

Warrior priests wait in the canoe to receive her. As the vessel, laden with gifts and stores for the queen, leaves the shore, the wind, as if ordered by the gods, fills the sails to their fullest. Pregnant with their cargo, they move out to sea. Ka'ahumanu gazes back to her sanctuary, thankful to be alive.

Many weeks later, on a cliff near the king's fishing pond in Kohala, John Young sits with Davis' old, dog-eared Bible, reading in a mild wind, the pages luffing.

Kamehameha, his forehead knitted with anguish, walks toward Young, his attendants remain at a distance.

Young looks up and rises. "Sir, I did not hear you coming."

The king puts up his hand in apology. "Olohana, I do not wish to stop your mind from a journey." At the king's gesture, Young sits back down. "I want you sit together me, Olohana." The king also sits.

"Ah. No – What I say is wrong English, yes?"

"My king, you could say, 'I want to sit together with you.'"

"Yes. 'Together. With you.'"

There is a silence in which each man hopes the other will speak. Finally, Kamehameha puts his hand on pages of the Bible resting on Young's lap. "Olohana, I see you look at the piles of leaves much times and after you have council with these gods, you have much aloha. Yes?"

"It is a wise king I serve. You see into hearts. True. I receive much counsel from these leaves. But, it is because they are alive, like you and me."

The king touches the book, grinning. "Olohana, this is trick. These dead leaves. No alive."

Young places his hand on the open Bible. "No, my king. To me, they are as alive as you and me. The spirit of the God of all gods, the one God who made you and made me, lives wherever these words live. I believe this." He points to the page. "These marks, this writing on the leaves, it goes from the heart of my God into my heart. Or your heart, if you want. And it calms the storms of my soul."

Kamehameha cannot fathom a god that powerful could be living in a dry clump of old leaves wrapped in leather. His hand comes down on Young's shoulder. "Olohana, you make me think much things. You bring much good. My people be more strong with help you give. But, Kamehameha have Ku-Ka-ili-moku. My god strong for me. Is good."

Young closes the book. "Sir, I would never have thought I could call Hawaii my home, but, I am surprised to be very content here. You are a good king."

Kamehameha knows enough English to know he is being complimented. "Olohana, no. You say Kamehameha good. But, I am not this. A good king would not have a rock in here." He taps his chest. "Olohana, my heart is with illness..."

"This rock, is it because your Ka'ahumanu is in Kau?"

The king looks down, the lump in his throat so big he cannot look up.

Young realizes the most powerful man in all the islands is capable of deeper feelings than he has been aware. "My king. Will you allow me to speak of this?"

The king throws him a look of cautious assent. "Maybe."

John is wary and taps his chest. "I also feel pain here when I see suffering. I think the only way to turn this rock in your chest back into your real heart is to send for Ka'ahumanu. It is not only you, but your people who see you suffering.

Kanaka E Loa'a ana. They have great aloha for you and Ka'ahumanu. Makahiki – this is true. Oiaio. They saw your love for each other for many years and want it to return, for you and for them. For all of us, sir."

The king shakes his head. "Olohana, you say my people much aloha Ka'ahumanu. But, I can no send, I do this and strong no more. My gods take power and Kamehameha lose Hawaii. Lose all mana. This I cannot do."

"You think they respect you more for sending her away forever? Or if you sent someone to kill her? You may keep your pride, but, they will respect you more, far more, if you forgive her.

"What you say?" The king cannot follow and Young can't stop.

"*Forgive* means to love again no matter what the person has done, because of a greater love. A love like the sea for the shore. It cannot be separated. That is what the god of these leaves means when he writes here." He begins to open the book.

The king rises. He's had enough. He is sorry he came to Olohana for encouragement. "I go to my fishpond. And my gods." He trudges off angrily.

Young watches him, crestfallen.

56

Lost Days

On the shores of Kau, Ka'ahumanu sits, staring upon the western bay, which leads back to Kohala, the place of her king and passion.

Ladies near her, make leis gossiping. They try to ignore the fact their queen sits like an empty gourd. One whispers, "She does not eat, she does not sleep, how will she live?"

She surprises them by speaking, though her voice seems dull and far away.

The grains of sand beneath my feet cannot equal my river of thoughts... memories of love and care

for my beloved and my people...this very earth
beneath me cries out for two hearts parted in
flesh but sewn with many singing days...
like parts of a wide flying net over the great sea,
strings tied to every other good heart in my
island lands.

The women have stopped their work.
Ka'ahumanu continues. She seems in a trance.

... the sun herself and husband moon
will lead me back to the place of love
and adoring eyes and embrace of hearts...

I give my life to the I'iwi bird
his blood red wings will cover me
he flies to the gods who see what hides
my heart resting deep in the nest of the king.
I am his prisoner. A willing prisoner. Only in
this love am I free.

The queen ends her mele. The women crowd
around and rock her.

Thick clouds of hot mist in the steamhut of the king rise as a naked group of men talk war and wipe sweat. Kamehameha, John Young, Isaac Davis, Kiana, Mapala and other chiefs discuss future battles on Oahu and Molokai. Slaves pour boiling water over rocks and larger clouds of steam billow up.

John Young, wipes his brow and sits next to the king, listening. He remembers the first time he was in such a hut in the first week of his captivity. He rubs large scars on his arms from wounds sustained over the two-and-a-half years he has been living under the reign of Kamehameha. He catches Davis's knowing glance and realizes he, too, must be thinking similar thoughts.

Breaking the lull in conversation, the king speaks in Hawaiian, "It is decided then. After the next harvest, we swiftly go and kill Kahekili. The trap must be set well. In that day there must be no retreating for him or Kalani-Kupule this time. The son and the father both must die. Their armies will not stand if we can achieve this one goal."

Kiana, rubbing down his tight stomach muscles with kukui nut oil, grins. "My king, we have trained for this year after year. It was only by shear chance he escaped last time. We will be ready this time. My army has never been so prepared. That is thanks to the instruction of Olohana and Akake and the new weapons."

The mariners smile at his bilious hypocrisy. Young watches Kiana, wishing he would trip himself up somehow, but ever since the night of the queen's infidelity, Kiana has been on his best behavior, never caught doing or saying anything that could possibly anger the king. He has been so solicitous and double-faced, that nearly all but the most stupid warriors and chiefs are sickened by his theatrics, which the king never seems to see through, so desperate is he to keep Kiana and his army under his power.

Kiana and his two chiefs ask permission to leave. After they are gone, Davis, Young, and the other chiefs continue to talk among themselves.

Kamehameha overhears a suspicious phrase spoken by one of the men to Ke'e au-moku. "What is that you are saying?"

Ke'e au-moku looks sheepish.

"Tell me what you speak of."

One chief reluctantly confesses, "My king, the women had a council last night. There was a rumor of a strange visitation."

The king is impatient. "What visitation?"

He struggles, knowing telling it could anger Kamehameha. "My king, there is some argument over this, but Nahena said the goddess, Hina, was seen near Ka'ahumanu's favorite papaya tree by her old handmaiden, the one too sick to go with her. It was said the goddess was angry the queen was still in Kau and was going to seek revenge upon our people if she is not forgiven. And the tree withered overnight. There is no fruit on it this morning. But, of course, it is only women's talk."

"Then why do you men chatter about it?" In a fury, the king throws the water bucket into the side of the hut. "Why is there is no escape from these endless conspiracies regarding this man's daughter?" He points to Ke'e au-moku, "Is there nothing else for old women and idle men to discuss?" He storms out.

Mapala, other chiefs and slaves follow behind him, leaving Young and Davis with Ke'e au-moku.

"The king needs help, sir." Davis is frustrated. "John and I and our wives have said everything we can think of."

Ke'e au-moku pours more water for steam. "I not know. Kamehameha not know. Ka'ahumanu not know. Kahunas not know. Gods know. They talk much on the wind, but king not listen. And I am just old man who is weak."

57

One Year Later

Arrival of Captain George Vancouver, Kealakekua Bay

On the windy west coast of Hawaii, British Captain George Vancouver is assailed by emotion as his vessel nears Kealakekua Bay for the third time in two years. He finds himself remembering with sudden and painful accuracy, the bloody death of his beloved Captain Cook on the far shore of this bay, fifteen years earlier. Captain Vancouver has been in the islands since Cook's death, but today there is something about coming to Kealakekua in February and the way the wind howls, and a glint of light upon the rocks where his Captain was killed, that is reminding him more severely than ever of the strange and swift altercation that led to the tragic death of his dear friend and mentor. The whole event sweeps though him with such shocking clarity, he is taken aback. He holds fast the starboard rail, his mind yet again, desperately trying some way to reach over all the warriors' hands and save Cook from their clutches and clubs.

George's bo'sun breaks the terrifying image, with a dispatch. "King Kamehameha sends word he will be happy to greet his 'magnificent' – that is his word, sir exactly, sir - 'friend' – Captain George Vancouver, at his wishes and convenience."

Vancouver, hearing this, suppresses the tide of bloody images and replaces them with a vision of such happiness as he has not had in many months. He knows this announcement from King Kamehameha is in a special code, a previously arranged message, not meaning at all what the actual words mean and connected to a labyrinthine plan and secretive circumstance by two forthright sailors, John Young and Isaac Davis.

Vancouver had been informed a week earlier upon arrival, that the king and his beloved queen had been apart for over a year. Her father, Ke'e au-moku, a respected man in the community, had taken him aside and explained the deep despair that has pervaded his heart and the entire social atmosphere on Hawaii, due to the disgraced state of the queen.

Young and Davis had also taken the captain aside and given their observations of the predicament. Beyond the king's personal devotion to Ka'ahumanu, there was a potentially greater issue. It is now the captain's concern as well as the two sailors, and a number of local leaders, that there are two or three maverick chiefs in the islands that could eventually use this circumstance to sabotage Kamehameha's future in the kingdom if he does not forgive his queen and unite their followers.

Had this young woman not been so powerfully loved by Kamehameha's people, it might have been easier to ignore the situation, or at least for Vancouver to keep out of it as a royal domestic matter to be avoided by foreign ship captains. But, through all the official ceremonies of this week and his private talks with the king, he has found him most forlorn and scattered in his thinking, completely unlike when he has known Kamehameha in previous visits over many years. This is to such a degree that he has asked the king to see if he could perhaps describe to him this inner trouble.

The king admitted to Captain Vancouver, that despite exiling his queen for her infidelity, his attachment to her and affection for her was unshaken, and the rift between them was clouding his ability to rule the kingdom. The people were continuing to send undercurrents of concern for her into the royal court and to the king himself. The most secret assertion from the king to George, was that he felt he needed her for his life even to continue, a confession which Vancouver was surprised and embarrassed to be told. This kind of love indeed was to be encouraged if there was any way to help. During the king's moments of surprising candor, he added that his own behavior, he supposed, was not exactly such as warranted his exiling her for infidelity. He even expressed a sort of internal conviction of her innocence, but he could not seem to figure a way out of this difficult conundrum and save face.

Kamehameha's pride had consistently thrown impediments in the way of any reconciliation. So, Captain Vancouver recently created a plan, which he is today conveniently placed in a position to attempt. He has put forth a possible social scenario that the king has apparently seen as viable, or at least worth a try.

At Kamehameha's "secret code" response from the bo'sun, Vancouver's mind is now awash with hopes for his domestic healing plan to proceed and perhaps succeed.

From what Isaac Davis has told him, it has been long the wish of the people to see Ka'ahumanu forgiven and restored to her former dignities. This desire is probably not a little heightened by the regard entertained also by Vancouver for the queen and the happiness and repose of what he describes this day in his Captain's log,

"...*due to these islands and my noble and generous friend, Kamehameha.*"

Captain Vancouver responds to his First Mate, "Ah! Tell the king all is ready. That is all. You may go."

The next morning, Vancouver sends an invitation through John Young, to Ka'ahumanu's father, Ke'e au-moku, to bring himself, his daughter, and a few members of their highly respected royal family to his ship's quarters for a brief visit that night. The queen was not to suspect any of the other part of George's plan, and his ship would remain safely

offshore enough for her to visit. His note to Young
and Davis reads:

Gentlemen,

*The meeting will not bring too much notice since
Ka'ahumanu is in effect, still in exile, but is
allowed to traverse the island on the water on
rare occasions and since her father has been so
friendly with myself and my crew in previous visits, it is not too unexpected that I would want to
see her as well as her family. The meeting will be
described as a casual event; one not mentioned
abroad and will be discreetly prepared for...*

58

Perfumed Wind

From her place on the dinghy slicing through calm waters, Ka'ahumanu's velvet brown eyes are set on the ship anchored across the bay, as she and her family are rowed from Kau on the western side of the island of Hawaii by Captain Vancouver's mariners around the end of the coast to his moorings in Kealakekua Bay.

Her long, delicate fingers nervously adjust the pile of leis made by her handmaidens as gifts for the kind "Kapene George", but her emotions are in control with her head held high and a serene smile in spite of her long exile and difficult circumstances.

Being accompanied by her father and mother is a great help, and she thinks that in any case, foreigners need to see the dignity of Hawaiians in every way possible. There are other gifts on trays included on the boat for Captain Vancouver and his crew.

Because the king has been spending some time in his palace huts and fish ponds in Kailua Kona village further north on the coast, he is closer to the queen than he has been in a long time, and Ka'humanu has added fears of some unexpected problems with him. She nearly rejected the invitation when it came from Vancouver, but she felt she must comply for the sake of her people under the auspices of Kamehameha.

The small hairs on the back of her neck jump when she sees in the far distance across the bay, the back of Kamehameha walking with his retinue and priests, leaving one of his personal fish ponds on that part of the coast. She quickly averts her eyes and tries to catch her breath, hoping her parents did not see him.

The dinghy slides up against the ship *Discovery*, and she turns her attention to the warm greetings flowing from all onboard. The Captain's kind gesture of waving to her as he leans over the side railing, is a relief and a welcome change from many humiliating experiences she has coped with since the tragic evening of her betrayal and exile.

The guests are ushered into the main salon where Captain Vancouver receives his flower leis, and he in turn, presents his guests with generous gifts of jewelry, pottery and linens which have been laid out for the Queen and her family.

Captain Vancouver's ship's log...

As was contrived between myself and the king, I suddenly stood up in the middle of my speech of compliments to my guests and, as if embarrassed, I announced I had forgotten one of my gifts. I immediately sent a message, a prepared symbol on a piece of paper wrapped around a rock in a beautiful length of cloth – which was the king's cue to arrive quickly with Young and Davis in tow.

While we continued our visit I received a planned message of his unexpected arrival. 'The king seems to be nearby and is coming aboard. What a nice surprise,' I told them.

All in the cabin seemed quite satisfied to think the king might come on board, except for the

*poor queen, who seemed to be much agitated at
the thought of being so suddenly in his presence.
The melodious voice of his royal person on the
deck upstairs sealed the queen's fate as there was
no way of escape, and social graces demanded
she stay in the cabin...*

As Ka'ahumanu pins her gaze to the floor
in panic and embarrassment, her father, one of
the conspirators in this plot, takes her hand and
presses it as he tries to comfort her with loving
words. However, it does no good, as Ka'a's heart
has jumped into her throat and is pounding so
hard she cannot focus. *I will pass out. I cannot
breathe. Oh, gods help me!*

"I come thank Kapene George for his mar-vel-
lous gift," booms the king in a vivacious manner
as he thunders down the passageway toward
Vancouver's main cabin.

Ka'ahumanu wants to melt into the wood
paneling behind her as the door is flung open
and the king appears, uncommonly jovial.

"My Kapene, you like my new word, 'mar-ve-
lous'? I just learn. Thank you for my – ahh – you
have other guests I see?" He registers surprise at
seeing Ke'e au-moku and family members, and
then presents the most realistic horror he can

muster upon seeing the queen. "I… oh, no… no…" He clutches his heart, in great thespian cleverness. He breathlessly recoils and tries to leave the room, but Vancouver has positioned himself at the door to prevent departure by either party. Young and Davis have stayed in the passageway to help. At that moment, Vancouver grabs the king's hand and the hand of the queen, and quickly joins them together, hoping the touch of flesh will produce results and save face for both.

After a moment of tremendous shock for everyone, including those in on the plan who could only pray for the best, Captain Vancouver glances at both lovers to see if the efforts have borne fruit. To his great joy, the reconciliation of king and queen is instantly secured as sounds that cannot be described, rise from both their throats, tears burst forth and escape down their cheeks and they embrace each other, forgetting everything and everyone around them. The feelings of all assembled and even of several sailors serving at the event, witnessed such an unexpected outpouring of passion, they were overcome by the beauty and impact of the reunion.

After this magical moment, the conversation begins again with the captain's awkward words, "Well, now. What a lovely surprise. It is my pleasure to be present for this unexpected reunion of two such fine people."

The others join in cheerfully, sharing any words they can think of to bring normalcy to the situation and put all at ease.

After a few glasses of fine wine, the event is considered a complete success. John Young and Isaac Davis even imbibed and are as happy as they have ever been since the day of their own ceremonies. They are hopeful this will finally create an end to the great unrest of the people of Kamehameha's Islands.

However, after a time of good humor and conviviality the guests prepare to leave the ship. Ka'ahumanu looks uncomfortable again. She takes Captain Vancouver aside, privately. "Kapene Van-koo-fer, my heart is aloha for you. You give my family much happy. You give father best face... he smile. 'Smile' is word?"

"Yes. It was my pleasure, your highness. I am smiling as well."

"Kapene, please, you make Kamehameha not beat Ka'ahumanu when go hut. I fear. I fear. You make Kamehameha promise, Kapene, you only say him this? Yes?"

Vancouver stares long enough at the young queen to see her real terror at the prospect of a beating from the king. He pats her shoulder. "Wait on top deck, Ka'ahumanu. I will speak to the king."

She turns from him with hope. Vancouver finds Kamehameha in the galley explaining how best to steam breadfruit to the ship's cook. The cook is much entertained by the explanation and personal visit by the now buoyant monarch.

Vancouver kindly dismisses the cook and escorts the king by the arm speaking carefully to him all the way down the passage during which the king assures him nothing of that sort will take place. Kamehameha is appalled, then saddened at such an idea. "Kapene, no. No, Ka'a will not be harm, no harm. Much aloha. All good." The king taps his heart in a gesture that indicates he is emotionally in peace.

Vancouver becomes convinced the king will not be a threat to her. He seems happy and relieved to have his queen back and is expectant that his people will finally respect him again.

They arrive on deck, where they encounter the slightly drunk Young and Davis and Ka'ahumanu's family waiting for the king. Despite Vancouver's assurances, Ka'ahumanu urges him most piteously to return with her and the king to the royal residence. Swept along by the anxiety in her eyes, he accompanies them onshore and toward the compound. The word has spread and people run out of their huts weeping and falling down with joy. They shout to each other, and sing as they prostrate themselves before the royal couple.

Vancouver is glad for the chance to see this display of love. He walks with them and stays to have the pleasure of seeing the queen restored to all her former honors and privileges the next day. At last, this seems to be enough evidence for her to have the captain confirm the happy process.

The outcome is also to the great satisfaction of the king's high chiefs, kahunas, throngs of Commoners and Young and Davis, who bring their wives to enjoy the event. Many trays of flowers arrive at the entrance of the king's residence. The aroma of pungent ginger, lofty pikake, and heavenly plumeria float in the air.

This unexpected reversal is much to the utter mortification of the culprit, Kiana, who by his scandalous report has been the cause of the unfortunate and nearly deadly separation. He is nowhere to be found. Nor are his comrades who were more than willing to carry out vengeance when the king was in his rage. But, they are not missed.

As Captain Vancouver leaves the king's huts, he is overtaken by a breathless handmaiden of

Ka'ahumanu's. He turns and greets her, sending his guard ahead to the ship. He feels a bit awkward as she speaks. He doesn't understand what she says. Then in silence she pointedly proffers a lei strung with exquisite pink flowers. The delicate, alluring young woman, stands in the glow of the rising moon and looks much like one of the delightful flowers she is holding. She says again, "Ka'ahumanu kena aloha Kapene." And from the sweetness in her eyes and the velvet tones of her voice, he knows the queen has sent her finest handmaiden to be a gift to him for the night. He stands in the path, enjoying her beauty for a moment. But, in spite of the generosity of Queen Ka'ahumanu, he declines with a soft word and polite tip of his hat. He receives the lei and says in his best Hawaiian, "Mahalo to Ka'ahumanu. Aloha ahi-ahi. Good evening." She stands, blinking at him. He walks down the slope into the night, caressed by the warm breezes, entertained by songs in the palms and revels in his ability to refuse such a pleasant prospect. After a quick sting of regret, he turns back to the maiden briefly, tips his hat a second time and amuses himself with the unexpected privileges of a virtuous sea captain.

Much later that night, long past when villagers are contentedly asleep, past even Vancouver's settling into slumber in his Spartan quarters, in the warm sleeping hut of the king, the fingers of Kamehameha, after much love-making, continue to gently stroke and please the hungry flesh of the queen of his heart. Ka'ahumanu, fast forgetting every lonely moment in exile, sweetly discovers fresh ways to bring pleasure to her forgiving king.

59

Letters from The Jackall & The Prince Lee Boo

O n a bright morning soon after the great reunion, Captain Vancouver, sits on deck of the *Discovery* and pens in his captain's logbook effusive compliments and high praise of John Young and Isaac Davis as well as their mutually satisfying friendship with King Kamehameha. He is methodical as he completes his entry. He cannot know at this time his sterling reputation and great voyages with the late Captain Cook will give his testimony of Kamehameha and the white mariners much credibility in Britain and throughout the world upon his return to Southampton.

Even though the mariners have thrown their lot in with the rising Hawaiian king and have planned never to return to their native lands, their humility, deep sufferings and valor become immortalized through the observations of one of the most successful of all sea-faring explorers in history. Moreover, by willing to help mend the destructive rift between the king and queen, Vancouver has solidified future happiness of the English sailors as well as the entire Hawaiian kingdom in ways he is not aware as he sails later into the eastern sea, leaving many warm-hearted and sweet memories in his wake.

Months pass as Kamehameha, his domestic affairs having taken such a happy turn, is finally free to focus on governing his people. He is making detailed preparations on the shore with a group of chiefs, Young, Davis and Kiana for his next assault on Kahekili at the end of the season. A runner arrives with news that Kahekili has just died at Waikiki, and his ruthless son, Kalani-Kupule, has taken over his father's kingdom.

Kamehameha is stunned he will not get to personally gut his arch enemy. *The gods have tricked me again.*

The islands of Oahu, Lanai, and Molokai are now under Kalani-Kupule's control. There had been news that Kahekili had made inroads back to Maui. So, with Maui in question and Kauai under rule by Kahekili's brother, the situation is tenuous at best. Even if Kamehameha has complete control of his island of Hawaii, he will never have the power to gain peace without taking the other islands completely. Kamehameha pronounces to the group, "Action should be taken soon while there is likely confusion and Kalani-kupuli's leadership could be vulnerable."

Kamehameha becomes silent to evaluate.

The season has been filled with many storms and getting armies ready is taking longer than expected, not to mention continuing the Fair American's transformation into being a part of a fast, fighting fleet of war canoes.

The king adds, "We will not be foolish. We will wait two moons to invade Oahu. We will leave when all is ready for war. They know we are coming. Let them wonder when."

Isaac Davis approves this plan, since he doesn't feel his division of the army is ready to fight on Oahu yet. Moreover, he is enjoying the unbridled attentions of his wife, Paloa, a woman deeply and madly in love with him. He returns her affection. She has even begun to write poems in English about Davis, charming him deeply. He is so inspired he has decided to try his hand at writing a journal about his adventures in Kamehameha's service.

John Young and Kaoana have had great joy in birthing a beautiful daughter, Fanny Kekela. Things have taken on a surprising semblance of normalcy. The kidnapped sailors-turned-royal-advisors are enjoying the spoils of war and aren't ready to risk their lives again so soon. They have a lot at stake.

Within a fortnight, Young is up in the mainsail in the bay, re-rigging the *Fair American* for battle with Davis and a crew of warriors. It's been difficult, because they are not experienced in turning a schooner into a Hawaiian war vessel, one that can be maneuvered fast as a part of a large flotilla. Young has been training his warriors to be the new crew, but these men have been fighting hand-to-hand on land, not being part of a crew to discharge a swivel cannon at the same time moving quickly through the water for a surprise attack. A heated discussion has ensued with Young and his men about a tricky problem lashing weapons to the rigging, when Opa, growing into a young man, stumbles down the makeshift dock shouting and waving a satchel. He gets to the schooner and hoists himself on deck.

"What on earth has you so excited, boy?" Davis guffaws. He tosses dried fruit to Opa, who gobbles and talks. "Akake! Olohana! The king send me! A ship! Give papers only you! Ship outside bay give bag to man in canoe. Ship much hurry out bay. Many in fear on the decks. Sail to Canton."

Young reads, *'Only For John Young or Isaac Davis'*.

Davis wonders, "Why would a ship do such a thing?"

Young opens a packet of papers. He looks up, shocked. "Isaac, this letter is to you and me directly from two sailors on two different vessels— the *Jackall* and the *Prince Lee Boo*. Listen – these men say, *'Both captains Brown and Gordon killed by Kalani-Kupule's men in a cunning plot to take their ships, arms, and ammunition…'* and then apparently the monsters have plans to invade this island, but, these sailors, Lamport and Bonallack, say they and their crews have *'taken the ships back from the attackers and now will sail away to Canton'*. They trust only us to warn Kamehameha of the attack coming here. This is some red work Kalani-Kupule is up to. He seems to have inherited his father's talent for ruthlessness. Opa, good job! Maika'i. But what flag did the ship fly? Britannee? China? Some other? Think. We must know."

"Britannee, sir," he chirps.

Young's jaw tenses. "That confirms it. We can trust them if it is an English flag. Let's get to the king." He hands the letters to Davis. "Isaac, what a bloody mess! We must get this ship able to move better in the water. I know as soon as the king hears this, no sand will be under his feet – he expects this ship to take him to Oahu. First, he must go to Maui to gather more warriors.

Davis puts the papers in the satchel. "I agree, even though Maui is won, the king must have support from villagers of Lahaina and Ka'anapali before taking Waikiki. That island must be secure before he can truly be king."

Young shouts to the group on the stern, "Mahalo, gents! We stop now – take news Kamehameha. War come from Kalani-Kupule."

Amazed, the men drop their tools, jump off the ship, and swim back to the village to prepare their families.

"A different lay of land on Oahu, Isaac. New

mountains we may have to climb – and been curious about Kahekili's gruesome house of bones. I
expect my curiosity will be satisfied quickly."

60

Swooping Hawk

Not since the victory on Maui has the king worn the royal yellow-feathered cloak. His demeanor radiates a new layer of commitment. He stands high above hundreds of assembled warriors, holds his long spear and makes an impressive image against the verdant mountains. He is flanked by Kahuna Lani, Young, Davis, Mapala, and Kiana.

Young stands near the king, listening to his strategy speech. He muses,

I am likely witnessing a call-to-arms as potent as Napoleon or Alexander or even his royal majesty

King George. I never was this close to my liege when I lived in England. And now I have mastered the Hawaiian language, I see how foolish I was to think Kamehameha a savage brute. In fact, he is a bold, brave, brilliant leader with vision and wisdom. It is true, I am often shocked by some of the barbaric customs and strange taboos in this violent society, but I know that for all its civilized laws, English life has harbored barbarity at times as well. Men of all nations need a code of morality in the midst of the evils that always grow. I hope to influence this king and these people in some Providential way. I am no longer a hapless victim, kidnapped and enslaved. I am a royal advisor with greater power than I ever thought possible. A ship's captain was my dream, but my position here makes me responsible for many more lives than I would have had on any ship in any ocean. Moreover, I enjoy the pleasures of a husband with a loyal wife. My future holds bright visions – that is, if I can manage somehow to stay alive in the next battle.

Kamehameha has been speaking, inspiring the hearts of his warriors.

"...Ku-Kaili-Moku has spoken. Those who do

not listen to his call are doomed to fail. Doomed and lost. The storms delayed us for a reason, my children! This warning we received has come to us for one purpose only. To sail swiftly, act boldly and silence forever those who would keep us from our destiny – to stop their evil attacks on our people and bring lasting peace. Do you hear me? Lasting peace! Are you ready to win this victory?"

The crowd shouts as one, "Victory – Kamehameha! Peace!" The king lifts his hand and trades the spear he holds for his carved scepter as Kahuna Lani steps forward, lifting the image of Ku-kaili-moku. "Look deep into his face. He asks you, will you destroy Kalani-Kupule and his army?" The crowd goes wild with weapons raised. Drums join in with chilling rhythm, rising to a fever pitch.

Young's heart pounds with sudden fear, a terror of losing all he has recently gained. He sees Kaoana, holding up his daughter to wave at him. He waves back.

Davis is in the throws of similar emotions. In the back of the assembly, Paloa watches Isaac. Her lips move soundlessly in a chant of appeal to her gods, and to Davis' *God of the leaves*, to bring him back safe – to bring back her king and his armies in a quick victory. Her fingers run along the edges of the Bible Davis gave her to read on lonely nights during a campaign from which he may never return.

The king raises his hand for quiet. "My people, I see you are driven by the same spirit as I am – by love for your land and our gods. But, when one is fighting, there is always the face of one who leads you through the howling and fearful cries of battle. I say to you in truth on this day that the one face I will ever see before me as I fight, the one face to light my way through, will be the face of my wise and loving queen, and your queen, Ka'ahumanu!"

A roar of joy explodes from the crowd and becomes a chant, "Ka'ahumanu – Ka'ahumanu – Ka'ahumanu!"

The generals part for her. The queen, resplendent in royal garb, eyes sparkling with pride and tears, is brought forth.

Her father and handmaidens present her to the king who takes her hand. He leads her to a platform built for her to watch the fleet. She smiles and lifts her hand. It is the signal for all warriors to take their places in the canoes.

Young is embraced by Ka'ahumanu. He speaks to her through shouts and cheers, "Gracious queen, we trust this island to your capable care 'til our victorious return."

Ka'ahumanu breaks into a bright grin. "I know it was you and Akake who do much to save my life. You must come back safe to your sweet families!"

Isaac Davis offers one last kiss to his wife and leaps on a skiff headed to the *Fair American*.

In the bay, the mariners and warriors-turned sailors wave as John calls out orders to the crew of the re-fitted schooner which catches the wind and moves fast to join the large war-canoes. Opa looks happy to be allowed on the ship and to sit next to one of the lashed guns.

61

Ma'alea Bay, Maui

Eleven hours later as the day ends, through heavy chop and white caps, the flotilla swoops into Ma'alea Bay, led by the king's war canoe. Kiana, his army, and the armies of two other chiefs have been sent to Molokai to lay claim for Kamehameha and meet up with Kamehameha's forces on the east coast of Oahu on the next day.

Through a scope, Kamehameha sees the last powerful chief loyal to Kahekili, waiting on the shore with a small army, gathered as soon as runners had informed him of the unexpected arrival of the king. The *Fair American*, with banners of Kamehameha's colors and the flag of Great Britain from Captain Vancouver, loaded with rows of warriors along its decks chanting and shouting, makes such a startling spectacle. The natives on shore are awestruck and unable to take a stand. They have no idea cannon are about to blast from the main deck.

John Young shouts the order, "Port cannon. Fire." *Boom*!

The group of warriors scatter like quail. The men in the Maui army retreat in horror. Within moments, the ferocity of Kamehameha's navy so overtakes the chief he raises his arms and shouts from a safe distance, "Allegiance to Kamehameha! Maui people all say, Allegiance to Kamehameha. We will serve you!"

"Mapala, tell him we accept," commands Kamehameha, "He may be full of treachery later, but he's a willing servant now. Olohana and Akake say it is best to let those who pledge service to me live and prove their loyalty in battle. Go ashore."

The entourage moves up the beach to the Maui king who shouts orders to his army. They lay down their arms. Many seem greatly relieved. All along the sides of the mountain hordes of common people run down the slopes to meet their new king with food and flowers. They shout with joy,

"Kamehameha! Ali'i Kane. Aloha a Kamehameha!"
The king feels the glow of victory rolling over him
like a huge, warm wave. He never thought this
would be so easy. Laughing, he makes eye contact
with Mapala, then to Young and Davis. They wave
and turn to their men, who shout back, "Oahu!
To Oahu!" It is a far more simple than anyone
had figured. Kamehameha officially retakes the
island of Maui. The king turns to the prostrating
warriors and commoners gesturing them to rise.

He speaks in gentle, but firm tones, "People
of Maui, hear me! I have come to free you from
the weight you have been suffering again under
an evil king. But, it is a new day – I will not make
slaves of you. You are my brothers. My friends. My
countrymen. I am going to Oahu to crush Kalani-
Kupule and Kahekili's House of Bones. We will all
earn our freedom and live in peace." A great cry of
victory spreads through the assembly. An elderly
kahuna, much respected by the commoners of this
island, comes walking and singing across the slope
toward Kamehameha. The warriors are concerned
for the safety of the king, but Kamehameha holds
up his hand. He believes this man has a good
message. He calls for silence. "Let us hear this holy
man!" Some women join the man's song. His new
subjects sing a heroes mele…

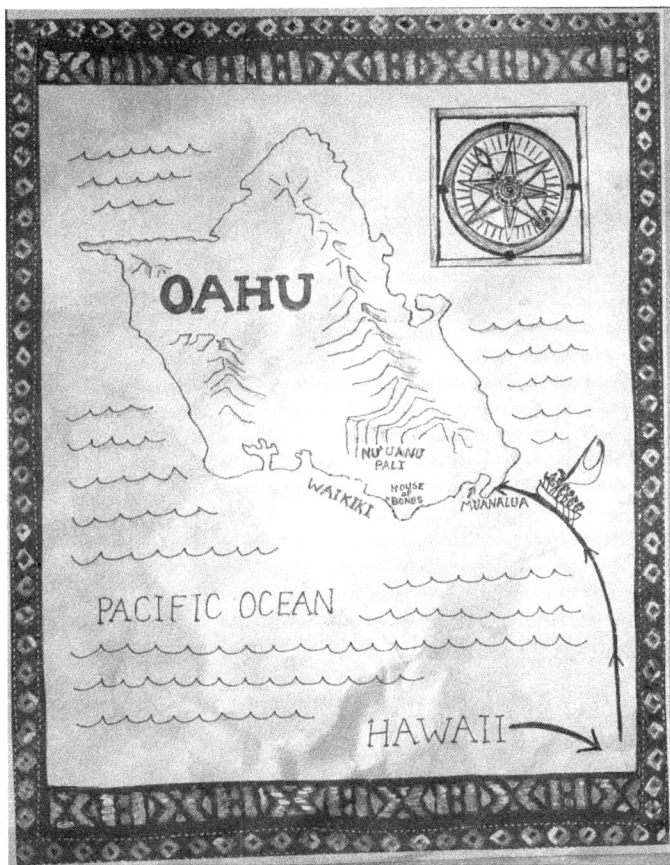

John Young's battle map to Oahu

That which is above shall be brought down.
That which is below, will be lifted up
The islands to be united,
The people shall stand upright.
Kamehameha. Kamehameha. Kamehameha.

The king smiles. He drinks in the sound and sweetness of their praise.

That night, they rest and prepare for their attack on Oahu. It is also a time of eating, drinking, and fellowship with their new countryfolk. The feeling of victory runs hot in their blood like good rum, or for John and Isaac, like the swirling embrace of fine grog at sea with sailors who have experienced great danger and yet survived. The two mariners see these warriors now as comrades-in-arms. They do not want even one man to be lost fighting in future battles. They love their families, wives and children, and the heartstrings have become thick.

So, on this night of easy victory, they do not care "how" or "why" these Maui islanders are so willing to surrender to Kamehameha. They are grateful for adding many warriors to the cause. Many Commoners and farmers join their camps along the shore, making the Hawaiian warriors feel welcome. They share tales of Kahekili's merciless tyranny over them for more painful seasons than any can count.

Dreams for the future grow around the fires. They make many vows, as men often do in the cauldron of war.

62

Oahu, The Gathering Place

The next morning in the Maui camp, the embrace of the octopus of strong drink from the night before has slowed many warrior regiments, creating late departure. The king did not drink intoxicating spirits, so rose early, found a glen to say his prayers and bathed in a nearby pool. He is having visions of a swift victory. He strides down the mountain trail and sees Young on the beach. He hurries to him. "Olohana. We win Oahu today, yes?"

"Yes!" Young throws his gear in a dinghy preparing to board the schooner. "My king, it is time for the reign of Kalani-Kupule to end. We will obliterate him utterly!

Kamehameha chuckles at a new word. "Aha!

Ob - blit - ter - No! *O - blit - er - rate?* He savors the word and likes it – then offers a crushing gesture with both hands – "Yes! Obliterate!"

"Yes – crush like a kukui nut. In Hawaiian, it is, *ho'o Ah*, yes?"

Kamehameha offers, " We say "ho'opau" Now you say."

"*Ho'opau*. Ha! You have greater command of English than I do Hawaiian. Opa declares he will obliterate Kalani-Kupule with you. He will make a brave warrior someday."

The king ponders. "Olohana, why leg with Opa not good for walking? In Britannee, no legs like this?"

"Oh, sir, in Britain, all manner of things go bad. Doctors try to fix them, like your kahunas. Many things cannot be helped, even in Britain. There is much suffering in the world everywhere I have visited." They walk down the beach to waiting vessels, enjoying each other's company, as hundreds of warriors fill canoes. "Olohana, you pray your god today?"

"Yes. You speak to yours?"

"Many words."

"My God sends greetings to wish you good fighting, and victory."

"I would like to see your god."

"No one can."

"You worship your god and never see him? This strange god, Olohana. He lives in those leaves?"

"Hard to explain. I see Him in all things. Not until I go to the other side will I see Him in the flesh." The king looks confused. Their conversation is swallowed up in shouts of warriors.

Hours later, in the bay of Muana-lua, eastern end of Island of Oahu, King Kamehameha's canoes are spotted by scouts on the road to Waialae. They hurry to report to king Kalani-Kupule in Waikiki. However, the landing of Kamehameha on this shore, once again, is uneventful. They see no resistance anywhere. They gather onshore to talk, wondering where the villagers are.

At the same time, miles away in Kahala, near the back of an ancient crater not far from Waikiki, Chief Kiana's war canoe has secretly pulled onshore. Kiana's adjutant waits with twenty men, as many other canoes wait offshore. The crater looms behind them, silhouetted in the afternoon sky. In a glen down the beach, Kiana and the disgraced Kona Chief, who had massacred young Captain Metcalfe and his crew of the *Fair American*, conspire. Sweat drips into Kiana's eyes. He speaks with deadly passion, "Listen, the only way it can work is if the king be taken first and killed or all will be lost. We must be sure he is dead."

The Kona Chief, having endured many seasons of humiliation and exile, as well as reprisals upon his people, has pretended to be repentant with Kamehameha, and has a true ally in the deceptive Kauai prince, General Kiana. After months of secret preparation, the two rebel chiefs are ready to attack.

"Let me strike him first," The Kona Chief snaps. He has had an unrelenting desire to kill Kamehameha since the day of his punishment. His public chastisement before foreigners has haunted him. Further, for Kamehameha to choose to favor "haoles", "ghostly creatures without souls", over a loyal servant such as himself, was a greater sin than all others. "However, Kiana, as soon as the king is dead, I and my men must destroy Akake, Olohana, and Mapala or the armies may rally behind them. Remember, Kalani-Kupule made it clear all four must be killed to achieve our purpose. He wants no leaders but ourselves, and his own chiefs."

Kiana puts a reassuring hand on the Kona Chief's shoulder. "Yes, but, you must be patient until the time is ripe. Continue hiding your feelings until we have heard the whole plan of attack from the king. You know how he can change suddenly. When we know his course of action, we will steal a moment to make our final plan. Guard your eyes and keep smiling. Kalani-Kupule is counting on us not to fail. Just wait. His armies will all be loyal to us before long."

The two men emerge from the trees. Their guards fall in behind them as violent breakers crash on the beach. A sleek, black mamo bird, a foot in length with hooked bill soars above the traitors and sees scouts from Kamehameha's army on the opposite slope. As is his habit, the bird often follows humans and calls to them. He is thought to carry messages from the gods. The bird screeches wildly to the king's scouts. But, they do not heed the mamo's shrill warning calls of treachery.

One of the scouts pulls back from the scope he's looking into. "There is General Kiana with his army, ready and waiting for battle," he observes. "Go report this good news." As they turn to go, the mamo bird circles and screams.

ᗧᗣ

An hour later, on the long beach on the leeward side of Oahu, Kamehameha and his personal guard move down the beach to observe the rows of warriors. His army gathers behind him, as well as battle canoes waiting for orders in the bay.

Kiana and his retinue arrive at the same time. He has marched over the hill from where the rest of his army waits. All appears to be well. The Kona chief and his legions are close behind. Kiana waves and smiles.

Kamehameha's bright yellow and red banners whip in the wind, sentries holding them proudly aloft. The sight of vast regiments and groups of special Polulu warriors with their long spears and the warriors with muskets is impressive to Kanlani-kupule's spies hidden in the underbrush high on a slope. They watch with wide eyes at the many armies coming together and row upon row of warriors stretching all the way up the side of the mountain. Beyond that, war canoes float in twenty lines at least a half-mile out to sea.

In the midst of the bay, the *Fair American,* arrives at full sail, with men in rows on the deck holding muskets and looking ready to fight. They trim sails and wait for orders. All eyes focus on the two men coming to meet onshore. Kamehameha stands with his warrior Kahuna Kaua, an aide of the ailing Kahuna Lani, who holds high the image of Ku-ka-ili-moku.

Kiana hurries to the spot where they are to confirm plans. His countenance is buoyed by anticipation of his long-awaited revenge. The two large warriors share a strong embrace. Then they clap forearms in a brotherly handshake.

Kamehameha's deep laugh exudes confidence, "My brother, it is a good day to take our future in our own hands."

Kiana returns the sentiment, thinking of his plans, "Yes, my king. We will do that, sir. We will."

"My friend. You should have seen that Maui Chief on the beach with his army as we entered his bay. I am sure his mouth was catching flies when he saw our ships coming with guns and cannon mounted, and men on the deck holding muskets. How did they take you in Molokai?"

"My king, the gods are truly with us. At Molokai, they put down their weapons and offered us anything we wanted! I see your landing here was good. And what a fine wind. We killed several spies when we arrived this morning. Their news of us coming will not reach Kalani-Kupule. Ha! I am sure he will be surprised. What is the final plan of attack? Or is the plan the same? Are you calling a meeting?"

"You are full of questions. I am glad you are so ready for this."

Kiana winks. "Yes, my king, I am. I have been waiting for this day for a long time. I have never been more ready."

The king chuckles and they walk down the beach. "But, Kiana, truly, how is the Kona chief? Is he with us all the way? Does he have hard feelings? You can be honest with me. He was very loyal in days gone by."

"My king, he is a changed man, I assure you. He was deeply sorry for what happened to the white sailors. He said when old captain Metcalfe treated him so cruelly, he wanted revenge. I can vouch for him, he will fight hard for you now."

Kamehameha is satisfied. "Listen. This is how it goes. I will take my men and Mapala will take his over the top of that ridge as we planned and we will come at them from the side, while you and your men and the Kona Chief go with the ship and my war canoes surprising them from the water. Kalani-Kupule will be so busy dealing with you, Olohana and Akake, they won't see us coming."

"This is a good plan. We will attack the beach at Waikiki, for that is where they say Kalani-Kupule is. And our forces will meet you there. Correct?"

Kamehameha takes his arm, "Make sure that Kalani-Kupule is dead. He is our first target. Captain Vancouver and Olohana are right. Once their leader is dead, we will offer them peace with us. I hope they take that offer quickly. Otherwise they will die."

Kiana looks deep in the king's eyes, "You can count on me, my king."

On the *Fair American* offshore, Isaac Davis shades his eyes and watches for Kamehameha's signal to head for Waikiki. Opa braids a knot for an additional shark's tooth on his warrior harness. He is confident in his ability to be a scout for the king upon landing at Waikiki. Young comes to Davis for a private moment. "It looks like all is well. But, I don't trust Kiana. It is foolish for the king to put him in charge of the Kona Chief.

"Yes, that bastard is as squinty-eyed to me now as ever. But, he fights like the devil and the king won't make a plan without him."

Kamehameha and Kiana finish their meeting and part – Kamehameha to the shore towards the *Fair American,* and Kiana to his waiting troops on the slopes. The king gives the signal to Young and Davis, who begin shouting commands to their crew. Kamehameha proceeds back toward his troops behind the dunes.

∋◐●

Less than an hour later, the *Fair American* rounds the end of the Oahu crater, the lead vessel in a flotilla of sixty canoes, some of which have cannon lashed to them, and warriors with muskets on board. They enter Waikiki Bay and expect to see islanders of Oahu busy at daily tasks, look up and suddenly see Kamehameha's fleet. This is not the case. The village is empty, not one sign of life other than chickens scratching and pigs in a pen.

Young looks away from his scope on the schooner and stares at Davis. "The village is empty – they got wind of us."

"Damn. Now what? We have to go get them? Who knows how much time they've had to hide in the underbrush."

Young is confused. "The plan was to surprise them. It looks like we must fight on land now. No way to get word to Kamehameha."

"He will find out soon enough. Dear God. What a bloody mess."

63

Valley of Tears

Kamehameha, leading his regiments on foot from the direction of Waialae, comes to a steep slope from which he can see a large portion of the sprawling Waikiki settlement of the heir to Kahekili, King Kalani-Kupule. He looks through a scope given him by George Vancouver. He searches the landscape and wonders why he has not heard cannon fire yet.

After a few moments of scanning the beach, huts and heiau, he comes to the same conclusion as other forces. He sees the *Fair American* in the harbor and warriors coming ashore with no resistance. The village is deserted. He sees Kiana's forces following behind. It enrages him that his surprise beach landing has failed. At Maui, the sight of his fleet alone had made such an impression there was no fighting or loss of life. But, here, where his greatest foe lives and prospers, his grand plan is in shambles. The worst has happened. He must fight in the underbrush and many men could be lost. He realizes someone warned Kahekili's son and has set a great trap for him. *But, which direction has the army gone?* There is nothing to do but get to Waikiki as quickly as possible and meet with Young, Davis, and Kiana.

"We have been found out, my children!" he exclaims from his perch on a rock overlooking Waikiki. The leaders of the regiments are confused. Their hearts sink. All are hushed. "We have an easy battle here, with only sand crabs to subdue. The spider and all his minions have taken to the hills. But, we will find them, we will pursue them, and kill them in their hiding places. My friends, if they will not choose to live with us in peace, they will choose death!"

Cries of passion spring from his men. He raises his seven-foot spear high for them to see all the way down the long rows of men. "Let us join our brothers near the shores. You will muster there and wait for orders. Prepare to win our goal at last."

Young, Davis, and their crew from the ship are joined by other warriors walking through the village. They are cautious and prepared in case some different trap has been set for them. There is an eerie silence. The much-feared House of Bones is indeed at the center of the village and is more grisly than had been described. It's layers of bones is a macabre and ghoulish reminder of the deadly reign of Kahekili. The old king's ruthless ways still seem to hold sway over this island.

Davis looks up and sees Kamehameha in the distance with his great height, spear and bright cloak, leading his men forward. The heads of the armies come together.

Kiana, followed by the Kona Chief, hurries to Kamehameha. "My king, they have vanished. Somehow, one of those scouts must have escaped!" Kamehameha is calm, aware of what he must do. All the generals form a circle. The king speaks slowly, partly in Hawaiian and partly in English, "You have searched the area and found nothing to reveal where they went?"

"No, my king," Young answers. "But, the terrain would suggest that valley." He points toward the gorge between Waikiki and the nearest mountains.

Kiana looks in another direction. "Oh, my king, I know Olohana to be great warrior, but I think

Kalani-Kupule would have gone toward Kalihi-Kai. One of the scouts, before we killed him, said that name when he was being tortured. We have heard they have much buried treasure there."

Kamehameha sadly believes Kiana. "We will march through the lowlands until we get close. Send scouts ahead to report back. We are wasting time. We must hope for some kind of surprise."

The Kona chief hurries to his adjutant and gives orders. Scouts are deployed. Young and Davis reluctantly follow suit. "My king," Young offers. "We have taken the cannon off the *Fair American*. At least we can take them with us to use on land. They will likely think we have many more guns."

"This is good Olohana. I had hope not need cannon on land. Bring cannon and ammunition from canoes and set up a chain of men to help you. We do not know how far in to the valley we have to go."

The armies form lines quickly and move into the low brush of the upper shores. As they move across, heading in front of the Nu'uanu Valley pass, all seems quiet. Opa and three other scouts run back to signal all is clear to where Kamehameha is heading. The forces move forward. Davis and Young and their men have fallen in behind Kiana and the Kona Chief and their regiments.

At that moment, from a long stretch of trees in front of the valley opening, a shout goes up, and hundreds of Kalani-Kupule's warriors storm them from the right flank. Kiana and the Kona Chief move quickly to Kamehameha's rear. They have a clear shot at him with their weapons – Kiana with a musket and the Kona Chief with his spear. The king is always protected by his personal guard. But the guards trust Kiana and the Kona chief and are blind to their intentions.

Opa, near the king, catches an evil look in Kiana's eyes and sees him move toward the king. "My king. Look out. Look out!" Opa throws himself in the way. Kamehameha spins around in time to see Kiana and moves barely enough to avoid a musket shot. But, the Kona chief's spear lands in Opa's side. Blood spurts from the boy's ribs. He goes down.

Seeing none of this, but hearing it, Young and Davis call to their warriors to take cover and shoot at will. They begin shooting at any enemy warriors they can discern, but must depend on the other warriors around them to go hand-to-hand while they re-load.

The worst possible trap has been sprung. To their further horror, they see some of Kiana's men turning and fighting Kamehameha's men.

Young can barely make out orders from the Kona chief to his men. "The king is dead! Kill the foreigners!" Young shouts to Davis, "We are betrayed – They have killed Kamehameha! Retreat! Back to the ship!" Davis, having understood just enough to know it is worse than they thought, is thrown into hand-to-hand combat with one of Kalani-Kupule's warriors. He fights for his life and can do no more at this moment.

The loyal warriors of Kamehameha realize they must fight Kiana, the Kona Chief and Kalani-Kupule's army. They grab the cannon. Those trained load and fire as quickly as possible in the direction of the Nu'uanu Valley opening. Kalani-Kupule's warriors are surprised by the power of the cannon and many retreat. But, waves of warriors who have poured in from Kalani-Kupule's army look to be more than Kamehameha's men can handle. The lines are broken in many places. Kiana's men and the Kona chief's are aware of the high stakes. They need to win a quick victory. The element of surprise is in favor of Kiana. It is a clear case of trusting the wrong man.

64

Retreat

Opa lies numb from shock and loss of blood as he watches the fighting around him move toward the opening of the valley. He sees Davis kill one of Kalani-Kupule's men and turn to fight one of Kiana's warriors. Ironically, it is a man Davis himself had trained and had thought of as a comrade. Opa's eyes are fixed on Davis. His lips form the Hawaiian words for *good-bye*.

Young has no time to re-load his musket, so he decides to fight as he was taught by Kamehameha, with short cudgel and knife. He works his way to where he last saw the king. All around Young are loyal warriors of Kamehameha. Young shouts, "Kiana is a traitor! Move to the valley! Kill them!" Kamehameha's men do their best. They were ready for Kalani-Kupule's army, but this surprise attack from their own ranks is a shock. They push forward.

Young takes on one man after another with his cudgel until he buys himself a moment to load his musket. From out of the tumult and shouting, he hears the boom of Kamehameha's voice, "Olohana!" He whirls around and sees Kamehameha and Kiana in a struggle. Both have lost their weapons in a furious fight to the death. Kamehameha is bleeding heavily. The shot from Kiana's musket has shredded his left arm. Young tries to intervene to shoot Kiana, but can't get clear aim when the men roll away from him, sand and dirt flying. When he can see again, Kiana has Kamehameha by the throat.

Young moves to take better aim. Kamehameha makes his battle cry sound from deep inside and, uses his legs to get balance. He rolls over, gets control, and grabs Kiana. Kamehameha strangles his enemy, shouting, "Traitor! No more… no more!" The Kona chief rushes in to help Kiana. He throws Young aside, but John slams him with a cudgel then grabs his knife and stabs him. The Kona Chief falls.

Kamehameha's thumbs press deeper into Kiana's neck. Kiana finally releases his grip, loses consciousness, and falls to the dirt, dead.

Davis rushes in to stop the bleeding of the king's arm. He rips his shirt for a tourniquet.

Young wants to help Davis but sees pandemonium in the valley.

Kamehameha's forces are confused and need leadership as they try to push back the enemy.

As Young fends off Kiana's warriors, he sees his men blasting the cannon on their own pushing many enemy warriors back in partial retreat. He shouts, "Keep firing. Don't stop, Pau Ahi!" as he gathers ammunition.

Kamehameha's regiments join up near the opening of the valley. They grab more weapons from supply warriors and women, forming a line all the way back to the ship. John knows once they get into the underbrush, it will be hard to get more supplies. He sticks another cudgel in his belt. He hears his cannon unit blasting and smiles.

From a rock above the mouth of the valley, the adjutant for Kalani-Kupule stands watching, trying to assess who is winning. Kalani-Kupule's remaining forces have come to the edge of the valley and are ready to be deployed. Through the trees, a messenger appears, his eyes wide with horror.

Kalani-Kupule also arrives demanding, "Kamehameha is dead. He is dead. Tell me!"

"No, sir, only wounded, he lives. Prince Kiana is dead and the Chief from Kona is missing." Another runner arrives. "My king. They are coming."

Kalani-Kupule looks in the direction of Kamehameha's army beginning to move up through the valley. "We have our fort on the ridge. Call the men to retreat there." They rush into the forest.

⌒⌒

The wide opening of the valley leading to the Nu'uanu Pali is a thick blanket of dark green on a steady rise from the sea up through trails to a small pass in the mountain that goes to the other side of the island. At the summit, sheer cliffs rise from the valley floor.

Young and Davis have stayed in a glen with Kamehameha. Davis finishes wrapping the tourniquet around the king's arm. The king evaluates. "We must catch Kalani-Kupule before he can get to the windward side. Do not let him get away!" He spits out instructions as he winces with pain. "Olohana, your men shoot cannon. Good! We find Kalani-Kupule! Hurry. Must go, Akake."

"Be still," Davis orders. "If you don't let me do this you will bleed to death, and we are all lost. Stand still!"

Kamehameha marshals his patience and allows himself a moment to watch Davis. "Yes, Kahuna Akake. You stop blood, good." A moment later, "Now I go?" Davis nods. The king grabs his spear, moves past his waiting pululu warriors and shouts back, "Follow me!"

The armies of Kamehameha storm the entrance to the valley and find little opposition. But, they can hear men running through the tangle of trees and undergrowth ahead of them, moving fast and out of reach. "What is better to cut them off?" Kamehameha asks Young.

"Get my cannoneers in front," Young suggests. "Maybe we can lob shots further up to where they run. They will be trapped."

"Yes. Go quick."

Young hurries ahead, leaping through under-brush. He finds his men and cannon and leads them to a higher spot on the right side of the valley. From above the retreating army they can shoot with better aim. The warriors in charge of the cannon hoist it up on a ridge, and prepare a round. Soon after comes the hiss of the fuse and, *boom!* They fire a shot over the trees to where Kalani-Kupule's men have disappeared. *Boom!* The training from Young and Davis is paying off. The cannoneers are a great team and able to work quickly.

Young scrambles to the next ledge. Through his scope, above the trees, he can see it is likely at least some of the cannon fire has landed to the left. That way has been blocked. The enemy is turning to the right. The cannonfire is diverting them from the pass.

Kamehameha shouts, "Cut them off! Oki! Make go right! Akau – Akau!" The king's troops hurry faster through the trees and swarm into the left side of the mountain. He is pushing the retreating forces away from the safety of the ridge fort and into the direction of the Nu'uanu Pali, one of the highest cliffs on the island of Oahu. If Kalani-Kupule's men were able to get to the ridge, the fight will be much harder for Kamehameha. The enemy regiments try to climb over blasted rocks to get to the mountain pass, but it has been blocked by rubble from cannonfire. The route Kalani-Kupule's men are now taking is the one which leads to the treacherous summit. The tide is turning.

65

Nu'uanu Pali

Kamehameha gathers the best fighters from his pululu guard and moves quickly to the front of the advance into the high valley. Minutes into the trek, he is out in front of the lines, using his amazing ability to strategize his next move while carrying weapons, nursing his wound, and fighting through the undergrowth. He calls to Young and his cannon warriors up on the ridge. "What you see Olohana?

"They are trapped I think, sir. The pass is blocked.

Kamehameha shouts, "Good! No way down. Push them to the Pali."

"What is the Pali?"

"High as sky. No way down but die."

"Sounds good, sir."

They hear more shouting and see some of Kalani-Kupule's warriors coming through the trees, desperate to escape or fight. The king shouts to his division commanders, "Run with me to them my brothers." He yells in his strange, curling tone, roaring and charging. Many in Kalani-Kupule's ranks are disorganized by Young's cannon attack and have lost connection with their leaders. Whole columns of the enemy are being forced to turn further up toward the Pali or face Kamehameha's army when they attempt to get back down. The enemy warriors know of the suicidal choice of retreating to the summit. Some turn and make a stand. Others run behind their lines to get to higher ground, hoping for a place to hide or some trail of escape they did not know of before.

Davis and his division move slowly up toward the king's men, gasping for breath, having brought more supplies. They join the fighting at the front. He dives into hand-to-hand combat. When he gets close enough to speak to Kamehameha, he shouts, "My king, is it true there is a cliff?"

"Yes, Akake, to push them over." He kills a man and moves into the undergrowth, fighting two more.

Davis is not sure he heard correctly, but he smiles with other warriors, feeding on the exhilarating thought they could win this battle. They double their efforts and push. The wind is picking up and cooler air is mixing with grey, mountain fogs, wrapping the two armies in ghostly mist as they ascend the steep trails.

Kamehameha, still bleeding despite the tourniquet, turns to see the route ahead. He hurries back to Young and grabs him. "Make cannon to keep shoot. Push to Pali." He points. "There, they run Pali. See?

Boom!" The concussion rattles the mountainous gorge. Young looks at his cannoneers. They get the idea Kalani-Kupule's troops will be forced to the summit. His men, filled with new hope, load and fire feverishly. He notices the king's wound. "My king, let me fix that arm. You are bleeding." The king bounds off in the direction where the steady stream of the enemy has gone. He runs toward them and roars, "Fight, you cowards. Fight! Where is your king?" He shakes his spear at them laughing wildly. Several enemy warriors turn and throw spears at him. He howls louder, catches them mid-air and throws them back with deadly results.

Davis and his company pull more sleds through the supply line up the mountain valley.

With difficulty, the regiment drags cannon balls, musket powder, food, and more spears to the fighting men on the front lines. Rivers of sweat pour down their faces. Isaac struggles with one of the sleds. "There lads, hurry. We must get to the fighting."

The Nu'uanu summit has dark mossy vegetation on either side of the sheer rock ledge, which creates a shelf dropping more than a thousand feet below. Kamehameha's forces are in control of the main trail and driving hard. The only way down the mountain is the one coming up. Kalani-Kupule's men, who have lived all their lives on Oahu, desperately try every possible route to get over the sharp and deadly lava rocks away from the edge of the cliff but it is in vain. Their only hope is to somehow hold off Kamehameha's army until dark when they might be able to sneak through undergrowth and work their way down.

Davis arrives at the ridge where Young and his warriors pound the escape route of the enemy. Young helps unload supplies. "This is a welcome sight. Maika'i lads! Isaac, strong company you've got," he shouts to Davis as he slaps backs and grabs whatever he can to ease their load. Davis pants and wipes sweat. "This had better be enough, John, to get us through the night. It is going to be impossible to find our way around this mountain once darkness comes."

Young snorts, "Isaac, don't worry. The king wants a full push all the way to the cliff up there in the light. He wants to move now in the light. Can your men keep up? He thinks we've got them trapped. But, we must push to the cliff."

He calls to his men, "A Nu'uanu. Wiki. Wiki Anone!"

Kamehameha gathers his special troops on the steep slopes. Another two hundred warriors have streamed up in groups of fifty and are ready to make the last advance. The king shouts directives. His army is becoming a furious tide, their blood lust rising. They know it will not be long before they call the victory. Percussive chants course through all divisions building their courage for the final assault.

66

End of the Trail

Young, catches sight of faces in the mass of men ready to storm the slope and sees the larger picture of what the outcome could be. He stiffens and shouts an order to his men to wait. He pushes his way toward Kamehameha. As he passes Davis he hollers to him over the chanting and singing. "Isaac, I am going to plead for the lives of those men before it's too late. Must ask for a chance to surrender." Davis yells, "Worth trying, but if they won't be loyal, they should be killed. Have we not had enough assassins, John?" Davis moves forward with his men, dragging sleds.

On the other side of the narrow pass, Kalani-Ku-pule is on the safe side of the mountain, but it is a path cut off from his army by cannon blasts. He shouts and rages as dozens of his private troops work in panic, attempting to re-open the pass. He hurls a stone at the tower of rocks, "It is impossible. He has his puppets, the white men – their guns and burning sand. Look what they can do. We needed to kill the king, seize the ship and weapons and we could not even escape! Kamehameha used all well. We failed." He realizes the futility of trying to open the pass.

His head chief tries to speak but, Kalani-Kupule shakes him off. He sits on the rubble. His mind reels. His ministers gather in a small circle near him, afraid to get too close. He lifts his hand, in a deliberate gesture, to make sure they all see it before he speaks, "It is... finished. I am finished."

His adjutant begs. "Most powerful king, we must try to get you to Kauai, where you might be safe."

"Go. Save yourselves. It is over."

The adjutant looks incredulously at his king. "But..."

"Leave me." He shakes his fist at his retinue. "Go!"

His highest chief kneels by him. "My leader, please come with us. We can take you safely down this path."

"Ha! For how long? Kamehameha will find me wherever I am. I see that now. No. It is only a space of a moon I have at best. But, you can swear allegiance to him when your time comes. You can live." He raises his hand again. "I cannot live under his rule. He must be rid of me. They all might talk of swearing to him and living, but, it will not be so for me. Now, if you want to live, go down that trail to the north shore, get in canoes and go around to Waikiki and land as if you were surprised at the attack. Say you were out at sea fishing and did not know. Swear your allegiance to Kamehameha. That is if he doesn't kill you first. It is your only hope. Get rid of all your fine cloaks and become Commoners. And pray they don't turn you into him. Go. And live."

With the sound of Young's cannons in their ears, the high chief, ministers and leading warriors hurry down through the undergrowth, stripping off their bright finery and the battle colors of Kalani-Kupule. From time to time, they turn back, only to see him look smaller and smaller, sitting on a rock.

At the summit of the Nu'uanu Pali, the wind howls like the voice of an angry woman. It has come up stronger. The first regiment of Kalani-Kupule's men arrives near the rock shelf at the cliff. It is about a hundred feet across, from which the largest expanse of the leeward side of the island can be seen. It is clear to the warriors there is no hope, no way out of any kind, only the sheer drop to the valley floor beneath. In the distance, wild waves and white caps roll into Waikiki far below.

Young comes onto the plateau of the summit and sees the tragic end waiting for the enemy. *"Oh, dear God, is there no other way? Must they all die like this?"* Nearby, Kamehameha fights while shouting directives for the assault. Young moves close enough to talk. "My king," Young shouts over the din. "Give them one chance. Tell them to lay down their arms, surrender and live!"

Kamehameha sees the seriousness in Young's eyes and retreats briefly to talk to him behind huge rocks. "Please, my king, remember, these men are your enemy today, but if they *know* they are beaten, they could serve you by the next moon. They may be even more loyal because they know you spared their lives. It is worth trying, sir. You promised Kapene Vancouver you would give them a chance. If it doesn't work, it will be on my head.

Try mercy. The mercy you gave Ka'a humanu. Your people will respect you more if you give them the chance. One chance. The meles around the fires of peace will praise you."

Kamehameha points toward the cliff. "Tell my conchmen go up on that rock. Once only will we give them chance. Live or die. Must choose. If surrender, live. If no, die. Go."

"Thank you, sir!" John ties the rest of his shirt around a spear to create a type of flag. He recruits two warriors with conches. Young talks to them as they climb a rock ledge above the fighting. He waves the makeshift flag while warriors blow the double conch alarm. It echoes across the gorge and the two sides cease fighting. John waits for many hundreds of men to quiet enough to hear. He shouts with all that is in him. "Ku'oko'a a Kamehameha – *freedom with Kamehameha*! Ha'awipio Kamehameha a ola – *surrender to Kamehameha and live.*"

The warriors with Young repeat the offer of mercy, shouting as loud as they can. The words bounce and roll across the armies, echoing in the rock walls, "Ha'awipio – *surrender.* Ha'awipio a ola – *surrender and live.*" Warriors below on the plateau shout the message through the enemy ranks. It is passed forward all the way to the edge of the Pali.

Kamehameha waits for response. A chief hands him some food which he shoves in his mouth and tightens the bandage on his arm. A slave brings him more spears, which are piled into his shoulder holster.

On the sheer cliff, word has spread to all of Kalani-Kupule's warriors. They gather and talk all at once. Some decide to surrender. But, as they move to do so, they are stabbed by those who disagree and thrown over the cliffs as examples to other warriors. Young watches in horror. Other warriors see this and shout in rage and panic. Soon general chaos ensues.

Above this Young hears, "Habakaka – *fight*! Habakaka mau loa – *fight forever*." The chant rises. Young's heart falls as he hears the result. The angry, fighting words spread quickly through the doomed enemy army. They muster to make a last stand, shaking with passion and fear. Kamehameha hears this. He knows John has just enough knowledge of the language to know what they say.

Young remembers the sound of dark bells he used to hear as a boy announcing the dead in his village. He had such hope he could be a good influence upon the souls in these islands in some way. His eyes meet Kamehameha's. He knows he

459

has done what he could and comes down from the ledge.

Kamehameha's army prepares the last charge at the enemy. A few of the warriors have surrendered without being killed by their comrades and are quickly rushed away as prisoners. The king gestures to Young that his offer was not in vain. He leaps over some rocks up onto a ledge above the hundreds of men poised for the signal. Kamehameha raises his spear. Higher it goes. He knows now, too, this is the deciding moment in his life – a moment for which he was born and chosen. Another mystical cry comes from his inner being as he lowers his spear, shaking it in rhythmic, hypnotic, motion. The wind seems to meet his command. It soars through the warriors, taking them forward as they charge up the slope. "A Nu'u – *to the highest place.* Lanakila – *victory.* Lanakila a Nu'uanu Pali – *victory at the highest cliff.* Hele-aku – *Go. Run to it.*" The king leaps off the rock and charges toward the precipice, leading his men, who rush in waves up the incline across the plateau, leading to the edge. As they reach the enemy warriors, a man attacks Kamehameha first, charging with a spear. The king dispatches him quickly. He yanks his spear out of the man and moves on, killing as many of the enemy as he can.

Young's men rush ahead, hungry for their revenge. John, seeing the necessity to fight, lunges into the bloodbath.

On the edge of the cliff, Kalani-Kupule's warriors dash forward in a line. Kamehameha's forces repel them in a fierce tide, compelling them to retreat further. A large group of enemy warriors go over the edge, into the jaws of the wind, screaming and clawing the air in panic.

Fighters on both sides turn in horror to see the sight, their eyes transfixed on men in mid-air, their legs, arms and spears going in every direction. But, the mysterious, mercurial wind, an ironic player on this field of war, arbitrarily lifts up two of the men, hurling them back, depositing them on the ledge like two leaves, rolling and tumbling in the wake of spectacular power. The sight mesmerizes every man in the battle. The event has a stunning effect. They see, in one overwhelmingly clear moment, the value of life deep in the eyes of those who were losing it. They realize they want to live. They run as far away from the ledge as they can, throwing down their spears and swearing allegiance to Kamehameha. Their desire to live is stronger than their fear of Kalani-Kupule's leaders.

However, there are others still dedicated to their position and willing to fight to the death.

Kamehameha's warriors are only too glad to dispatch them.

Davis and his men arrive at the battle on the cliff. As they do, they hear warriors in the army of Kamehameha shouting back, "Ho'opau Hakaka – *cease fighting.* Kaua pau – *war over.* Ho'opau, ho'opau – *cease.* Lanakila, lanakila – *victory!* The men's faces are flushed with joy as they careen across the slope and repeat over and over the thrilling announcement. Visions of their loved ones and children rush back into their minds, as well as the need for water, food and rest. Davis, hearing the news, feels an intake of air filling his chest. He shouts to his men, "Rest. Ho'omaha eia – *rest here.* I go, hele, a Kamehameha!"

On the Pali, John Young pushes to the edge where the men had fallen to their deaths. He looks over briefly then back to the two men who had been blown back onto land. He joins several warriors sitting with them, talking to them, as they lie, still in shock, mumbling words and gesturing to an unseen god.

In Hawaiian, Young orders them taken as prisoners, but given water and food. He gazes at them, not just as captured enemy, but with mercy, an experience nearly unknown to them. Young sees them as Mana'oi saw him two years before in a hut on the edge of Kealakekua Bay. He gets one of his men to translate to them their future will be much better in the hands of Kamehameha. He also hopes he is planting a seed of thought in their minds that white men are not necessarily the evil, soulless beings their people have been led to believe. Everything is different. John wipes blood from his face and looks round. The fighting has stopped and for the first time, he notices how high on the mountain they are.

The king commands his regiments to carry wounded men, of both armies, back down to Waikiki. To others he orders to camp on the slopes and rest before coming down.

"Olohana, lanakila."

Young beams. "Aha. You have not bled to death, sir. A miracle."

Kamehameha grabs John's face. "Olohana, where Akake?"

"Right behind you."

Kamehameha sees Isaac and two of his generals moving toward him, smiling.

He teases, "You sailors, you talk of gods? You see much makani wind today. Makani spit back men to earth. Can your god do this? Ha-ha!"

Young sniffs. "What makes you think it was not Him? He is certainly God of the wind."

463

A silence falls over the king as well as his close leaders. For a moment they are drawn to the sprawling vista and expanse of farms across the coastal plain below. They move to the cliff's edge. Isaac gestures with a grand bow. "King Kamehameha the Great, I believe you are now king of the richly bountiful island of Oahu as well as Hawaii and other islands. Myself and my men congratulate you."

Kamehameha understands the history he is making. "I see great lanikila for my people. I want peace..." His face darkens. "Akake, I not have true aloha at Oahu before see broken bones of Kalani-Kupule. He escape. Other side of mountain."

Mapala, the loyal general, speaks firm and clear, "He will not escape, my king. Ku-ka-ili-moku will be satisfied." Kamehameha nods to him. "He has earned his death." He opens his arms, "All my brothers, the island is won. You fought with me when you could have gone with Kiana. I am grateful to my soul. Akake and Olohana, speak true. We must have trust with Oahu people. I will destroy House of Bones and see if they come out from where they hide." They begin to move toward the slope.

67

Sacrifice

The *Fair American* stands like a sentinel in Waikiki Bay. Men load stores and goods from Kahekili's huts into the ship and many waiting canoes. On the shores, hundreds of wounded men are being tended by women and elder men.

Davis arrives on deck from the small captain's quarters and holds the last bottles of secret grog hidden in the wall below decks. He is aware of pounding drums onshore. He looks in the direction of Kahekili's huts in the horseshoe of the harbor. He can just make out a large group of men beginning to form there. He dashes to the waiting canoe, jumps in, and orders the man to take him ashore.

Once on the beach, Davis moves through the on-lookers – warriors, and old people of the village who have come out of hiding to watch Kamehameha's men tear down the terrifying house. Coming closer, the ghoulish sight is worse than Davis had imagined. More than a thousand skulls, some with obsidian and shell eyes in menacing or soulful expressions, some attached and left to dry with jaws gaping, blanket the structure which stands at least twelve feet high and sixteen feet across. On a second glance, it is clear there were also perhaps thousands of leg bones and other bones shoring up the walls. After being astonished at its hideous and shameful reality, Davis is aware of how easily this one structure could have continued to enslave the people of Oahu and beyond, to hold them in fear of being an addition to its decoration.

How clever and imaginative a butcher Kahekili was. Not that Kamehameha doesn't have some flaws, which he does, but by comparison, I am grateful, even happy to think how much worse my fate might have been had I fallen into the hands of that monster's son.

After carefully felling the walls of the structure, the warriors, helped by villagers who have come out of hiding, begin to place skulls, bones and any other human remains, in a huge pit away from the sea. Many old women and men, tears streaming, come out of the underbrush, one by one, laying garlands of flowers or ti leaves next to various skulls. Some also bring rocks wrapped with leaves.

John Young has made a makeshift cross and wrapped flowers around it. He buries it next to other signs of sacred wood-carvings the old men bring.

Davis, after being on the detail of burying remains, asks one of the leaders supervising the work, "Where has the king gone?"

Young looks up. "I have not seen him for at least an hour."

Davis explains, "I wanted to be dismissed to look for a friend. I believe he is dead. I want to find him and bury him as well."

As Davis turns to go, Kamehameha appears on the horizon, his arms full. Isaac squints to see what the king might be carrying. As he gets closer, they see he has the body of Opa. Davis swallows hard. He puts his shovel down and moves toward the king whose face bears dried tears.

The warriors whisper. "This was the youth who died protecting the king." Word spreads. Quickly, a line forms of men on either side of the king, wanting to see the brave boy. By the time the king gets to Davis, a crowd is growing. The king offers the boy to Davis, who takes the body of his friend. "You train Opa well, Akake. He great warrior." At these words, the king's voice breaks slightly.

Davis forces a smile, unable to stop his tears. "He was so often alone on a point, for hours. Watched for ships coming. He wanted to be first to call when they came. I will bury him out on that point, so he will always welcome you when you come to Oahu."

As the mariner carries his friend, other warriors and villagers follow, creating a funeral procession that young Opa would have been pleased to see. He carries the boy past the now leveled House of Bones, past a long grove of palms, and out to land's end.

68

Home

The next dawn, John Young wakes in his bunk on the *Fair American*. His eyes pop open at the sound of a woman's lilting song floating across the water. He wonders if he is still dreaming or if it is real. He looks for Davis in the other bunk, but it is empty. He gets up swiftly and grabs a handful of food. He limps on deck gingerly protecting his wounds. He blinks at the oddly pink and amber dawn and squints, not trusting this sweet morning. It is as if none of the horrors of the days before had ever been. Even the air is perfumed with plumeria instead of the stench of death. He stares at the long curve of shore known as Wai-kiki and sees villagers already up, taking on tasks of the day in a graceful dance of normalcy. He blinks again. He decides to embrace the seeming goodness of the world as he slips into a canoe to search for Davis.

Out on the point, Isaac wakes to the brilliant crest of orange sun breaking the horizon. It is enough to illuminate his work completed in the dark of the previous night before he fell asleep. He sees something incomplete on the wooden marker he has carved. He grabs his blade and completes the task.

Young paddles a bit faster, recognizing Davis on the point. "Isaac!" he calls, but Davis doesn't hear him.

Young hauls the canoe on shore. Davis looks up at his approach.

"Good morning," Davis says with refreshing calm.

"Aye, mate. Yer up early. Did you sleep at all?" He walks up from the shore. "Brought you some biscuit."

Davis places the marker in the hole he has dug, lifts a shovel and brings down a few blows on the wooden plaque to secure it. Young sees the small mound of fresh dirt. He respectfully doffs his cap and comes to the grave. He reads the carving.

REST IN PEACE

Here lies Opa, Faithful Warrior
And servant of King Kamehameha
Who died saving our king.
His body was crippled, but, not his mind.
And as the Bard says,
"None be deformed, but the unkind."
1795, battle of Nu'uanu Pali

"We sail home today," Young mumbles as the sun continues to rise.

"Indeed," Davis replies, scratching his head. "Home."

Pau – The End

The Kingdom of Kamehameha

King Kalani-Kupule was caught with little resistance shortly after the battle of the previous day. He went to his death by sacrifice at the royal temple dedicated to Kamehameha's beloved war god, Ku-Ka-ili-moku on the island of Hawaii.

King Kamehameha, after the battle of Nu'uanu Pali, ruled all of the islands of the Hawaiian chain, except Kauai, from 1795 until 1806, when that island was also added to his realm. The circumstances of that additional island joining the kingdom are questionable, but resulted in a continued peaceful reign in Hawaii of the king and his lady regent, Ka'ahumanu.

As a peacetime king, he ruled with surprising wisdom and justice and became known throughout the world as *Kamehameha The Great* and even *The Napoleon of the Pacific.*

Kamehameha's rule over all the islands with his beloved Ka'ahumanu spanned twenty-five years until he died of old age in 1819. However, to the disappointment of his advisor, John Young, and other Europeans living in the islands, Kamehameha never turned away from his war god, Ku-ka-Ili-moku, nor the concept of human sacrifice. Near the end of his life, he discovered a long kept secret, that it was likely, but never proven, that his most hated enemy, King Kahekili, may have been his real father.

Ka'ahumanu, the ever clever and wise queen, survived her king, and ruled for thirteen more years after his death until her passing in 1832. The year after the king's death, in1820, she sent to Boston to implore missionaries to come tell her people about the God of Olohana, the god of grace. During her reign, she became a Christian, and with the help of Kamehameha II, ended the entire Kapu system of worship, tearing down the temples of the old gods. She thereby finally created a path of liberty for her country's women, as well as allowing for freedom of conscience for all her people. Some joined her beliefs and some chose other paths.

Under Kamehameha, John Young became an honored chief, and was named the first governor of the island of Hawaii. Much later, his grand-daughter, Emma Rook, served briefly as Queen of Hawaii.

Both John Young and Isaac Davis fought in several more battles for their king and were well-respected by Hawaiians throughout the island kingdom as wise chiefs and friends.

After King Kamehameha's death, John Young served under Ka'ahumanu as an advisor until his death in 1835 at age 93.

Isaac Davis also never left Hawaii. He became a Hawaiian chief under Kamehameha and was named the first governor of the island of Oahu. He served faithfully until he heard of a plot by some of Kamehameha's inner circle to kill the young king of Kauai on a state visit. He then warned Kamehameha, who stopped the plot. But, in revenge, the faction wanting to kill the Kauai king poisoned Isaac Davis. His murder was deeply grieved by Kamehameha and the entire court. His children were adopted by John and Kaoana Young.

It is not clear when the slave system ended, but it is assumed that after the king's death in 1819,

Ka'ahumanu likely helped it fade and allowed every Hawaiian the opportunity to move through all echelons of their society.

Author's Note

The following are words from the tombstone of John Young, located on the island of Oahu, near the bottom of the trail leading to the Nu'uanu Pali:

*Beneath this stone are deposited
the remains of
John Young (of Lancastershire, England),
The friend and companion-in-arms
to KAMEHAMEHA I,
who departed this life December 17th 1835,
in the 93rd year of his age,
and the 46th of his residence
on the Hawaiian (Sandwich) Islands*

In the Bishop Museum in Honolulu, Hawaii, are the few entries in one of John Young's surviving personal journals. Most of Mister Young's effects were destroyed in storms and during floods. Only several pages remain. On them the verses below were found amongst routine entries of lists of food brought and services performed by people living on the lands given to John Young by Kamehameha I after he became supreme monarch of the islands.

King Kamehameha, during his reign, called the inhabitants of the big island of Hawaii, *Olohana's People*. Two hand-written entries follow listings of weather and gifts of homage regularly paid to him. The poem was in his own hand. It is as follows:

Life is the time to serve the Lord
Then I insure the great reward.
And the lamp holds out to burn,
The vilest sinner may return.
Life is the hour that God has given
To scape from hell and fly to heaven
The day of Grace. And mortals may
Secure the blessings of the day.

The living know that they must die
But all the dead forget to sigh,
Their memory and their senses gone
Alike unknowing and unknown.

Their hatred and their love is lost
Their envy buried in the dust.
They have no share in all that is done
Beneath the circuit of the sun

Then what my desires to do
My hands with all my might pursue

Since no device nor works is found,
Nor faith, nor hope, beneath the ground.

There are no acts of pardon passed
In the cold ground to which we hiest
But, darkness, death and song despair
Pine in eternal silence there.

Whence the hopes, the sons of men
On their own works have built.
Their hearts, by nature, all unclean
And all their actions, guilt.

Let graces and gentles stop their mouths
With a murmuring word…
And the whole race of Adam stand
Guilty before the Lord.

And a few pages later… a prayer…

Almighty God, who has given us grace at this
time with one accord,
to make our common supplications unto thee
and doth promise that
when two or three are gathered together in thy
Name, that thou wilt
grant their requests.

Fulfill now, Oh Lord, the desires and petitions of thy servants as may
be most expedient for them, granting us in this world, knowledge of
Thy truth, and in the world to come, life ever-lasting Amen....

The following is written by Laura Fish Judd as an introduction to a letter by John Young

John Young, Senior, was an important personage during the wars with Kamehameha I (1790—1796) and it was owing in a great measure to his energy and skill that the conqueror succeeded in subjugating the hereditary kings of each island and uniting them under his own supreme control.

Mr. Young, "*Olohana*", did a great deal in building the heiau at Kawaihae and attended the sacrifices but continued to exert his influence in favor of the overthrow of idolatry. He was closely identified with the councils of the nation for a period of forty years.

The following letter of John Young's tells his own story:

Kawaikai, Island of Hawaii, November 27, 1826

Whereas it has been presented by many persons that the labors of the missionaries in these islands are attended with evil and disadvantage to the

479

people, I hereby cheerfully give my testimony to the contrary.

I am fully convinced that the good which is accomplished and effected is not little. The great radical change already made for the better in the manner and customs of this people has far surpassed my most sanguine expectations. During the forty years that I have resided here I have known thousands of defenseless human beings in their exterminating wars. I have seen multitudes of my fellow-beings offered in sacrifice to their idol gods. I have seen this large island, once filled with inhabitants, dwindled down to the present few in numbers through WAR and DISEASE and I am persuaded that nothing but Christianity can prevent them from total extinction. I rejoice that true religion is taking the place of idolatry, that good morals are superseding the reign of crime, and that a code of Christian laws is about to take the place of tyranny and oppression. These things are what I have long wished for, but have never seen till now. I thank God that in my old age I see them and humbly must feel them too.

Signed,

John Young, 1826

Cultural System of
the Hawaiian Islands

1790—1796

Ancient Hawaii was a caste society and culture much like Hindus in India. People were born into specific social classes; social mobility was not unknown, but it was extremely rare. The main classes were:

- Ali'i. [A–lee-ee] This class consisted of the high and lesser chiefs of the realms. They governed with divine power called mana. This could be equated with Kshatriyas in India who had the same role in the society.

- Kahuna.[ka-hoona] Priests conducted religious ceremonies at the heiau and elsewhere. Professionals included master carpenters, boatbuilders, chanters, dancers, genealogists, physicians, and healers. Much like Brahmins in Hindu society.

- Maka āinana.[mika–eena] Commoners farmed, fished, and exercised the simpler crafts. They labored not only for themselves

and their families, but to support the chiefs
and kahuna. Much like vaishyas in Hinduism.

- Kauā. [kow –va] Slaves. They are believed to
have been war captives or the descendants
of war captives. Marriage between higher
castes and the kauwa was strictly forbidden.
The kauwa worked for the chiefs and were
often used as human sacrifices at the luak-
ini heiau.They were not the only sacrifices;
law-breakers of all castes or defeated political
opponents were also acceptable as victims,
much like shudras in Hinduism.

REGULATIONS REGARDING WOMEN IN KAMEHAMEHA'S HAWAII OF THIS PERIOD:

Women could not ride in boats, catch fish, or
speak to the gods except through male intermedi-
aries or on rare occasions. They could not eat many
local foods, including pork, bananas, and certain
fish, and they were barred from eating with men
or from cooking their food in the same oven as
the men.

However, while women were banned from
attending the councils of religious and political
power and were subject to many other constraints
stemming from the *kapu* system, they still had

a great deal of personal autonomy and relative sexual egalitarianism.

Hawaiian women often acted in opposition to the interests of their men if it suited them. They controlled their own property and engaged in commerce on their own grounds.

The *kapu* system began to crack as foreign sailors reached the islands.

It was Ka'ahumanu who passionately ended the kapu system after Kamehameha died in 1819, allowing women to have the same rights as the men. The people of the islands loved their Regent, and she ruled in peace and prosperity.

Chris Weatherhead,
Folly Beach, South Carolina,
July 15, 2019

Selected Bibliography

Beaglehole, J.C., Edwards, Phillip,
The Journals of Captain Cook,
The Penguin Group, 1999

Beckwith, Martha,
Hawaiian Mythology,
University of Hawaii Press, 1970

Kuykendall, Ralph S.,
The Hawaiian Kingdom, Volume I,
1778 – 1854, Foundation and Transformation,
University of Hawaii Press, Honolulu, 1980

Malo, David,
Hawaiian Antiquities (Moolelo), Translated by
Dr. Nathaniel B. Emerson, 1898, Published
by The Bernice P. Bishop Museum, printing
1951

McBride, L.R.,
The Kahuna, Versatile Mystics of Old Hawaii,
The Petroglyph Press, Hilo, Hawaii, 1972

Pukui, Mary K. & Alfons L. Korn,
The Echo of Our Song, Chants &
Poems of the Hawaiians.
The University Press of Hawaii, 1973

Papa Ii,
>   *Fragments of Hawaiian History,*
>   Translated by Mary Kawena Pukui, Bishop
>   Museum Press,1959

Pukui, Mary Kawena, Elbert, Samuel H.,
Mookini, Esther T.,
>   *Hawaiian Dictionary, Hawaiian-English,*
>   *English-Hawaiian,*
>   University of Hawaii Press, Honolulu, Hawaii,
>   1975

Vancouver, George,
>   *A Voyage of Discovery to the North Pacific and*
>   *Around the World,*
>   Volume One, London, J. Stockdale 1798 &
>   1801

Valeri, Valerio, Translated by Paula Wissing,
>   *Kingship and Sacrifice, Ritual and Society in*
>   *Ancient Hawaii,*
>   The University of Chicago Press, 1985

Glossary

Ali'I – Persons of royal dynastic families given respect for their relation to their ancestors.

Haole – A Hawaiian term for caucasians when they arrived in the 18th Century, and for others from foreign lands who behaved in questionable ways that made them have "no spirit or soul". In modern times it has various connotations.

Kahuna – A respected person who has authority over society morally as a priest, healer and teacher. They were also masters of many crafts.

Kapu – (or Tabu) – A forbidden action based on a code of laws and regulations. This system covered lifestyle, roles, politics and religion. An offense against Kapu law was often a capital offense, but also often denoted a threat to spiritual power, or theft of mana.

Kauva – A member of the slave/outcast class, from birth.

Ku-a-ili-moku – The war god of King Kamehameha, which was created or carved in several forms.

La'au make – A deadly poison substance.

Lua – Ancient Hawaiian martial art; some holds could fracture, paralyze or kill instantly.

Mana – Spiritual power in any person or thing.

Mamo – A native yellow bird, now extinct. The bright yellow feathers were used in royal capes and helmets.

Mele – A story told in voice and physical movements by male or female, often a piece of history, poem or statement honoring a hero. The word, "mele" also means "poetic language".

Pali – A precipice. The Nu'uanu Pali precipice on the island of Oahu is 1,168 feet high.

Tapa Or Kapa – Cloth made from bark made in the islands of the Pacific Ocean. Hawaiian kapa is the only type that can be as large as a king size blanket and yet have no seams where pieces were joined together to get such a size. The print is stamped on in many varied styles.

Mahalo – An offering of thanks.

Note: Conch shell usage – A shell trumpet was used to announce religious and secular events or warnings of impending danger.

About the Author

Chris Weatherhead was born in Glendale, California, the daughter of WWII hero pilot and his wife, a former Hollywood singer. The family traveled extensively, and Chris was able to study various cultures, living briefly in the Dominican Republic, Tokyo, Japan, London, England and several regions of the United States.

She began writing at a young age but chose to be a professional actress, screenwriter and producer, while studying with Brewster Mason, a leading actor of the Royal Shakespeare Company in London.

Chris performed in major projects in New York City and Hollywood, starring in many productions and prime-time series before directing two American Revolutionary War docudramas about unsung heroes of South Carolina. Both films have won many international awards. She resides in South Carolina with actor/writer/director husband, Clarence Felder. They have one daughter, Helen, a middle school teacher. Filmography available on IMDB.com.

List of Illustrations